The Divine Reality
God, Islam & The Mirage of Atheism

By Hamza Andreas Tzortzis

FB PUBLISHING
SAN CLEMENTE

Published by:

FB Publishing
645 Camino De Los Mares
Suite 108-276
San Clemente CA 92673
Visit our website at www.FBPublishinghouse.com

Book Design: Ramit Kumar

ISBN: 978-0-9965453-8-9
First Edition

Printed in the United States of America

In the name of God, the merciful, the giver of mercy.

All praise and gratitude is due to God, the Lord of everything that exists. May God's peace and blessings be upon His final Prophet and Messenger, Muhammad ﷺ.

For my family.

Their love, patience, and enduring compassion deserve eternal gratitude.

Preliminary notes

In the Islamic tradition when the Prophet Muhammad ﷺ is mentioned by name or title the honorific phrase 'ﷺ' is used. It is a sign of love and respect. The phrase denotes 'May God's peace and blessings be upon him'. This phrase has been used throughout this book.

The word God has been used throughout this book. However, in the Islamic tradition the name of God is Allah. Arabic linguists suggest that the name Allah comes from the word *Al-Ilah*, which means The-Deity. The name Allah has no plural and is genderless.

Acknowledgements

Undoubtedly this book would not have been possible without God. I praise and thank Him. Once you finish reading this book you will realise that everything depends on God and He alone is worthy of perfect praise and gratitude.

The Prophet Muhammad ﷺ taught that the person who has not thanked God has "not thanked people."[1] In this light, there are a number of people to whom I owe thanks for helping and encouraging me to write this book.

First among them are my family. I cannot ever forget the love, patience, support, encouragement and sacrifices of my wife and children. My neglect and isolation was endured and overlooked by the people I love. The fact that God gave me such a family is something that deserves eternal gratitude.

I would like to show my appreciation to my brother Spyros Tzortzis. He was an early intellectual inspiration in my life. We shared the same bedroom for over two decades. His ability to think outside of the box and explore new ideas planted intellectual 'seeds' in my mind, the fruit of which is this book. I would like to thank my sister Haris Tzortzis. She has always supported me and never defined me by my faults, always by my strengths. My mother Androula Tzortzis is one of the most loving people that I know. Her undying love, energy and support have shaped who I am. My father Petros Tzortzis has always been my hero. His patience, tolerance, love, humility and wisdom have inspired me. I can never repay my parents. Anything I say cannot truly express the gratitude that is due to them. I pray that God guides and protects my family, and that He grants them long, healthy lives full of joy, love and piety. I pray that He continues to unite us in love.

I want to thank my friend Imran Hussein. Imran reviewed the book and provided significant input. His contribution to Chapter 3 was extensive. I am also extremely grateful to my friend Subboor Ahmad, who provided important contributions and moral support.

I want to express my deepest gratitude to Abu Hurayra. He is one of the smartest people I have had contact with. Although we have never met, due to our similar interests we have exchanged ideas. He reviewed the book at its early stage and his input was beyond significant. Without his incisive criticism and contribution this book would not have been possible.

I would like to thank the author and academic Safaruk Chowdhury. Our friendship has inspired me to pursue further studies in Islamic thought and philosophy. His review of the book and scholarly contribution was extremely helpful.

I would like to thank Asif Uddin, who spent hours researching various Islamic classical texts. His input and corrections helped shaped the character of the book.

I am ever grateful to my friend Adnan Rashid. His review of the book and his contribution to Chapter 14 was extensive.

I would also like to express my gratitude to Dr. Atif Imtiaz and Sharif Randhawa for their important suggestions and advice.

I would like to thank Umm-Talha bint Abi-Bilal who did a last minute review of the entire manuscript.

I am grateful to Ghazi Mannai, Fahad Tasleem, Dr. Mohamed Ghilan, Anthony Green, Salahuddin Patel, Joni Molla, Esa Khan, Abdullah Mekki, Moseen Khalid, Zeenat Bibi, Abu Zakariya and Umm Zakariya for their noteworthy support and contributions.

Finally, I would like to thank John Paine for his editorial work and FB Publishing for their support and making this book become a reality.

There are many more people whom I should show my appreciation and gratitude to. However, anyone that has been left out, know that your reward is with God, and what is from Him cannot be compared to anything in this world.

Contents

Preface
My Journey

What is the point of writing a book about God, Islam and atheism? Philosophers, thinkers and academics from various religious backgrounds have already written books on similar topics, so why reinvent the wheel? To explain this, let me elaborate a little on the journey that I have taken so far in my life.

I was born in London to Greek parents. Both of them came to the UK in the seventies for different reasons. My father mainly wanted to escape life in Athens. My mother did not have much of a choice; she was a refugee driven out by the Turkish invasion of Cyprus in 1974. My parents suffered many hardships, but with love, patience and determination they have become now two of the happiest, most loving, compassionate and tolerant people I know. I am eternally grateful to have them in my life.

Despite all their setbacks, what concerned my father the most was solving his version of what people call an existential crisis. He was in search of answers to life's key questions. His journey led him to acquire an array of books. At home, I had access to a wide range of literature, from *The Power of Positive Thinking* to *The Science of the Mind*. My father was always immersed in his books and constantly shared his ideas with us. I was the middle of his three children, and none of us had mature enough minds to comprehensively grasp what he was saying.

Being brought up in this background, I picked up my father's existential anguish, and I began to ask questions about the basis of my own existence. I still remember how, at around the age of eleven, I would go into the bath and sit in the tub for a while, crying. I felt so lonely. What occurred to me was that I was the only one conscious of my existence (*see Chapter 7*). Only I knew what it was like to be me, whether I was alone in the bath or playing with friends in the park. This created a sense of doubt about the existence of other people's conscious lives. Were they really conscious? Did they exist in a real sense? What were they feeling? What were their conscious experiences when I was not there to witness them?

Later in life, I learnt that this was a form of solipsism, which is the view that *you* can only be certain that your mind exists. Nevertheless, it was a profoundly lonely experience, which I believe was the emotional driving force to find answers to very important questions in my life. This experience instilled within me that the concept of truth is very important. In my search for truth, I used to engage with my friends and ask them questions about their beliefs. I was so fortunate to have connections with people from myriad ethnicities and cultures. This was one of the blessings of being brought up in the London borough of Hackney.

I felt that without knowing the truth, life seemed unreal and illusory. Many psychologists have acknowledged that human beings want to be right and seek to learn from social norms when they are unsure about things. From this perspective the search for truth is very important as it offers the possibility of shaping who we are or the person we want to be.

I felt that not searching for the truth was tantamount to lying to myself, or accepting a lie. Therefore, the search for truth was a means of trying to be more sincere with my own existence, as I would be seeking to establish the truth of this life and my place within it. For me, holding on to the sceptical view of the truth, which argues that there is no truth, was self-defeating. This is because the concept that there is no truth is actually a claim itself, so how could I claim that scepticism is true but everything else is not? This is the inconsistency of the sceptical view; a sceptic would claim the truth of scepticism but would deny all other truths. Consequently, no matter what position I held, I still had to accept a truth.

When I first learnt about Islam, two aspects fascinated me. The first was the certainty that emanated from my Muslim friends. The second was their social and spiritual practices; both eventually led me to accept Islam. This is not the space to go into detail about my conversion, but there was a point when, although I was intellectually convinced in the rational foundations of Islam, that still was not enough for me to embrace Islam. So I started adopting two practices. First, I started to learn some chapters of the Qur'an in Arabic and pray several of the five daily prayers that Muslims carry out as part of their spiritual practice. When I used to prostrate, which is a part of the Islamic prayer, I would talk to God, asking for His guidance. I did this after receiving a spiritual insight of my brother's friend, Amir Islahi. He was studying medicine at university, but he would visit my college campus and give us advice. Since I had Muslim friends, I would listen to him; echoing the words of the Prophet Muhammad ﷺ, Amir once said that you are closest to God during prostration, so speak to Him.

I found this profound because the face reflects who we are. Many times it represents our ego and vanity, yet Muslims humble themselves and acknowledge that they are nothing compared to God. In that submission they find themselves servants of the One that created them. In prostration, the physical station of humility and egolessness, Muslims speak to God. So I started talking to Him too, and begged for guidance. Dr. Amir Islahi is now my friend, but I do not think he knows the impact of those few words he spoke to me over 15 years ago.

Second, I began to have more conversations with a school friend of mine, Moynul Ahmed. He would come to my house and speak to me about Islam, and I would ask him questions. However, early on in the process I was intellectually convinced, but my heart was dead. Nothing I knew about the truth of Islam had been internalised. In this struggle to combine what I knew with what I felt, I met Moynul outside my house and sat in his car on 4 October 2002. To be honest, I do not really remember what he told me, but I remember how I felt. He expressed a profound and poetic description of the certainty of death. I cannot recall the exact words; to do so would be like catching a black cat in the dark. However, it hit me hard and somehow opened a door that seemed to have been locked, allowing my certainty in the truth of Islam to affect my heart.

Human beings do not enjoy thinking about death. It creates the realisation within us that all of the attachments we have built in this world will cease to be. Significantly, it awakens us to the brutal fact that we will no longer exist on this planet. We have to face the reality of an inevitable personal apocalypse. There have been many philosophical theories about death. For example, some thinkers have held that death is like a permanent sleep. Others have explained that death is to be considered part of life, something which every person must come to terms with in order to live well; part of what is involved in accepting our finitude. Some thinkers have claimed that death is a transition from this life to an afterlife, which includes the eternal life of bliss via Divine mercy, or pain because of our insistence on rejecting the mercy and guidance of God.

Whatever our views on death are, we can all agree is that it is a subject that we do not think about enough. This may sound morbid, but there is a profound benefit in reflecting on death—it brings about the realisation that life is short. Pondering our finite nature helps diminish our egos and our selfish desires no longer seem that important. Our ephemeral attachments to the material world are put into perspective and our lives are questioned—all of which offer great benefit. As the 11th century theologian Al-Ghazali said, "...in the recollection of death there is reward and merit."[2] Contemplating death provokes thought and gives us a window of opportunity to reflect on the nature of our existence.

Considering death answered questions on how I should view life. It taught me to measure how much importance I should attach to material things. In viewing my life through the lens of death, I entered an emotional and intellectual space where I could assess my situation on this planet. How did I come to be? What should I be doing here? Where am I going? Death was the driving force behind these critical questions, because the moment I recognised that this life is short, that one day I will breathe my last, it put everything into perspective.

To understand what I went through, I want you to reflect on death; imagine you are here one minute and the next you are no more. You have probably experienced loved ones that have passed away; how did you feel? Did you feel loneliness, emptiness and lack of attachment to the things you used to take so seriously? Now, if you were to taste death this instant, as every human being eventually will, what would that mean to you? What would you do differently with your life if you were given the chance to go back? What thoughts and ideas would you take more seriously? What would your outlook be if you could relive your life having experienced the tragic reality of death?

The sad thing about death is that we cannot go back. This realisation weighed heavily on my mind. Deeply reflecting on death led me to the conclusion that life is short and that I wanted to transform it for the better without delay. The very next morning I took a taxi to London Central Mosque and embraced Islam. The date was October 5, 2002.

My need to know the truth transformed into a desire to tell others about the truth. In my naivety, I would latch onto anything that I felt supported Islam and its rational foundations. I would study the works of various Christian philosophers because nothing of that sort was accessible to Muslims in the English language—most profound Islamic intellectual writings are in Arabic. This inevitably made my learning process hard. Adopting the arguments espoused by Christian philosophers was not the best way to imbibe Islamic theism. Although the two faiths have a lot in common, there are huge and subtle differences.

Throughout my years as a Muslim, I have learnt things the hard way. I have made many mistakes and errors, and much of this book consists of the lessons that I have learnt. Many of my mistakes are available for all to see on the Internet. This process of trial and error has had its benefits as well as its negative consequences. The negatives are that all of my blunders, slip-ups and oversights are available for all to see. However, by reading this book, you can learn from my mistakes and you do not have to learn things the hard way. Trial and error have refined, developed and strengthened the arguments I have adopted. This journey has also made me appreciate that tolerance and compassion are among our highest virtues. These experiences also challenged my views on my own faith, and helped open the door to find out that Islam is a compassionate tradition. Through the Prophet Muhammad's ﷺ teachings, I understood compassion beautifies everything. ﷺ

I have tested my ideas and arguments with some of the brightest atheist minds in the world. I have debated prominent atheist academics and thinkers from a wide range of intellectual backgrounds. Some of my interlocutors have been Professor Simon Blackburn, Dr. Brendan Larvor, Dr. Stephen Law, Professor Richard Norman, Dr. Nigel Warburton, Professor Peter Simons, Professor Lawrence Krauss, Professor Graham Thompson, Dr. Peter Cave and Dan Barker. I have even had a brief street discussion with Professor Richard Dawkins, but unfortunately we were interrupted and Dawkins made a quick exit. The topics we have debated range from *Can we live better lives without religion?* to *Can consciousness be best explained by God's existence?* And *Islam or Atheism: Which Makes More Sense?*[3] These debates have facilitated improvements to my arguments. It has been a huge blessing, and those who are familiar with my work have seen that I have evolved from mirroring the arguments of analytical philosophers to developing positions rooted in the Islamic tradition. This does not mean I have 'thrown away the baby with the bathwater'. As you will see in this book, I have kept all the sound, universal and robust arguments while giving them an Islamic flavour, as well as refining them to ensure that they are theologically and rationally coherent.

Completing my postgraduate degree in philosophy at the University of London has proven to be very beneficial. My ability to critically challenge and support philosophical views has improved. I am currently continuing postgraduate studies in this field and it is my intention to use what I have learnt to articulate an intelligent and compassionate case for traditional Islam to a wide range of audiences. These academic experiences have shaped and influenced the logical flow and content of the arguments presented in this book. They have also strengthened my view that Islamic theology, thought and philosophy—grounded in the Qur'an and the prophetic teachings—are intuitive, coherent and robust.

No other book available in the English language articulates an intelligent and nuanced case for Islamic theism while addressing the incoherence of atheism. This is not to praise this book; rather, it highlights the lack of writing on this topic. During my lectures at the hundreds of university campuses I have visited all around the world, I have interacted with thousands of Muslim and non-Muslim students and academics. These interactions, in addition to the rise of atheism, have made it quite clear that people have an intellectual thirst concerning the Islamic view of God, the role of revelation and the personality of the Prophet Muhammad ﷺ. This book aims to quench that thirst, thereby providing an English reader with a coherent set of arguments for God's existence, oneness, and why He is worthy of our worship, including a compelling case for the Qur'an and the prophethood of Muhammad ﷺ. It also responds to and addresses a wide range of academic and popular arguments and objections that favour the denial of the Divine.

This book contains a combination of universal and Islamic arguments for God's existence, the Qur'an and the prophethood of Muhammad ﷺ. Many of these arguments have been tried and tested with academics and thinkers over the years. Each chapter has relevant Islamic references to show the Islamic basis for each argument, which ensures that they are not only philosophically sound but Islamically coherent. Approximately fifty percent of the references in this book come from the Islamic tradition; this includes references from the Qur'an, the Prophetic Traditions[4] (known as *hadith*; *ahadith*, pl), and the Islamic scholarly tradition. This book does not just focus on Islamic theism and a response to atheism; it addresses a key argument for the Divine authorship of the Qur'an and explains how, by looking at the life experiences, teachings and impact of the Prophet Muhammad ﷺ, we can only conclude that he was the final messenger of God. Significantly, it elaborates in detail on why God is worthy of our worship, which is the reason for our existence.

Irrespective of whether you consider yourself a Muslim, atheist or sceptic, I invite you to read this book with an open heart and mind. I truly believe that if you respond to this invitation, one of the conclusions you will reach is that atheism is an intellectual mirage and that the Islamic conception of God is coherent and true. Once you read this book you will see that the phrase 'intellectual mirage' is an apt description for atheism. A mirage is an optical illusion that we experience due to atmospheric conditions. Likewise, the conditions that facilitate the denial of the Divine are based on false assumptions about the world, incoherent arguments, pseudointellectual postulations that veil emotional issues and, on occasion, egocentricity. Atheism is not based on a commitment to reason; in many ways, it is its adversary (*see Chapter 3*).

Chapter 1
Atheism
Its Definition, History and Growth

The best place to start may be with a definition. Atheism linguistically means 'not a theist'; in other words, someone who does not believe in a God or gods. The prefix *a* means none or not, and theism, coming from the word *theos*, denotes a 'belief in the existence of an intervening God or gods'. Both come from Greek, but relying on the literal meaning is not enough to explain the implications of the term. So what does disbelief in a God or gods imply? Does it indicate that the one who describes himself as an atheist has positive arguments in favour of atheism? Does it mean that they are currently not convinced by any theistic arguments? Or does it mean that they just do not believe in any gods?

Academics have not reached a consensus on a definition for atheism, but my concern is not with philosophical hair-splitting. My focus is a practical one.[5] Let's address the first question I raised: *Does it indicate that the one who describes himself as an atheist has positive arguments in favour of atheism?* In this sense, an atheist is someone who makes a knowledge claim—that there is no God. Nevertheless, such a claim requires justification. The claim is a positive assertion, and it requires some sort of argument to back it up. Therefore, this type of atheist must provide evidence for their position.

This leads us to the second question: *Does it mean that the atheist is currently not convinced by any theistic arguments?* This seems to be far removed from atheism and is entering into the realm of agnosticism. Holding such a position would imply that if a good argument were offered for God's existence, they would have to accept it.

Finally, we have the question: *Does it mean that the person is someone who just does not believe in any gods?* If an atheist disbelieves based on mere choice, in the absence of any rational investigation, then how does that differ from any other belief, whether it is the belief in fairies or astrology?

From my experience the question *Why do you believe in no gods?* is an excellent conversation starter with an atheist (*see Chapter 4*). Depending on the response I receive, I clearly know if they are agnostics, atheists who believe without any positive evidence, or if they have found an argument against God. If they are agnostics, then the best strategy is to provide good reasons for why you believe God exists. If they are sincere, and the argument is valid, then they should accept the existence of the Divine. If they believe in no gods without evidence, then what I find useful is to get them to question and think about their beliefs. I would ask them: *What evidence do you have to reject God's existence?* I would also show them the negative implications of just believing in something based on mere choice without any reasoning or intellectual basis. If they claim to have found evidence against God's existence, I would ask them for the evidence. In that case, as a Muslim, it would be my job to show how the evidence they have provided is false or misunderstood, while at the same time presenting a case for why God does exist.

So here's a summary of what it practically means to be an atheist. Firstly, there is the negative assertion that one is simply a disbeliever in a God or gods. Secondly, there is the view that the current arguments for God's existence are not convincing, which implies agnosticism. Finally, there is the positive assertion that there are no gods. Such an assertion requires an argument. From my experience, regardless of the hair-splitting debates on this issue, many atheists are atheists simply because they are not convinced by any argument in favour for the Divine. This means that most atheists are not really atheists at all, but closet agnostics. So there is hope, and all one has to do is offer a good argument for theism. It is important to note that the practical definitions I have proposed here are not binary; there are varying degrees of each type of atheist. Atheists can also be described as having one or a combination of these definitions.

If only it was that easy. Human beings are not intellectual robots. An array of emotional, social, spiritual and psychological factors determines which worldview we adopt. Unravelling the vast number of variables that lead to certain decisions or beliefs is impossible. However, from my experience, atheism is not a strict intellectual decision born out of reason and science. On the contrary, atheism is deeply rooted in psychology (although I appreciate this applies to some and not all atheists).

Misotheism: hatred of God

Although not considered a form of atheism, I thought it would be of great interest to elaborate on another type of rejection of the Divine. Rather than rejecting God's existence, this perspective involves a hatred of God and wish that He not exist. Known as misotheism, coming from the Greek *misos,* meaning hatred, and *theos* meaning God, this religious rebellion has been lurking in the dark. It is time some light was shed on this denunciation of God, which some might argue is the psychological basis for certain types of atheism. Associate Professor Bernard Schweizer has written a book on the topic; after sifting through a number of literary works of prominent thinkers and writers, including Algernon Charles Swinburn, Zora Neale Hurston, Rebecca West, Elie Wiesel, Peter Shaffer and Philip Pullman, he concludes that they seem to struggle with the idea of a compassionate and merciful God in a world of evil and suffering. He indicates that the motivation for their hatred of God is due to being "generally motivated by admirable humanistic impulses"[6]. Schweizer indicates that the misotheist is emotionally and psychologically troubled. He argues that it is "quite true that the psychologically, emotionally, and physically wounded are most likely to turn away from God"[7] and that it is "by no means certain that more effective forms of ministering would help douse the fires of misotheism or block the path to atheism"[8]. Although these thinkers and writers represent different types of misotheists, they all question God's role in human suffering:

> "The situation is different for the misotheist. To him, the incompatibility of widespread evil with the image of a benevolent God is a real problem, not merely a case of hair-splitting theological arguments. Misotheists are genuine accusers of God, and they will hold him accountable for random evil and undeserved suffering. Thus, atheists and misotheists come to the question of God's role in human suffering from opposed directions: the unbeliever would say that the misotheist makes an invalid claim based on fiction. To the misotheist himself, precisely because he is a believer, God is not a scapegoat but an accomplice or an instigator of evil."[9]

Schweizer's study is quite nuanced. He categorises misotheism into agnostic misotheists, absolute misotheists and political misotheists. To summarise the professor's main point, the misotheist is motivated by a key question: *What has humanity done to deserve God and all the evil and suffering that He allows to occur?* From my experience, I would contend that quite a few atheists are closet misotheists. One question to ask that usually testifies to this conclusion is: *If God did exist, would you worship Him?* (*see Chapter 15*). The response from many atheists that I have encountered would be no, and they frequently cite the amount of 'unnecessary' and 'gratuitous' evil and suffering in the world. Although I empathise with their concern and anguish at the suffering inflicted on fellow sentient beings, atheists and misotheists alike suffer from a veiled type of egocentricism. This means they make special effort not to see the world from any perspective other than through their own eyes. However, in doing so, they commit a type of emotional—or spiritual—fallacy. They anthropomorphise God and turn Him into a limited man. They assume that God must see things the way we see things, and therefore He should stop the evil. If He allows it to continue, He must be questioned and rejected.

Comparing man with God exposes their inability to understand things holistically. The misotheist would probably at this point exclaim that this means man has more compassion than God. This further highlights their inability to see things from beyond their perspective, and reveals their failure to fathom that God's actions and will are in line with a Divine reason that we cannot access. God does not want evil and suffering to happen. God does not stop these things from happening because He sees something we do not, not because He wants evil and suffering to continue. God has the picture and we merely have a pixel. Understanding this facilitates spiritual and intellectual tranquillity because the believer understands that ultimately all that occurs in the world is in line with a superior Divine wisdom that is based on superior Divine goodness. Refusing to accept this is actually where the misotheist falls into the quagmire of arrogance, egocentricism and ultimately, despair. He has failed the test, and his hatred of God makes him forget who God is, and dismiss the fact of Divine wisdom, mercy and goodness (*see Chapter 11*).

Atheism and Philosophical Naturalism

Before I discuss the Islamic definition of atheism, this chapter is a good opportunity to introduce a concept that will be referred to in many chapters of this book. Like atheism, philosophical naturalism denies the Divine and the supernatural. Therefore, it is not surprising that most atheists adopt philosophical naturalism as a worldview. Philosophical naturalism is the view that all phenomena within the universe can be explained via physical processes. These physical processes are blind and non-rational. Philosophical naturalists reject all supernatural claims and some argue that if there is anything 'outside' the universe it does not interfere with it. Atheists, according to Professor Richard Dawkins, are philosophical naturalists. As stated by Dawkins, an atheist "believes there is nothing beyond the natural, physical world".[10] However, some atheist academics are not naturalists. Although these atheists deny the Divine, they affirm the existence of non-physical phenomena. For the theist, this type of atheism is—generally speaking—easier to intellectually engage with because they do not dismiss non-physical phenomena. In this respect there is some common ground with theism. It is important to note that most atheists who assert evidence against God's existence—or argue that there is an absence of strong evidence for the Divine—adopt philosophical naturalism, implicitly or explicitly. Nevertheless, most of the arguments presented in this book can still be used toward atheists who do or do not adopt philosophical naturalism.

Islamic definition

The traditional Islamic term for atheism is *ilhaad*, which literally means 'deviation', best translated as 'godlessness'. The term *ilhaad* comes from the Arabic word *lahad*, which is used to describe a type of Islamic grave where a hole is dug and a side pocket is made for the deceased. In this sense the *lahad* is a deviation from the main hole that is dug. Linguistically, this implies that atheism is a deviation of what is natural and rational. The Prophet Muhammad ﷺ taught that all human beings are born with an innate nature or primordial state that essentially acknowledges God and has an affinity to worship the Divine (*see Chapter 4*).[11] This Prophetic teaching provides a clear basis for the Islamic belief that atheism is unnatural and an aberration of the human psyche.

According to Islamic theology, God's names include The-Creator (*Al-Khaaliq*), The-Sustainer (*Al-Muqeet*), and The-Originator (*Al-Mubdi*). Atheists reject these names as they deny the idea of a creator for the universe. The Islamic doctrine of God's oneness, known as *tawheed*, considers denying any of God's names and attributes as a form polytheism (*see Chapter 15*). Therefore, from the Islamic point of view, atheists are considered polytheists. It is not surprising to see that the Qur'an affirms that those who reject a creator "are not certain"[12] and describes those who reject monotheism as "fools"[13], which implies that polytheists and by extension atheists are irrational, imprudent and unwise. In summary, the Islamic description of atheism is that it is an unnatural worldview based on uncertainty and irrationality.

This definition of atheism is not neutral. It positively assumes the existence of a God or a creator. This is not unusual, as the Qur'an does not accept atheism to be the default position. The Divine book constantly refers to natural phenomena. These verses are used as a premise for the reader or listener to conclude that God is worthy of our worship because He created the universe with wisdom, purpose, precision and beauty. These verses also evoke an appreciation of God's majesty, power, glory, mercy and love. Although at least two verses directly address atheism (*see Chapter 5*), much of the Qur'an that pertains to the empirical world not only provides a basis for intellectual arguments, but serves as a powerful sign to conclude that the universe and everything within it was created with a Divine wisdom, power and purpose. This in turn should propel one's mind and soul to conclude that God is worthy of our worship and love (*see Chapter 15*). This Qur'anic strategy is a clear indication that atheism, and the related question *Does God exist?* is not the starting point; rather, it is the unnatural position that denies reality (*see Chapter 4*).

A brief history of atheism

In Islamic history

Atheism was not a major social and intellectual threat until the emergence of the 8th century Dahriyya. These thinkers were empiricists who believed that all knowledge could only be acquired via the empirical method. They believed that the cosmos was eternal and composed of four qualities, which were responsible for everything that existed. They argued that everything had always existed and did not require any creator or maker.[14]

According to *Kitab al-Aghani* by Faraj al-Isfahani, Abu Hanifa, the famous jurist and founder of one of the traditional schools of thought, debated a Dahri in the 8th century. Abu Hanifa was known to have intellectually hammered the Dahriyya in public debates (*see Chapter 8*). Many of the Islamic scholars responded to the claims of the Dahriyya, including Al-Ghazali, Ibn al-Jawzi, al-Jahiz, Muhammad b. Shabib, Ibn Qutayba, and Abu 'Isa al-Warraq.[15] In Al-Ghazali's book, *Kimiya'-yi sa'adat,* he describes the Dahriyya as reductionists who do not have a holistic understanding of the universe and its purpose. He asserts that they are like ants on a piece of paper that cannot lift their eyes from the ink or the pen they see before them, and fail to see who is writing.[16]

The Islamic history of atheism clearly shows an environment of intellectual discussion and debate, which could only have been facilitated by mutual respect and tolerance. The Qur'an makes it absolutely clear that having myriad beliefs is part of God's will, and that there should never be any form of compulsion but mutual respect and tolerance:

> "And had your Lord willed, those on Earth would have believed— all of them entirely. Then, would you compel the people in order that they become believers?"[17]

> "There is no compulsion in the religion."[18]

The Islamic thinker and scholar, Dr. Jaafar Idris, aptly summarises Islam's stance on other beliefs:

> "Existing peacefully with non-Islamic beliefs is an essential Islamic principle that is clearly stated in many Qur'anic verses, and that has been practiced by Muslims throughout their history. It is not something that Muslims impose on their religion or something that they have to resort to because of exceptional external circumstances. It is a requirement demanded by the nature of the religion...."[19]

The intellectual heritage of Islam should provide confidence for Muslims who are exposed to contemporary challenges that confront the rational foundations of their religion. Many of the answers to so-called new objections from atheist and secular thought have already been dealt with by Islam's classical scholarship. From this perspective, Muslims are standing on the shoulders of giants. Their only concern should be accessing that wealth of knowledge and learning how to contemporise it, using a language that is modern, relevant and applicable.

In the West

Atheism was not a popular movement in antiquity, and it did not have a substantial following. According to historians, all we have in this period are individuals (cases of exception) "who dared to voice [their] disbelief or bold philosophers who proposed intellectual theories about coming into existence of the gods without, normally, putting their theories into practice or rejecting religious practice altogether."[20] The first use of the term atheism can be traced back to the Greek scholar Sir John Cheke in a translation of Plutarch's *On Superstition*. In France during the 1600s, atheism inspired polemical writings and socio-political measures against its worldview.[21] Atheism was perceived as a threat even as early as the 1700s in Britain. The celebrated playwright and essayist Joseph Addison wrote a book titled *The Evidence of the Christian Religion,* which had a section against atheism. In this part of the book, he describes atheists in the following way:

"There is something so ridiculous and perverse in this kind of Zealots, that one does not know how to set them out in their proper colours. They are a sort of gamesters who are eternally upon the fret, tho' they play for nothing. They are perpetually teizing their friends to come over to them, though at the same time they allow that neither of them shall get anything by the bargain. In short, the zeal of spreading atheism is, if possible, more absurd than atheism itself... They are wedded to opinions full of contradiction and impossibility, and at the same time look upon the smallest difficulty in an article of faith as a sufficient reason for rejecting it...

I would fain ask one of these bigoted Infidels, supporting all the great points of Atheism, as the causal or eternal formation of the world, the mortality of thinking substance, the mortality of the Soul, the fortuitous organization of the Body, the motions and gravitations of matter, with the like particulars, were laid together and formed into a kind of Creed, according to the opinions of the most celebrated Atheists; I say, supporting such a Creed as this were formed, and imposed upon any one people in the world, whether it would not require an infinitely greater measure of faith, than any set of articles which they so violently oppose. Let me therefore advise this generation of Wranglers, for their own and for the public good, to act at least so consistently with themselves, as not to burn with Zeal for Irreligion, and with Bigotry for Non-sense."[22]

Addison's words, although colourful, indicate the kind of passionate and fierce discourse on religion in the 1700s. Although atheism was not a popular movement in Britain, the seeds of disbelief had already been planted and some of their fruits were already growing.

Although Addison's representation of atheism is a biased social commentary on the emerging discussions of his time, the 17th and 18th centuries were marked by significant intellectual achievements that paved the way for an academic type of scepticism and a form of non-dogmatic atheism. There were many philosophers and thinkers responsible for this. In 1689 the Polish thinker Kazimierz Lyszczynski denied the existence of God is his *De non existential dei*. Lyszczynski maintained that God is a creation of man and that humans created the concept of God to oppress others. In 1674 Matthias Knutzen, who had a large following across Europe, produced writings in support of atheism. In the 1700s the likes of David Hume and Voltaire presented arguments and ideas that would provide the necessary intellectual seeds for atheism to take root. Voltaire argued for deism, which is a philosophical and theological position which asserts that a single creator exists, but rejects the role of revelation and the authority of religious knowledge. David Hume wrote a corpus of material on the issue of God and religion. He argued that the idea of God was incomprehensible. He also contended the idea of God's necessary existence, and attempted to expose the weakness and limitations of the argument from design (*see Chapter 8*). Hume argued that the existence of evil and suffering in the world proved to be intellectually challenging. Echoing the ancient philosophers, his argument did not deny God; it did, however, question the degree of evil and our inability to justify it from a human perspective (*see Chapter 11*). Hume's attack on the religious idea of miracles had significant influence. He maintained that belief in miracles would only be rational if the probability of the eyewitnesses to be mistaken is greater than the probability of them occurring. Although this is not an exhaustive account of the thinkers, writers and philosophers that helped cement atheism in popular culture and academic discourse, it gives an insight to the history of rejecting the Divine in the West during that period.

During the 19th century, an important figure in the fight to make atheism acceptable was Charles Bradlaugh. A member of the British parliament, he fought a long battle to make atheism acceptable to society. Although he did not achieve his goals, by the end of the 19th century he paved the way for others to continue the battle for acceptability and respect.[23] Bradlaugh wrote many essays, including *Humanity's Gain from Unbelief*, *A Plea for Atheism* and *Doubts in Dialogue*.[24] Bradlaugh, a defender of scepticism and atheism, used his writings to remove "some of the many prejudices prevalent, not only against actual holders of Atheistic opinions, but also against those wrongfully suspected of Atheism".[25] Bradlaugh's activism was not solely focused on convincing British society to accept atheism; it was also dedicated to show that atheism makes humanity happier and increases the well-being of man. He wrote in his essay, *Humanity's Gain from Unbelief*, "As an unbeliever, I ask leave to plead that humanity has been a real gainer from scepticism, and that the gradual and growing rejection of Christianity—like the rejection of the faiths which preceded it—has in fact added, and will add, to man's happiness and well-being."[26]

The 1920s saw the emergence of the logical positivists. Inspired by achievements in science, this radical philosophical movement maintained that statements can only be meaningful if they can be verified empirically. They argued that if one utters a statement that refers to something that is beyond the reach of the senses, then it is nonsense. The logical positivists argued that there is nothing that transcends the physical world. Statements are either analytical or synthetic. Analytical statements are statements that are true by definition. For example, the statement 'the ball is red' is true because it is red. Synthetic statements are statements that are true by experience. For example, the statement 'the ball is bouncing' can be verified by looking at the ball bouncing. In light of this, the logical positivists created an empirical measure of meaning. This criterion essentially argues that for any statement to be meaningful, it must be verified by physical experience. For this reason, many questions pertaining to God, metaphysics, morality and history were considered meaningless. Therefore, atheism was the default position, as God could not be verified via physical experience.

Post 1960s saw the death of logical positivism. One of the key reasons for its demise was the fact that it was self-defeating. The logical positivists' criterion for meaning was that any statement had to be verified by physical experience; however, the criterion itself could not be verified by physical experience. Consequently, the criterion itself was meaningless.

After the demise of logical positivism, the academic world saw the intellectual resurrection of theism. *Time* magazine in 1980 commented on the rise of intellectual theism: "In a quiet revolution in thought and argument that hardly anybody could have foreseen only two decades ago, God is making a comeback. Most intriguingly, this is happening not amongst theologians or ordinary believers, but in the crisp intellectual circles of academic philosophers, where the consensus had long banished the Almighty from fruitful discourse."[27]

One reason for the intellectual revival of theism was the intriguing scientific discoveries of the mid-20th century. These include the 'Big Bang', which postulates a cosmic beginning to the universe. This was a departure from conventional thinking that postulated the universe was static and eternal, needing no creator (*see Chapter 5*). In the 1970s cosmologists discovered the intriguing phenomenon of fine-tuning, which explicitly demonstrated that the universe's laws and arrangement seemed designed and fine-tuned so that complex conscious life, like human beings, could exist (*see Chapter 8*). Near the beginning of the 20th century we had an utterly inadequate understanding of biology's nuts and bolts. We thought cells—the building blocks of organisms—were just homogenous blobs of protoplasm. In 1953, however, James Watson and Francis Crick demonstrated the double helix structure of DNA, the information-storage device of the cell. Following this discovery, the molecular biological revolution continued, unearthing more and more fascinating, sophisticated features at the microscopic level. Crick (even he was an atheist) was so impressed with the apparent design in the DNA that he became convinced that this could not have happened by chance, and that some sort of extra-terrestrial intervention was involved.[28] These discoveries and progresses in science, as well as their philosophical implications, progressively brought theism back onto the intellectual and academic discussion table. Today, theism is a perfectly respectable position.

To this date, numerous academic publications have attempted to answer the God question. This has trickled down to the popular level, where many books have been written on the topic. Social media has millions of posts on the issue.

The growth of Atheism

In spite of these factors, atheism is now one of the fastest-growing social and intellectual movements. The past twenty years have featured an increase in people who describe themselves as atheists or non-religious. This movement, also known as new atheism, has begun to articulate a case for atheism and secularism (generally considered the political manifestation of atheism). Modern atheist writers and academics, including Richard Dawkins, Sam Harris, Christopher Hitchens and Dan Dennet, have extensively promoted this movement. Their books have become bestsellers, and thousands have viewed their public lectures. However, some would argue that their rhetoric has been nasty, circular and quite unnuanced.

The late Christopher Hitchens argues "religion poisons everything"[29], Sam Harris asserts "the days of our religious identities are clearly numbered"[30] and Richard Dawkins maintains that God is "delusion".[31] Notwithstanding these similarities, atheists do not form a homogenous group. Certain atheist academics actually disagree with the new atheist discourse. For instance, the philosopher Tim Crane writes:

> "It seems to me that many of the claims made by the new atheists are simply not true, and that their view of the role of religion in world affairs is in many ways mistaken... going on in this way about

religion is not a very sensible approach to tackling the problems of the world... it is surprisingly difficult... to change people's beliefs. But if there is one thing which should be obvious here, it is that the way to do it is (generally) not to tell them that they are stupid, irrational or hopelessly ignorant."[32]

The prominent atheist philosopher Michael Ruse exclaimed, "I think Dawkins is ignorant of just about every aspect of philosophy and theology and it shows." Ruse does not hold back in assessing the success of the new atheists' strategies in addressing intelligent design and Christianity, describing them as:

"...absolute disasters in the fight against intelligent design—we are losing this battle... what we need is not knee-jerk atheism but serious grappling with the issues—neither of you are willing to study Christianity seriously and to engage with the ideas—it is just plain silly and grotesquely immoral to claim that Christianity is simply a force for evil, as Richard claims—more than this, we are in a fight, and we need to make allies in the fight, not simple alienate everyone of good will."[33]

Despite 'internal' fighting, the new atheist movement has been very successful in promoting its ideas and worldview. In England and Wales, 25.1% of the people describe themselves as having no religion, with a substantial increase on UK campuses.[34] In Europe, 46% of the people do not believe in the traditional concept of God, and 20% state that they do not believe there is a spirit, God or life force.[35] Half of Chinese people consider themselves atheists.[36] Professor of Sociology Phil Zuckerman argues that atheism in many societies is growing.[37] He also asserts that atheists come in fourth place after the main world religions: "...finally, nonbelievers in God as a group come in fourth place after Christianity (2 Billion), Islam (1.2 Billion), and Hinduism (900 Million) in terms of global ranking of commonly held belief systems."[38]

The Muslim world is not immune to this growing social movement. According to Win-Gallup International, 5% of Saudis consider themselves convinced atheists, and over 19% consider themselves non-religious.[39] The

Arab world has seen a rise in atheism with more books on the topic being translated into the Arabic language. Muslims in the West are facing similar problems. There is an increase in apostasies, with apostates declaring themselves as atheists. This problem manifests itself at different levels of the Muslim community, but an immense change is occurring on university campuses. The popularisation of atheist publications and social media, coupled with aggressive and fervent activism, has created an environment of intellectual challenge and peer pressure. A Muslim on campus who is not equipped with the adequate spiritual, intellectual and theological tools to address these challenges can be misguided onto the irrational path of denying the Divine.

One of the main reasons that I have written this book is to provide people with these tools to show that Islamic theism is coherent and true, and atheism is an intellectual mirage.

Chapter 2
Life Without God
The Implications of Atheism

Atheism is not simply an intellectual position that exists in a bubble. If its claims are true, then one would have to make some inevitable existential and logical conclusions that are very bleak. Under atheism, life is ludicrous. The following discussion may not provide a rational case for God, nor does it follow that God exists simply because life without God seems absurd. However, it does provide the fertile ground in which the rational arguments in this book take root.

As discussed in Chapter 1, most atheists are philosophical naturalists who hold that there is no supernatural and everything in the universe can be explained in reference to physical processes. Atheism combined with philosophical naturalism is a recipe for existential disaster. The formula is simple: no God, which includes the associated concepts of Divine accountability, equals no hope, value, purpose, or eternal happiness.[40] This conclusion is not an outdated religious cliché; it is a result of thinking rationally about the logical and existential implications of atheism.

No hope

Hope is defined as the feeling or expectation and desire for something to happen. We all hope for good lives, good health and a good job. Ultimately, we all hope for an immortal blissful existence. Life is such an amazing gift that no one really wants his or her conscious existence to end. Similarly, everyone desires that there will be some form of ultimate justice where wrongs are made right, and the relevant people will be held accountable. Significantly, if our lives are miserable, or experience pain and suffering, we hope for some peace, pleasure and ease. This is a reflection of the human spirit; we hope for light at the end of the dark tunnel, and if we have tranquillity and joy, we want to keep it that way.

Since atheism denies the Divine and the supernatural, it also rejects the concept of an afterlife. Without that, there can be no hope of pleasure following a life of pain. Therefore, the expectation for something positive to happen after our lives is lost. Under atheism we cannot expect any light at the end of the dark tunnel of our existence. Imagine you were born in the third world and spent your whole life in starvation and poverty. According to the atheist worldview, you are merely destined for death. Contrast this with the Islamic perspective: all instances of suffering that happen in our lives are for some greater good. Therefore, in the larger scheme of things, no pain or suffering we undergo is meaningless. God is aware of all our sufferings, and He will provide recompense (*see Chapter 11*). According to atheism, however, our pains are as meaningless as our pleasure. The immense sacrifices of the virtuous and the distress of the victim are falling dominoes in an indifferent world. They occur for no greater good and no higher purpose. There is no ultimate hope of an afterlife or any form of happiness. Even if we lived a life of pleasure and immense luxuries, most of us would inevitably be doomed to some form of evil fate or an incessant desire for more pleasure. The pessimist philosopher Arthur Schopenhauer aptly described the hopelessness and ill fate that awaits us:

> "We are like lambs in a field, disporting themselves under the eye of the butcher, who chooses out first one and then another for his prey. So it is that in our good days we are all unconscious of the evil fate may have presently in store for us—sickness, poverty, mutilation, loss of sight or reason... No little part of the torment of existence lies in this, that Time is continually pressing upon us, never letting us take breath, but always coming after us, like a taskmaster with a whip. If at any moment Time stays his hand, it is only when we are delivered over to the misery of boredom... In fact, the conviction that the world and man is something that had better not have been, is of a kind to fill us with indulgence towards one another. Nay, from this point of view, we might well consider the proper form of address to be, not *Monsieur, Sir, mein Herr*, but *my fellow-sufferer, Socî malorum, compagnon de miseres*!"[41]

The Qur'an alludes to this hopelessness. It argues that a believer cannot despair; there will always be hope, and hope is connected to God's mercy, and God's mercy will manifest itself in this life and the hereafter:

"Certainly no one despairs of God's Mercy, except the people who disbelieve."[42]

Under atheism, justice is an unachievable goal—a mirage in the desert of life. Since there is no afterlife, any expectation of people being held to account is futile. Consider Nazi Germany in the 1940s. An innocent Jewish lady who just saw her husband and children murdered in front of her has no hope for justice when she is waiting for her turn to be cast into the gas chamber. Although the Nazis were eventually defeated, this justice occurred *after* her death. Under atheism she is now nothing, just another rearrangement of matter, and you cannot give reprieve to something that is lifeless. Islam, however, gives everyone hope for pure Divine justice. No one will be treated unfairly and everyone shall be taken to account:

> "On that Day, people will come forward in separate groups to be shown their deeds: whoever has done an atom's weight of good will see it, but whoever has done an atom's weight of evil will see that."[43]

> "God created the heavens and the Earth for a true purpose: to reward each soul according to its deeds. They will not be wronged."[44]

Atheism is like a mother giving her child a toy and then taking it back for no reason. Life, without a doubt, is a wonderful gift. Yet any pleasure, joy and love we have experienced will be taken away from us and lost forever. Since the atheist denies the Divine and the hereafter, it means that the pleasures we have experienced in life will disappear. There is no hope of a continuation of happiness, pleasure, love and joy. However, under Islam, these positive experiences are enhanced and continued after our worldly life:

> "They will have therein whatever they desire and We have more than that for them."[45]

> "The people who lived a pious life will have a good reward and more...."[46]

"Verily, the dwellers of Paradise that Day, will be busy in joyful things... (It will be said to them): *'Salāmun'* (Peace be on you), a Word from the Lord, Most Merciful."[47]

No value

What is the difference between a human and a chocolate bunny? This is a serious question. According to many atheists who adopt a naturalistic worldview, everything that exists is essentially a rearrangement of matter, or at least based on blind, non-conscious physical processes and causes.

If this is true, then does it really matter?

If I were to pick up a hammer and smash a chocolate bunny and then I did the same to myself, according to naturalism there would be no real difference. The pieces of chocolate and the pieces of my skull would just be rearrangements of the same stuff: cold, lifeless matter.

The typical response to this argument includes the following statements: "we have feelings", "we are alive", "we feel pain", "we have an identity" and "we're human!" According to naturalism these responses are still just rearrangements of matter, or to be more precise, just neuro-chemical happenings in one's brain. In reality everything we feel, say or do can be reduced to the basic constituents of matter, or at least some type of physical process. Therefore, this sentimentalism is unjustified if one is an atheist, because everything, including feelings, emotions or even the sense of value, is just based on matter and cold physical processes and causes.

Returning to our original question: *What is the difference between a human being and a chocolate bunny?* The answer, according to the atheist perspective, is that there is no real difference. Any difference is just an illusion—there is no ultimate value. If everything is based on matter and prior physical causes and processes, then nothing has real value. Unless, of course, one argues that what matters is matter itself. Even if that were true, how could we appreciate the difference between one arrangement of matter and another? Could one argue that the more complex something is, the more value it has? But why would that be of any value? Remember, nothing has been purposefully designed or created, according to atheism. It is all based on cold, random and non-conscious physical processes and causes.

The good news is that the atheists who adopt this perspective do not follow through with the rational implications of their beliefs. If they did, it would be depressing. The reason that they attribute ultimate value to our existence is because their innate dispositions, which have been created by God, have an affinity to recognise God and the truth of our existence (*see Chapter 4*).

From an Islamic point of view God has placed an innate disposition within us to acknowledge our worth, and to recognise fundamental moral and ethical truths (*see Chapter 9*). This disposition is called the *fitrah* in Islamic thought (*see Chapter 4*). Another reason we can claim ultimate value is because God created us with a profound purpose, and preferred us to most of His creation. We have value because the One who created us has given us value.

"Now, indeed, We have conferred dignity on the children of Adam... and favoured them far above most of Our creation."[48]

"Our Lord! You have not created all this without purpose."[49]

Islam values the good and those who accept the truth. It contrasts those who obey God and thereby do good, and those who are defiantly disobedient, and thereby do evil: "Then is one who was a believer like one who was defiantly disobedient? They are not equal."[50]

Since naturalism rejects the hereafter and any form of Divine justice, it rewards the criminal and the peacemaker with the same end: death. We all meet the same fate. So what ultimate value do the lives of Hitler or Martin Luther King Jr. really have? If their ends are the same, then what real value does atheism give us? Not much at all.

However, in Islam, the ultimate end of those who worship God and are compassionate, honest, just, kind and forgiving is contrasted with the end of those who persist with their evil. The abode of the good is eternal bliss and the abode of the evil is Divine alienation. This alienation is a consequence of consciously denying God's mercy and guidance, which inevitably results in spiritual anguish and torment. Clearly, Islam gives us ultimate value. However, under atheism, value cannot be rationally justified except as an illusion in our heads.

Despite the force of this argument, some atheists still object. One of their objections involves the following question: *Why does God give us ultimate value?* The answer is simple. God created and transcends the universe, and He has unlimited knowledge and wisdom. His names include The-Knowing and The-Wise. Therefore, what He values is universal and objective. Another way of looking at it is by understanding that God is the maximally perfect Being, which means He is free from any deficiency and flaw. Therefore, it follows that what He values will be objective and ultimate, because this objectivity is a feature of His perfection.

Another objection argues that even if we were to accept that God gives us ultimate value, it would still be subjective, as it would be subject to His perspective. This contention is premised on a misunderstanding of what subjectivity means. It applies to an individual's limited mind and/or feelings. However, God's perspective is based on unlimited knowledge and wisdom. He knows everything; we do not. The classical scholar Ibn Kathir states that God has the totality of wisdom and knowledge; we have its particulars. In other words: God has the picture, we merely have a pixel.

Seyyed Hossein Nasr, Professor of Islamic studies at George Washington University, provides an apt summary of the concept of human rights and dignity—which ultimately refer to value—in the absence of God:

> "Before speaking of human responsibilities or rights, one must answer the basic religious and philosophical question, 'What does it mean to be human?' In today's world everyone speaks of human rights and the sacred character of human life, and many secularists even claim that they are true champions of human rights as against those who accept various religious worldviews. But strangely enough, often those same champions of humanity believe that human beings are nothing more than evolved apes, who in turn evolved from lower life forms and ultimately from various compounds of molecules. If the human being is nothing but the result of 'blind forces' acting upon the original cosmic soup of molecules, then is not the very statement of the sacredness of human life intellectually meaningless and nothing but a hollow sentimental expression? Is not human dignity nothing more than a conveniently contrived notion without basis in reality? And if we are nothing but highly organized inanimate particles, what is the basis for claims to 'human rights'? These basic questions know no

geographic boundaries and are asked by thinking people everywhere."[51]

We have value, but what value does the world have?

If I were to put you in a room with all your favourite games, gadgets, friends, loved ones, food and drink, but you knew that in five minutes you, the world and everything in it would be destroyed, what value would your possessions have? They wouldn't have any at all. However, what is five minutes or 657,436 hours (equivalent to 75 years)? It is mere time. Just because we may live for 75 years does not make a difference. In the atheist worldview it will all be destroyed and forgotten. This is also true for Islam. Everything will be annihilated. So in reality the world intrinsically has no value; it is ephemeral, transient and short-lived. Nonetheless, from an Islamic perspective the world has value because it is an abode for getting close to God, good deeds and worship, which lead to eternal paradise. So it is not all doom and gloom. We are not on a sinking ship. If we do the right thing, we can gain God's forgiveness and approval.

> "There is terrible punishment in the next life as well as forgiveness and approval from God; so race for your Lord's forgiveness...."[52]

No purpose

> "I do not know why we are here, but I'm pretty sure that it is not in order to enjoy ourselves."[53]

These are the words of influential philosopher Ludwig Wittgenstein. Like many philosophers, he did not have an answer to the question: *What is the purpose of life?* But he did indicate that life is not just a game. Other people, however, have argued that the question is false. There may be nothing we should be bothered about. We should carry on living and not worry about why we are here. The Nobel Prize winner Albert Camus explained this attitude in the following way: "You will never live if you are looking for the meaning of life"[54]. Camus was basically saying that the important thing is to live a life that works for you, regardless of any truth behind your existence.

In light of these differing views, we must ask: *is it reasonable to believe we have a purpose?* To help answer this question, let us take the following illustration into consideration:

You are probably reading this book sitting on a chair, and you are wearing some clothes. So I would like to ask you a question: *For what purpose?* Why are you wearing the clothes, and what purpose does the chair have? The answers to these questions are obvious. The chair's purpose is to allow us to sit down by supporting our weight, and our clothes fulfil the purpose of keeping us warm, hiding our nakedness and of course making us look aesthetically pleasing. Our clothes and the chair are lifeless objects with no emotional or mental abilities, and we attribute purpose to these. Yet some of us do not believe we have a purpose for our own existence. Naturally, this seems absurd and counter-intuitive.

Having a purpose for our lives implies that there is a reason for our existence—in other words, some kind of intention and objective. Without a purpose we have no reason to exist, and we lack a profound meaning for our lives. This is the perspective of naturalism. It dictates that we merely spring from prior physical processes. These are blind, random and non-rational. The logical conclusion of this indifferent view on our existence is that we are riding on a sinking ship. This metaphorical ship is our universe because, according to scientists, this universe is heading towards its inevitable demise and will suffer what they call a 'heat death'. Human life will be destroyed prior to this heat death as the Sun will eventually obliterate the Earth.[55] Therefore, if this ship is going to sink, I ask you, what is the point of reshuffling the deck chairs or giving a glass of milk to the old lady? The Qur'an represents humanity's intuitive stance on this issue: "Our Lord! You have not created all this without purpose."[56]

Nevertheless, various disputes emerge from this discussion. First, an atheist can argue that a purposeless worldview gives us more freedom to create purpose for ourselves. To further explain, some of the existentialists have argued that our lives are based on nothing, and from this nothingness we can create a new realm of possibilities for our lives. This rests on the idea that everything is intrinsically meaningless, and therefore we have the freedom to create meaning for ourselves in order to live fulfilling lives. The flaw with this approach is that we cannot really escape meaning. Denying purpose for the basis of our existence while attributing some made-up purpose to our lives is, by definition, self-delusion. It is no different in saying, "Let's pretend to have purpose."

Another disagreement consists of the Darwinian claim that our purpose is to propagate our DNA; as the famous atheist Richard Dawkins proposes in his book, *The Selfish Gene*, our bodies have developed to do just that.[57] The problem with this view is it relegates our existence to a random accident via a lengthy biological process. This renders the human nothing more than a by-product, an incidental being that emerged via the random collision of particles and the random rearrangement of molecules.

Islam's view on the purpose of our lives is intuitive and empowering. It elevates our existence from products of matter and time to conscious beings who choose to have a relationship with the One who created us (*see Chapter 15*). Atheism and naturalism provide no ultimate purpose for our existence.

No happiness

"[A]nd a happy future belongs to those who are mindful of Him."[58]

The pursuit of happiness is an essential part of our human nature. All of us want to be happy—even when sometimes we cannot pinpoint exactly what 'happiness' is. This is why if you were to ask the average person why they want to get a good job, they would probably reply, "To earn enough to live comfortably". However, if you questioned them further and asked why they want to live comfortably they would more than likely say, "Because I want to be happy". If you then asked them, "Why do you want to be happy?" They would be stuck for an answer, because happiness is ultimately an end, not a means. It is the final destination, not necessarily the journey. We all want to be happy, and there is no reason why we want to be happy other than happiness itself. This is why we endlessly seek ways to help us achieve that final happy state.

The journey that people seek varies from one person to the next. Some dedicate years to adding qualifications and career credentials to their names. Others work tirelessly in gyms to achieve a perfect figure. Those who desire the love of family often end up sacrificing their lives to the care of their spouse and children, while some party their weekends away with friends, seeking a release from the relentless cycle of work. The list is endless. It begs the question: *What is true happiness?*

To help answer this question, imagine the following scenario: While reading this, you are sedated against your will. Suddenly you wake up and find yourself on a plane. You're in first class. The food is heavenly. The seat is a flatbed, designed for a luxurious, comfortable experience. The entertainment is limitless. The service is out of this world. You start to use all of the excellent facilities. Time starts to pass. Now think for a moment, and ask yourself the question: *Would I be happy?*

How could you be? You would need some questions answered first. Who sedated you? How did you get on the plane? What is the purpose of the journey? Where are you heading? If these questions remained unanswered, how could you be happy? Even if you started to enjoy all of the luxuries at your disposal, you would never achieve true happiness. Would a frothy Belgian chocolate mousse on your dessert tray be enough to drown out the questions? It would be a delusion, a temporary, fake type of happiness, only achieved by deliberately ignoring these critical questions.

Now apply this to your life and ask yourself, *am I happy?* Our coming into existence is no different from being sedated and thrown on a plane. We never chose our birth, our parents or where we come from. Yet some of us do not ask the questions or search for the answers that will help us achieve our ultimate goal of happiness.

Where does true happiness lie? Inevitably, if we reflect on the previous example, happiness really lies in answering key questions about our existence. These include: *What is the purpose of life? Where am I heading after my death?* In this light, our happiness lies in our inwardness, in knowing who we are, and finding the answers to these critical questions.

Unlike animals, we cannot be content by reacting to our instincts. Obeying our hormones and mere physical needs will not answer these questions and bring happiness. To understand why, reflect on another example: Imagine you were one of 50 human beings locked in a small room with no exit. There are only 10 loaves of bread, and there is no more food for another 100 days. What do you all do? If you follow your animalistic instincts, there will be blood. But if you try to answer the question, *how can we all survive?* it is likely that you will, because you will devise ways to do so.

Extend this example to your life. Your life has many more variables, which can result in almost an infinite number of outcomes. Yet some of us just follow our carnal needs. Our jobs may require Ph.Ds. or other qualifications, and we may wine and dine with our partners, but all of that is still reduced to the mere instincts of survival and procreation. Happiness cannot be achieved unless we find out who we really are and search for answers to life's critical questions.

However, under naturalism these questions do not have any real answers. *Why are we here?* No reason at all. *Where are we going?* Nowhere. We will just face death. We all need to answer the fundamental question of why we are here. In Islam, the answer is simple yet profound. We are here to worship God (*see Chapter 15*).

But worship in Islam is quite different from the common understanding of the word. Worship can be shown in every act that we do. The way we walk and talk to each other, the small acts of kindness we do each day. If we focus on pleasing God by our actions, then our actions become an act of worship.

Worship is not merely limited to directing our acts of worship to God alone, like the spiritual acts of prayer and fasting. Worshipping God also means loving, obeying and knowing Him. Worshipping God is the ultimate purpose of our existence; it frees us from the 'slavery' to others and society. God, in the Qur'an, presents us with a powerful example:

"God puts forward this illustration: can a man who has for his masters several partners at odds with each other be considered equal to a man devoted wholly to one master? All praise belongs to God, though most of them do not know."[59]

Inevitably, if we do not worship God, we end up worshipping other 'gods'. Think about it. Our partners, our bosses, our teachers, our friends, the societies we live in, and even our own desires 'enslave' us in some way. Take, for example, social norms. Many of us define beauty based on social pressures. We may have a range of likes and dislikes, but these are shaped by others. Ask yourself, why are you wearing these trousers or this skirt? Saying you like it is a shallow response; the point is, *why* do you like it? If we keep on probing in this way, many will end up admitting "because other people think it looks nice". Unfortunately, we've all been influenced by the endless adverts and peer pressure that bombard us.

In this respect we have many 'masters' and they all want something from us. They are all 'at odds with each other', and we end up living confused, unfulfilled lives. God, who knows us better than we know ourselves, who loves us more than our mothers love us, is telling us that He is our true master, and only by worshipping Him alone will we truly free ourselves.

The Muslim writer Yasmin Mogahed explains in her book, *Reclaim Your Heart,* that anything other than God is weak and feeble, and that our freedom lies in worshipping Him:

"Every time you run after, seek, or petition something weak or feeble... you too become weak or feeble. Even if you do reach that which you seek, it will never be enough. You will soon need to seek something else. You will never reach true contentment or satisfaction. That is why we live in a world of trade-ins and upgrades. Your phone, your car, your computer, your woman, your man, can always be traded in for a newer, better model. However, there is a freedom from that slavery. When the object upon which you place all your weight is unshaking, unbreakable, and unending, you cannot fall."[60]

The next question is: *Where are we going?* We have a choice: to embrace God's eternal, unbounded mercy, or to run away from it. Accepting His mercy, by responding to His message, and obeying, worshipping and loving Him will facilitate our eternal happiness in paradise. Rejecting and running away from God's mercy necessitates that we end up in a place devoid of His love, a place of unhappiness—hell. So we have a choice. Either we decide to embrace His mercy or try to escape from it. We have the free will to choose. Even though God wants good for us, He does not force us to make the right choices. The choices we make in this life will shape our lives after we die:

"...and when that Day comes, no soul will speak except by His permission, and some of them will be wretched and some happy."[61]

"There they will stay—a happy home and resting place!"[62]

Since our ultimate purpose is to worship God, we must establish our natural balance to find out who we really are. When we worship God, we free ourselves, and find ourselves. If we do not, we are forgetting what makes us human (*see Chapter 15*):

"And be not like those who forgot God, so He made them forget themselves."[63]

In summary, atheism cannot provide profound answers for our existence, and therefore real happiness can never be achieved. If someone argues that they are happy under atheism, I would argue it is a drunken type of happiness. They only sober up when they start thinking deeply about their own existence. Even if they have attempted to find the answers and have settled with not knowing—or being sceptical about the available responses—they will still not achieve ultimate happiness. Compare the person who knows why they exist and where they are going with the one who does not. Their conditions are not the same, even if they both claim to be happy.

This chapter has clearly shown the logical implications of denying God. While atheists are emotionally justified in believing their lives have a sense of ultimate value, hope, happiness and purpose, the point is clear: intellectually they are groundless. Even Richard Dawkins appreciates the logical implications of naturalism. He argues that under naturalism, everything is meaningless and based on pitiless indifference:

"On the contrary, if the universe were just electrons and selfish genes, meaningless tragedies like the crashing of this bus are exactly what we should expect, along with equally meaningless *good* fortune. Such a universe would be neither evil nor good in intention. It would manifest no intentions of any kind. In a universe of blind physical forces and genetic replication, some people are going to get hurt, other people are going to get lucky, and you won't find any rhyme or reason in it, nor any justice. The universe we observe has precisely the properties we should expect if there is, at bottom, no design, no purpose, no evil and no good, nothing but blind, pitiless indifference."[64]

A universe made up of non-rational, blind, cold physical stuff is not concerned with our emotions. Only God can provide the intellectual justification for the things that define our humanity.

Chapter 3
Adversaries of Reason
Why Atheism is Irrational

Imagine you are a taxi-driver and one day you receive a call to pick up two passengers from the train-station. You are quite close so you arrive before the scheduled time. The passengers' train arrives and after a few moments they get into your car. You exchange greetings and then you ask them where they want to go. They request that you take them to their office, which is about 9 miles away. You start the car and begin to drive. After some time you drop them off at their office.

Now rewind the story. Imagine that just after the passengers get into your car, you put on a blindfold. In this scenario, would you be able to drive your passengers to their destination? The answer is obvious. You could never drive them to their destination because you are blind; you cannot see because of the blindfold. However, what if you insisted that you could drive your vehicle with your blindfold on? Wouldn't your passengers describe you as irrational, if not insane?

The taxi-driver who can see represents Islamic theism, and the taxi-driver who has a blindfold on represents atheism.

Introducing the argument

Before I explain why the taxi-drivers in this story are analogies of atheism and Islamic theism, let me provide you with some essential background information. Both Muslims and atheists assume that they have the ability to reason. This means that we are able to form mental insights. We "see" our way to a conclusion in our minds. Our minds take premises or statements and "drive" them to a mental destination; in other words, a logical conclusion. This is a key feature of a rational mind.

So why is atheism like a taxi-driver with a blindfold on? Most forms of atheism imply philosophical naturalism, which demands that reason (and everything else) must only be explained via blind, non-rational, physical processes. However, just as you cannot drive passengers to their office with a blindfold on, physical processes that are blind can never "drive" any premises in our minds to a mental destination. Therefore, atheism is in effect equivalent to rejecting reason itself, because it invalidates its own assumption. Our ability to reason simply does not fit within the naturalistic worldview, because rationality cannot come from blind, non-rational physical processes. To maintain that it can is the same as believing that something can come from nothing. From this perspective atheism is irrational. Atheism invalidates the thing that it claims to use to deny God: reason.

So why is Islamic theism like a taxi-driver who can see? Our ability to form mental insights fits within Islamic theism because this ability makes sense (i.e. is explained adequately) if it was given to us by the Creator Who is All-Seeing, The-Knowing and The-Wise. A thing cannot give rise to something if it does not contain it, or if it does not have the ability (or the potential) to give rise to it. In other words, rationality can only come from rationality. This is why our ability to form mental insights can come from the Creator.

The argument in this chapter asserts that our ability to reason is assumed by both atheists and theists. This assumption, however, fits nicely within Islamic theism and does not fit or make sense under atheism. Therefore, it would only be rational to accept Islamic theism over atheism. This chapter will examine these assertions in detail.

However, before I elaborate, the dialogue below is a summary of what will be discussed in this chapter:

Atheist: "There is no evidence for the existence of God. Belief in God is irrational."

Muslim: "That's an interesting assertion. Before we continue, can I ask you, do you believe that you have rational faculties? In other words, do you believe you can reason?"

Atheist: "Obviously. Any rational person would deny God. There's simply no evidence."

Muslim: "Okay, great. So can I ask, how do you explain your rational faculties under atheism?"

Atheist: "What do you mean?"

Muslim: "Well, do you believe all phenomena can be explained via physical stuff? And do you believe that there is no supernatural?"

Atheist: "Sure."

Muslim: "Physical stuff is just blind and non-rational. So how can rationality come from non-rationality? How can anything arise from something that does not contain it or have the potential to give rise to it? How can we form mental insights based on blind physical processes? In this light, how can you explain your ability to reason?"

Atheist: "Well, we have a brain that has evolved."

Muslim: "Okay, and according to atheism an evolved brain is based on physical stuff too, no?"

Atheist: "Yes, but our brains have evolved to be rational, because the more you know about the world the more likely you are to survive."

Muslim: "That's not true; holding non-rational beliefs about the world can lead to survival too."

Atheist: "So what? We both assume reason to be true, so it's not an issue."

Muslim: "Well, for me it isn't. But under atheism your ability to reason does not make sense. Atheism has invalidated the very assumption that it claims to use to deny God. So it is absurd to be an atheist since atheism nullifies reason itself."

Atheist: "No, you have to prove God to me first."

Muslim: "That's a cop-out, because your use of the word 'proof' assumes your ability to reason. However, you are not justified in making such an assumption because rationality is nullified under atheism. Rationality cannot come from non-rationality. From this perspective, atheism is irrational. However, rationality can come from rationality. This is why Islamic theism explains best why we can use our reason, as it came from the Creator Who is All-Seeing, The-Knowing and The-Wise."

What is reason?

In the context of this argument, reason refers to the fact that we have rational faculties. We can acquire truth, we desire to discover, and we can infer, induce and deduce. A significant aspect of our rational faculties is the ability to come to a logically valid conclusion. When we reason logically, our conclusions will be based on our rational insight; we see that the conclusion follows. This "seeing" cannot be established empirically. In other words, we have a mental insight that the conclusion follows logically; it is logically connected to its previous premises.

Deductive arguments are a good example to explain our rational insights. Deductive arguments are where the premises guarantee the truth of the conclusion. A deductive argument is *valid* if its conclusion follows necessarily from its premises. It is *sound* if it is valid and its premises are true or rationally acceptable.

Consider the following deductive argument:

1. All bachelors are unmarried men.
2. John is a bachelor.
3. Therefore, John is an unmarried man.

We know that (3) necessarily follows from (1) and (2) based on our insight. We are also justified in believing in the truth of premises (1) and (2). Nothing in the physical world can prove why (3) is connected to the previous premises; in other words, why it logically follows. You may never have met John before and you may never have had contact with a bachelor. However, your rational faculties perceive that the conclusion follows necessarily from these premises, regardless of any of your physical experiences. Reason clearly has a transcendent dimension.

To drive this point home, consider the following deductive argument:

1. John has observed 5 modifus.
2. The 5 modifus John has observed are yellow.
3. Therefore, some modifus at least must be yellow.

This is a valid argument; the conclusion necessarily follows from the premises. John has observed 5 yellow modifus, so it necessarily follows that at least some modifus must be yellow (whether they are all yellow or not, if there are more than 5 modifus in existence, is not deducible from these premises; either is possible). Given premises (1) and (2), (3) must follow. However, why do we agree that the conclusion (3) necessarily follows from these premises? Why do we believe in the logical validity of the conclusion, although we have no idea what a modifu is? (By the way, I have made the word up). It is because the logical flow of the argument occurs in our minds regardless of any personal inferences we might ever have formed from our own experiences. We have achieved an insight into conclusion (3) without any external, material data. We have achieved an insight into something that is not based on our experience (we do not know what a modifu is). In actual fact, if the word "yellow" was replaced with "zellow" (another made-up word), the conclusion would still necessarily follow; some modifus (at least 5) must be zellow.

Not only have our minds come to a conclusion that is not based on any external evidence; our minds have also directed and driven our insight to conclude that (3) must follow from (1) and (2). Our minds have taken premises (1) and (2) and driven or directed our insight to conclude (3). However, being driven or directed to a mental destination or endpoint is not a characteristic of a physical process. Physical processes are blind, random and have no intentional force directing them anywhere. This means that we cannot use physical processes to account for our ability to achieve an insight into a conclusion.

Reason: an assumption of science

The human mind has a distinctive quality; we can distinguish between right and wrong, truth and falsehood, beauty and vileness. This clearly separates us from animals. Our mental abilities have enabled us to progress and advance. In fact, we must trust our rational faculties before we can even begin to conduct science. One of science's key assumptions is that our minds have the ability to reason. Without such an assumption we could never use words such as evidence, fact, truth and proof.

The human practice of science rests on the assumption that we can reason. This means that the existence of reason cannot be fully accounted for by any type of scientific explanation. For example, when a scientist attempts to address a testable hypothesis or an answerable question, there is an assumption that the results can be rationalised. Scientists also accept that they have the ability to assess the logical validity of a scientific explanation. This obviously assumes that the scientist can use her reason before she performs any science.

This does not mean that science cannot provide any partial explanation at all for our ability to reason. However, it is unable to justify reason from a foundational point of view. Attempting to demonstrate how reason emerged via some physical process does nothing to explain its transcendent dimension. This includes the ability to come to a logically valid conclusion that is determined by an insight in one's mind. This is why relying solely on a scientific explanation is inadequate: it fails to account for the fact that we see the conclusion in our minds, without it being based on anything we can verify empirically. Science can only deal with what can be observed in some way. Since science requires reason in order to begin to explain reason, to argue that it can somehow justify our ability to reason would be tantamount to arguing in a circle. Science is a useful tool to help us understand the world, but it has many limitations (*see Chapter 12*).

At this point one might argue that assumptions do not need to be explained or accounted for, because assumptions are taken to be true without evidence. This is a valid point. However, there is a difference between valid and invalid assumptions. For an assumption to be valid it must make sense to the concept or theory that it supports. However, if an assumption that aims to support a worldview cannot fit within that worldview, then the assumption cannot be presumed. For example, science rests on the notion that there is "consistency in the causes that operate the natural world"[65]. If scientists were to always conclude that physical causes are inconsistent, then that assumption would need to be dismissed or changed. If philosophical naturalism (and even science) maintains that reason can be explained via random, non-rational physical processes, then how can an atheist—who adopts naturalism—account for such an assumption when it clearly cannot fit within the perspective of naturalism? Naturalism actually denies reason, because rationality cannot come from non-rational physical processes. Mental insights cannot come from blind physical processes. Therefore, atheists must change their worldview or dismiss the idea that we are rational.

Under atheism we cannot justify our rational faculties

Most atheists are philosophical naturalists; naturalism asserts that there is no supernatural, and that physical processes can explain all phenomena. According to naturalism, if we probe the most basic levels of reality we see that everything is the result of blind, random, non-rational physical processes; subatomic particles, atoms and molecules are whizzing around without any direction, guidance or intended outcome. Physical stuff has no purpose; nothing is intentionally driving these physical processes. If this is the case, though, how can we claim our minds have the ability to achieve mental insights? How can we claim the ability to reach a conclusion? A key part of being able to reason is to have rational insights, to see in one's mind that something logically follows from something else. This is where naturalism fails, as it asserts that all phenomena are based on random, non-rational physical processes.

The ability to take premises and "drive" them towards a mental destination is invalidated if one postulates that the ability comes from blind, non-rational physical processes. A thing cannot give rise to something if it does not contain it, or if it does not have the ability (or the potential) to give rise to it. For example, I cannot give you $500 if I do not have the money, and I cannot raise the amount if I am jobless with bad credit (this principle will be used throughout this book). Likewise, if physical processes do not contain rationality, then how do they give rise to it? Physical processes by definition do not contain rationality, and they do not have "insight". They cannot see the conclusion that follows from an argument. Physical processes are not purposefully or intentionally driven or directed. Therefore, to even suggest that rationality can come from non-rational physical processes is exactly the same as believing that something can come from nothing.

Consider the following example. Similar to the story at the beginning of this chapter, imagine there are two bus-drivers. The first has good eyesight and is an experienced driver. The second bus-driver is blind and inexperienced. The first driver starts his journey and picks up two people called "Premise 1" and "Premise 2". Their final destination is "Conclusion". He sees the destination on his map and as the journey is coming to an end he clearly observes the final stop. The second driver is escorted to his bus at the bus station. Waiting on the bus are "Premise 1" and "Premise 2". Their destination is the same as in the first scenario. The driver manages to start the bus. However, do you think he will reach the destination? Just like the taxi-driver with the blindfold, he will never reach the final destination. Physical processes suffer the same problem. They are blind. They cannot explain reason because a feature of rationality is the ability to derive insight or reach a conclusion, and one cannot obtain insight from something that is blind. To assert such a thing is the equivalent of saying something can arise from nothing.

From this perspective, atheism—because of its naturalistic perspective—is not only irrational, but an adversary of reason. It invalidates the thing that is required to make any claim about God: reason itself. Since rationality cannot come from non-rationality, it follows that naturalism cannot explain our ability to reason.

Despite this argument, there are a few possible objections. These will be discussed at the end of this chapter. However, one key objection argues that computer programmes have the ability to reason deductively: computer programmes are made up of physical stuff; therefore, physical processes can explain rationality. This contention will be addressed in detail at the end of this chapter. However, the main point is that computer programmes do not have "insights"; in particular, they do not have *meaningful* insights. Human rationality involves the ability to establish meaningful conclusions. The very fact that we can question the implications or the meaning of a conclusion (even if we do not know its meaning, as in the case of the modifus above) indicates that human rationality involves meaningful insights. Computer programmes do not have these meaningful insights. In actual fact, a computer system is based on syntactical rules (the manipulation of symbols), not on semantics (meaning). This will be explained further later.

Can Darwinian evolution justify our rational faculties?

According to naturalists our minds have evolved to be rational. Naturalists argue that it was advantageous for our ancestors to have known the truth about their environments. Having an ability to distinguish between truth and falsehood was necessary for their survival. Despite the fact that naturalism invalidates the assumption that we have the ability to reason, Darwinian evolution seems a plausible explanation on the surface.

However, when we scratch a little deeper we run into a myriad of problems. Even Charles Darwin himself had his doubts about this matter. He understood that our ability to acquire truth could not be accounted for if it had only evolved from lower life-forms. He wrote in a letter in 1881: "But then with me the horrid doubt always arises whether the convictions of man's mind, which has been developed from the mind of the lower animals, are of any value or at all trustworthy. Would anyone trust in the convictions of a monkey's mind, if there are any convictions in such a mind?"[66]

Now let's see whether naturalistic evolution can provide a lifejacket with which to rescue human rationality. When we use the term *naturalistic evolution*, we are referring to the idea that the evolutionary process is free from Divine intervention; according to this idea, our minds evolved to be rational because our ability to reason and attain true beliefs is necessary for survival. There are several problems with this claim. Firstly, our ability to distinguish between truth and falsehood is not a requirement for survival. Secondly, achieving mental insights is also not a requirement for our continual existence. Evolution is about the ability to survive, not about the ability to make logically valid conclusions. Finally, our ability and desire to discover—which is a necessary feature of a rational mind—is often detrimental to our survival.

One of the key features of our rational minds is their ability to attain truth and discard what is false. We also have mental insights, and the ability to see a conclusion based on previous premises. These are the very processes we use when we engage in science. Now the question to ask is: *Can naturalistic evolution account for these abilities?* The answer is no. All we need to do in order to disprove this idea is show that false beliefs can lead to survival. In that case, there is no need for the evolutionary process to result in rational faculties.

So can false beliefs result in survival? It does not take long to work out that countless false beliefs do. An individual who believes that all insects with red markings on their bodies are poisonous will avoid all insects with red markings and survive. However, this belief is false, as many insects with red on their bodies are harmless, the common ladybird being the most obvious example. Someone else might avoid all fungi because he or she believes they are poisonous, and by doing so survive. However, we know that some fungi, like button mushrooms, are completely healthy and nutritious to eat. Professor of Philosophy Anthony O'Hear provides a similar example to show that evolution can produce false rather than true beliefs, thereby showing that non-rational beliefs can lead to survival:

"A bird may avoid caterpillars with certain types of colouring because they are poisonous; but it will also avoid non-poisonous caterpillars with similar colours, and may be credited with a false belief about the poisonousness of the harmless caterpillar. Of course, the survival chances of the bird are increased by its avoidance of the caterpillar type which includes both noxious and harmless caterpillars. Having a false belief, then, about a particular caterpillar will be a by-product of a survival-producing disposition. Given that the harmless caterpillars have evolved through mimicry of the poisonous ones, we have here an evolutionary explanation of falsehood, reinforcing the general point that there is no direct way of moving from evolutionary workings to truth."[67]

Our desire to discover also poses a problem for evolution. There is no need for evolution to result in abilities that allow us to understand the laws of physics or engage in mathematics. It just does not make sense that we should end up with minds that have the ability to understand the universe. Cockroaches and beetles survive extremely well, and have done so for millions of years, yet we do not see them sitting over coffee discussing the existential and logical implications of atheism (or anything else, either).

Think about this for a moment: Imagine a rocket containing 500,000 kilogrammes of fuel, about to be blasted into space at 17,500 miles per hour. What drives an astronaut to board this shuttle, unknowing of whether or not he will return or even reach space? Is this desire to explore and discover conducive to his survival? What drives a climber to ascend Mount Everest, enduring cold and harsh conditions, not knowing if he will reach the summit? Isn't he designed to put his survival first? What drives a monk to isolate himself, remain celibate and devote himself to discovering inner peace? Does not this go completely against survival and reproduction? Indeed, the desire to discover is powerful in humans and in many cases overrides our desire to survive. We see many cases of people cutting themselves off from the very things that are conducive to their survival, and in doing so achieve true happiness and peace.

So how can we explain our desire to discover, resulting in activities that are detrimental to survival? The answer is, we cannot. These desires do not make sense if one adopts naturalistic evolution. In conclusion, our higher levels of rationality and desire to learn often lead us to spend time in 'superfluous' activities which do not aid survival and reproduction, such as art, spirituality, philosophy or designing novel contraceptive techniques. Natural selection should have eliminated all of these, because such behaviours have no adaptive benefits. Because the Darwinian evolutionary mechanism explains only "survival and reproduction", it cannot account for our ability to reason, nor for its most conspicuous characteristic: the desire to discover.

It should be clear from these two problems that the Darwinian theory of evolution, which is geared towards survival, not truth, is an inadequate explanation of our ability to reason and desire to discover. Academics have recognised these problems and have made some startling remarks. Biologist John Gray states:

> "If the human mind has evolved in obedience to the imperatives of survival, what reason is there for thinking that it can acquire knowledge of reality, when all that is required in order to reproduce the species is that its errors and illusions are not fatal? A purely naturalistic philosophy cannot account for the knowledge that we believe we possess."[68]

DNA discoverer Francis Crick said, "Our highly developed brains, after all, were not evolved under the pressure of discovering scientific truths, but only to enable us to be clever enough to survive and leave descendants."[69]

Cognitive scientist Steven Pinker wrote, "Our brains were shaped for fitness, not for truth. Sometimes the truth is adaptive, but sometimes it is not."[70]

Although Sam Harris, outspoken atheist and neuroscientist, believes that science will eventually give us answers, he admits that "...our logical, mathematical, and physical intuitions have not been designed by natural selection to track the Truth."[71]

In summary, when atheists claim to have used their rational faculties to prove that God does not exist, it is a form of intellectual hypocrisy. To account for the fact that they have a rational mind, they have to deny atheism or deny reason itself. The intellectual irony is that their ability to reason is best explained by the existence of God.

Islamic theism: the best explanation

I could not give you a loaf of bread if I did not have one in the first place or if I did not have the ability to obtain or make one. This is based on the following rational principle: A thing cannot give rise to something else if it does not contain it, or if it does not have the ability to give rise to it. For instance, non-rational forces cannot give rise to rationality, as they do not contain it in the first place. Physical processes are non-rational because they do not have any "insight". They cannot see a conclusion following from previous premises. God makes sense of the fact that we have rational minds, because rationality *can* come from the Creator Who is All-Seeing, The-Knowing and The-Wise. If in the beginning of the universe there had been only non-rational, blind, random, physical matter and processes, then no matter how they were arranged they could not give rise to rationality. However, if in the beginning there was a creator with the names and attributes mentioned above, it follows that the universe can contain conscious beings with the ability to reason. From this perspective, atheists actually need God to account for their rational faculties. Therefore, the existence of a Creator Who is All-Seeing, The-Knowing and The-Wise is the best explanation for a universe with conscious organisms who have the ability to reason.

Islamic theism provides a beautiful and simple answer to the main questions raised in this chapter. God created us and gave us rational minds with a desire to discover in order to aid us in fulfilling our purpose. One way God does this is by directing us towards His creation, wherein lie His signs (i.e. clues, hints, indications). By pondering and reflecting over these signs we can appreciate His majesty and creative power, for which appreciation and acknowledgement then naturally lead us to worship Him (*see Chapter 15*).

God via His knowledge, power and will created the universe and our minds, hence explaining our ability to reason and discover the interconnecting principles of the cosmos. This brings to mind a beautiful verse of the Qur'an: God says, "We will show them Our signs in the horizons and within their own selves until it becomes clear to them that it is the truth. But is it not sufficient concerning your Lord that He is over all things a Witness?"[72]

God continuously encourages us to ponder, to use our minds:

"Then do they not reflect upon the Qur'an, or are there locks upon [their] hearts?"[73]

"So will you not reason?"[74]

These verses signify that we have the ability to reason and ponder on the natural world to attain truth. God also says in the Qur'an: "Indeed, in the creation of the heavens and the Earth and in the alternation of the night and the day are signs for the people of understanding."[75]

From this we can draw a comprehensive conclusion. God gave us rational minds and the desire to discover so that we can use our rational faculties to understand the universe in all its beauty, which in turn leads us to worship the One Who created it (*see Chapter 15*). God placed within us the very tools required for us to engage in disciplines such as science, yet the irony is that when some of us find this God-given gift, they use it to challenge God Himself (*see Chapter 12*).

There are some key objections to this argument that will be addressed below.

God of the gaps

The "god of the gaps" objection asserts that a gap in scientific knowledge about a particular phenomenon should not give rise to belief in God's existence, or reference to Divine activity, because science will eventually progress far enough to provide an explanation. This objection cannot be applied to the argument presented in this chapter because it does not address a gap within scientific knowledge; it addresses the foundations of science. The ability to reason is required *before* any science can take place. To argue that science will eventually explain its own assumptions is tantamount to arguing in a circle. This discussion is beyond the realm of science, as we are discussing the foundational assumptions of science itself. Hence the "god of the gaps" objection is in this case misplaced.

This is a presuppositional argument

Presuppositionalism is a form of argument that asserts that we cannot account for reason without the Christian worldview. The assertion maintains that you cannot use reason if it is unaccounted for. However, the atheist can—and rightly does—throw the argument back at the Christian. The atheist can ask why the Christian believes he has accounted for his ability to reason. If the Christian replies that the Christian worldview accounts for his ability to reason, then the atheist is within his right to ask how, and the argument can go round in circles.

The argument in this chapter is not a presuppositional one. It accepts the assumption that we have the ability to reason, and it does not argue that before you use your reason you need to account for your ability to reason. The argument answers the question: *Given that we accept the fact that we can reason, what worldview best explains our ability to do so?* It argues that the best way to explain our ability to reason is by God's existence, and that naturalism—and by extension, atheism—invalidates the assumption that we have the ability to reason. Therefore, atheism must be rejected.

Rationality can arise out of complexity

Emergent materialists argue that a system of complex physical processes undergoing complex interactions can give rise to properties or phenomena that do not exist in the individual components that comprise the system. The emergent materialist will cite the history of science: when something was deemed 'mysterious' it was later demystified when the underlying complex processes were understood. Therefore, the emergent materialist responds to the argument from reason by postulating that our ability to reason—more specifically, the ability to achieve an insight into a conclusion—is based on complex processes in the brain. Once these processes are understood, our ability to reason will have been explained.

A common example that emergent materialists cite is water, H_2O. Water is made up of hydrogen and oxygen, which are gases, yet when combined chemically they form the life-sustaining liquid. Water has properties that hydrogen and oxygen do not. Examples like these provide the emergent materialist with the confidence to argue that a property can arise from a system of complex processes even though it is not present in the components of that system. Nevertheless, this example is misplaced because the argument articulated in this chapter is not a case of a physical thing bringing into existence another physical thing (like gases hydrogen and oxygen giving rise to water's physical properties). On the contrary, what requires explaining is a nonphysical property (having a mental insight into a conclusion) arising from physical ones (blind physical processes). If the complex processes that underpin brain-activity were understood, and all of their causal interactions were mapped out, how would that explain our ability to reason? It would still not answer the question: *How can we acquire truth using our ability to form insights with minds allegedly based on prior blind, random, physical processes?*

To simply refer to complexity does not explain anything, and it is tantamount to saying "it just happens". It seems to me that emergent materialism is a weak attempt to fill the gap created by a naturalistic worldview (Chapter 7 explains how emergent materialism cannot explain subjective conscious experiences).

The wider implication of adopting emergent materialism is that we allow theories that cannot explain the physical relations or processes of a system. If one argues that complexity can explain new properties—without explaining how they emerge—then why should we expect a theory to explain anything? Merely waiting for our scientific understanding to improve is not an argument. This is equivalent to explaining to a trainee builder that you can build a house by having many bricks. This is not true; other things are also required to build a house, such as cement, a design, bricklayers, plumbers, electricians, tools, etc. In conclusion, emergent materialism is not a coherent theory; it is an incoherent attempt to fill the gap left by naturalism.

Computers are rational; therefore, physical processes can explain rationality

A common objection to the argument that rationality cannot arise from physical processes is the alleged ability of computer programmes to engage in deductive reasoning. A key feature of rationality is that, in a valid deductive argument, a conclusion necessarily follows. Since computer programmes are based on physical processes and exhibit a key feature of rationality, physical processes can account for our ability to reason, the argument goes. This is another misplaced contention. As highlighted in this chapter, human reasoning is based on having mental insight. Computer programmes cannot "see" anything. Humans not only have insights; our insights are also meaningful. We have the ability to understand and question the meaning of the conclusions we come to. Computer programmes are not characterised as having meaningful insights. Computer programmes are based on syntactical rules (the manipulation of symbols), not semantics (meaning).

To understand the difference between semantics and syntax, consider the following sentences:

- I love my family.
- αγαπώ την οικογένειά μου.
- আমি আমার পরিবারকে ভালবাসি.

These three sentences mean the same thing: *I love my family*. This refers to semantics, the meaning of the sentences. But the syntax is different. In other words, the symbols used are unalike. The first sentence is using English 'symbols', the second Greek, and the last Bangla. From this the following argument can be developed:

1. Computer programmes are syntactical (based on syntax).
2. Minds have semantics.
3. Syntax by itself is neither sufficient for, nor constitutive for semantics.
4. Therefore, computer programmes by themselves are not minds.[76]

Imagine that an avalanche somehow arranges mountain rocks into the words *I love my family*. It would be absurd to say that the mountain knows what the arrangement of rocks (symbols) means. This indicates that the mere manipulation of symbols (syntax) does not give rise to meaning (semantics).[77]

Computer programmes are based on the manipulation of symbols, not meanings. Likewise, I cannot know the meaning of the sentence in Bangla just by manipulating the letters (symbols). No matter how many times I manipulate the Bangla letters, I will not be able to understand the meaning of the words. This is why for semantics we need more than the correct syntax. Computer programmes work on syntax and not on semantics. Computers do not know the meaning of anything.

Professor John Searle's Chinese Room thought-experiment is a powerful way of showing that the mere manipulation of symbols does not lead to an understanding of what they mean:

"Imagine that you are locked in a room, and in this room are several baskets full of Chinese symbols. Imagine that you (like me) do not understand a word of Chinese, but that you are given a rule book in English for manipulating the Chinese symbols. The rules specify the manipulation of symbols purely formally, in terms of their syntax, not their semantics. So the rule might say: 'Take a squiggle-squiggle out of basket number one and put it next to a squiggle-squiggle sign from basket number two.' Now suppose that some other Chinese symbols are passed into the room, and that you are given further rules for passing back Chinese symbols out of the room. Suppose that unknown to you the symbols passed into the room are called 'questions' by the people outside the room, and the symbols you pass back out of the room are called 'answers to questions.' Suppose furthermore, that the programmers are so good at designing the programs and that you are so good at manipulating the symbols, that very soon your answers are indistinguishable from those of a native Chinese speaker. There you are locked in your room shuffling your Chinese symbols and passing out Chinese symbols in response to incoming Chinese symbols... Now the point of the story is simply this: by virtue of implementing a formal computer program from the point of view of an outside observer, you behave exactly as if you understood Chinese, but all the same you do not understand a word of Chinese."[78]

In the Chinese Room thought-experiment the person inside the room is simulating a computer. Another person manages the symbols in a way that makes the person inside the room seem to understand Chinese. However, the person inside the room does not understand the language; they merely imitate that state. Professor Searle concludes:

> "Having the symbols by themselves—just having the syntax—is not sufficient for having the semantics. Merely manipulating symbols is not enough to guarantee knowledge of what they mean."[79]

The objector might respond to this by arguing that although the computer programme does not know the meaning, the whole system does. Professor Searle has called this objection "the systems reply"[80]. However, why is it that the programme does not know the meaning? The answer is simple: it has no way of assigning meaning to the symbols. Since a computer programme cannot assign meaning to symbols, how can a computer system—which relies on the programme—understand the meaning? You cannot produce understanding just by having the right programme. Searle presents an extended version of the Chinese Room thought-experiment to show that the system as a whole does not understand the meaning: "Imagine that I memorize the contents of the baskets and the rule book, and I do all the calculations in my head. You can even imagine that I work out in the open. There is nothing in the 'system' that is not in me, and since I don't understand Chinese, neither does the system."[81]

Atheism does not—and cannot—have a monopoly on reason. It is a shame that there is a growing perception that atheists are rational and that atheism is based on reason. Nothing could be further from the truth. Blind, random physical processes cannot account for our ability to reason. This is why atheism invalidates the very thing it claims to use to reject the Divine. However, according to Islamic theism, we live in a rational universe created by the All-Seeing, The-Wise and The-Knowing Creator, who gave us the ability to reason. This is coherent and accounts fully for our rational faculties; nothing else will (indeed, nothing else can). Maintaining that blind, random physical processes can make sense of our ability to see, think and learn is irrational. Those who persist in this thinking are in fact adversaries of reason. They are no different from a taxi-driver putting on a blindfold and insisting that he can drive his passengers to their destination.

Chapter 4
Self-Evident
Why Atheism Is Unnatural

Imagine one evening you receive a call from David, one of your old school friends you used to sit next to during science lessons. You haven't spoken to him for years, but you remember the weird questions he used to ask you. Although you found him pleasant, you were not a fan of his ideas. Reluctantly you answer the phone. After a brief exchange of greetings, he invites you to have lunch with him. You half-heartedly accept his invitation. During lunch he asks, "Can I tell you something?" You reply positively, and he begins to express to you something that you haven't heard before: "You know, the past—like what you did yesterday, last year, and all the way back to your birth—didn't really happen. It's just an illusion in your head. So my question to you is, do you believe the past exists?" As a rational person you do not agree with his assertion and you reply, "What evidence do you have to prove that the past does not exist?"

Now rewind the conversation, and imagine you spent the whole meal trying to prove that the past is something that really happened.

Which scenario do you prefer?

The reason you prefer the first scenario is because you—like the rest of the reasonable people out there—regard the reality of the past as a self-evident truth. As with all self-evident truths, if someone challenges them, the burden of proof is on the one who has questioned them.

Now let's apply this to a theist-atheist dialogue.

A theist invites his atheist friend for dinner, and during the meal the atheist asserts, "You know, God does not exist. There's no evidence for his existence." The theist replies with a barrage of different arguments for God's existence. However, has the theist adopted the right strategy? Before we present a positive case for God's existence, shouldn't we be probing why questioning God's existence is the assumed default question? It shouldn't be: *Does God exist?* Rather, it should be: *What reasons do we have to reject*

His existence? Now, do not get me wrong. I believe we have many good arguments that support a belief in God, and these are discussed in this book. The point I am raising here is that if there are no arguments against God's existence, then the rational default position is the belief in the Divine. Otherwise, it would be tantamount to questioning the reality of the past without any good reason to do so. From this perspective atheism is unnatural.

Self-evident truths

We consider many beliefs to be self-evidently true. This means the belief can be described as natural or true by default. Some of them include:

- The uniformity of nature
- The law of causality
- The reality of the past
- The validity of our reasoning
- The existence of other minds
- The existence of an external world

When someone questions these truths, we do not blindly accept their conclusions, and we usually reply, "What evidence do you have to reject them?"

These truths are self-evident because they are characterised by being:

- **Universal:** Not a product of a specific culture, they are cross-cultural.
- **Untaught:** Not based on information transfer. They are not acquired via information external to your introspection and senses. In other words, they are not learnt via acquiring knowledge.
- **Natural:** Formed due to the natural functioning of the human psyche.
- **Intuitive:** The most easy and simple interpretation of the world.

Let's apply the above features to the belief that the past is real.

The reality of the past is a self-evident truth because it is universal, untaught, natural and intuitive. It is a universal truth because most—if not all—cultures have a belief in the past, from a point of view that the past was once the present. The belief in the past is also untaught because when someone first realises that the past was an actual state of affairs, it is not based on someone telling them or any type of learning. No one grows up being told by his or her parents that the past was real. This belief is acquired via their own experience. The reality of the past is also natural. People with normal rational faculties agree that the past consists of things that happened. Finally, the belief that the past once happened is the simplest interpretation of our experiences and it is based on an innate understanding of the world. To claim that the past is an illusion raises more problems than it solves.

God: a self-evident truth

Just like the belief that the past was once the present, the existence of God is also a self-evident truth. What is meant by 'God' in this chapter is the basic concept of a creator, a nonhuman personal cause or designer. It does not refer to a particular religious conception of a deity or God. The following discussion explains why the belief in this basic idea of God is universal, untaught, natural and intuitive.

Universal

The basic underlying idea of a creator, or a supernatural cause for the universe, is cross-cultural. It is not contingent on culture but transcends it, like the belief in causality and the existence of other minds. For example, the idea of other people having minds exists in all cultures, a belief held by most rational people. The existence of God or a supernatural cause is a universally held belief and not the product of one specific culture. Different conceptions of God are held in various cultures, but this does not negate the basic idea of a creator or nonhuman personal cause.

In spite of the number of atheists in the world, the belief in God is universal. A universal belief does not mean every single person on the planet must believe in it. A cross-cultural consensus is enough evidence to substantiate the claim that people universally believe in God's existence. Evidently, there are many more theists than atheists in the world, and this has been the case from the beginning of recorded history.

Untaught

Self-evident truths do not need to be taught or learnt. For example, for me to know what spaghetti is, I require information of western cuisine and Italian culture. I cannot know what spaghetti is merely by reflecting on it. By contrast, you do not require any information, whether from culture or education, to know a creator for things exists. This may be the reason why sociologists and anthropologists argue that even if atheist children were stranded on a desert island, they would come to believe that something created the island.[82] Our understanding of God differs, but the underlying belief in a cause or creator is based on our own reflections.

Some atheists exclaim, "Believing in God is no different than believing in the spaghetti monster". This objection is obviously false. Self-evident truths do not require external information. The idea that monsters exist, or even that spaghetti exists, requires information transfer. No one acquires knowledge of monsters or spaghetti by their own intuitions or introspection. Therefore, the spaghetti monster is not a self-evident truth; thus, the comparison with God cannot be made. Diverting our attention from the context of this chapter, this objection also fails, as there are many good arguments for God's existence and no good arguments for the existence of a spaghetti monster.

Natural

Belief in some type of supernatural designer or cause is based on the natural functioning of the human psyche. The concept of God's self-evident existence has been a topic of scholarly discussion in the Islamic intellectual tradition. The classical scholar Ibn Taymiyyah explained that "affirmation of a Maker is firmly-rooted in the hearts of all men... it is from the binding necessities of their creation...."[83] The 12th century scholar Al-Raghib al-Asfahani similarly asserts that knowledge of God "is firmly-rooted in the soul".[84] As well as the Islamic position, a wealth of research in various fields supports the conclusion that we are meant to see the world as created and designed.

Psychological evidence

The academic Olivera Petrovich conducted research concerning the origins of natural things, such as plants and animals, and she found that pre-schoolers were about seven times more likely to say God created them rather than humans.[85] In her popular interviews, including private correspondence I have had with her, Petrovich concludes that the belief in a non-anthropomorphic God seems to be natural, and that atheism is an acquired cognitive position.[86] Petrovich is publishing a book called *Natural-Theological Understanding from Childhood to Adulthood* in 2017 that will address this issue further. Psychologist Paul Bloom argues that recent findings in cognitive psychology indicate that two key aspects of religious belief—belief in designer, and belief in mind-body dualism—are natural to young children.[87] In the article *Are Children 'Intuitive Theists'?* Professor Deborah Kelemen explored research that suggested young children have a propensity to think about natural objects in terms of purpose and intention. Although more research is required and it only tentatively suggests evidence to support 'intuitive theism', Kelemen's summary further indicates the conclusions we have been discussing in this chapter:

> "A review of recent cognitive developmental research reveals that by around 5 years of age, children understand natural objects as not humanly caused, can reason about non-natural agents' mental states, and demonstrate the capacity to view objects in terms of design. Finally, evidence from 6- to 10-year-olds suggests that children's assignments of purpose to nature relate to their ideas concerning intentional nonhuman causation. Together, these research findings suggest that children's explanatory approach may be accurately described as intuitive theism."[88]

Recent research by Elisa Järnefelt, Caitlin F. Canfield and Deborah

Kelemen, titled *The divided mind of a disbeliever: Intuitive beliefs about nature as purposefully created among different groups of non-religious adults,* concluded that there is a natural propensity to see nature as designed.[89] This conclusion was grounded in three studies. Study 1 was based on a sample of 352 North American adults. The sample included religious and non-religious participants. The procedure involved a speeded creation task which was "a picture-based procedure devised to measure adults' automatic and reflective tendencies to endorse natural phenomena as purposefully made by some being"[90]. The participants were randomly assigned either to a speeded or an unspeeded condition. All of the participants were presented with 120 pictures on a computer. They were then to judge whether "any being purposefully made the thing in the picture" and respond yes or no by pressing the relevant keys on a keyboard.[91] Study 2 was based on 148 North American adults "who were recruited via the email lists of atheist and other explicitly non-religious associations and organizations"[92]. The same speeded creation task of Study 1 was given to the participants in Study 2. Study 3 was based on 151 Finnish atheist adults "recruited via the email lists of student associations and organizations all around Finland"[93]. This group was given a similar speeded created task. The results were fascinating. In their discussion the academics conclude that atheists saw things as purposefully made:

"Consistent with Study 1 and Study 2, Study 3 revealed that non-religious participants in Nordic Finland, where non-religiosity is not an issue and where theistic cultural discourse is not present in the way it is in the United States, default to viewing both living and non-living natural phenomena as purposefully made by a non-human being when their processing is restricted. Interestingly, comparisons across the different groups of non-religious participants in all three studies showed that, despite the absence of prominent theistic cultural discourse, non-religious Finnish participants were more likely than North American atheists to fail in suppressing their overall level of creation endorsement. This pattern of results shows that ambient theistic cultural discourse is therefore not the only factor that explains people's tendency to endorse purposeful creation in nature."[94]

The general conclusions of this research include the fact that the results "lend empirical support to the proposal that religious non-belief is cognitively effortful"[95] and that "the current findings suggest that there is a deeply rooted natural tendency to view nature as designed".[96] In other words, non-belief is intellectually exhausting, and seeing things as designed is part of what makes us human. The study suggests that theism is innate. However, as with most research, "many questions remain regarding possible connections between these early developing design intuitions".[97]

Much more research is required in both cognitive and developmental psychology to form any definitive conclusions. However, the above studies support the view that the belief in God is natural.

Some objectors may cite research that suggests that children from religious backgrounds have difficulty distinguishing between reality and fantasy at a young age. This research cannot undermine the aforementioned conclusions because the studies only focused on religious narratives and not the concept of things requiring a designer or creator.[98] Even so, the fact that religious children may have difficulty distinguishing between reality and fiction is still metaphysically neutral, because to suggest that it supports atheism rather than theism assumes that atheism is true and theism is fiction. Such research would not invalidate the findings mentioned above. It must be pointed out that some of the research I have presented above has cross-cultural implications, which means that regardless of the participants' theist and atheist backgrounds, they had a tendency to have theist-like intuitions.

Another contention includes that since some of the research shows that atheism is cognitively effortful—which implies that more thought is required—then it indicates that it is the most rational position. This objection is based on a false inference. The evidence can also suggest that atheism requires adopting false assumptions about the physical world (*see Chapter 12*); hence it becomes mentally taxing as a result.

I have not included all of the relevant research here. The discussions can be quite complex and although there are contradictory studies, they are—in my view—less conclusive. The main objective of this discussion is to show a growing trend in the research that supports the view that the belief in God's existence is natural.

Sociological and anthropological evidence

Professor Justin Barrett's research in his book, *Born believers: the science of children's religious belief,* looked at the behaviour and claims of children. He concluded that the children believed in what he calls "natural religion". This is the idea that there is a personal Being that created the entire universe. That Being cannot be human—it must be divine, supernatural:

> "Scientific research on children's developing minds and supernatural beliefs suggests that children normally and rapidly acquire minds that facilitate belief in supernatural agents. Particularly in the first year after birth, children distinguish between agents and non-agents, understanding agents as able to move themselves in purposeful ways to pursue goals. They are keen to find agency around them, even given scant evidence. Not long after their first birthday, babies appear to understand that agents, but not natural forces or ordinary objects, can create order out of disorder... This tendency to see function and purpose, plus an understanding that purpose and order come from minded beings, makes children likely to see natural phenomena as intentionally created. Who is the Creator? Children know people are not good candidates. It must have been a god... children are born believers of what I call natural religion...."[99]

Intuitive

The existence of a creator is the most intuitive interpretation of the world. It is easy to understand without explicit instruction. Human beings have an affinity to attribute causes to things all the time, and the entire cosmos is one of those things (*see Chapters 5 and 6*). Not all intuitions are true, but evidence is required to make someone depart from their initial intuitions about things. For example, when someone perceives design and order in the universe, the intuitive conclusion is that there is a designer (*see Chapter 8*). To make that person change their mind, valid evidence is required to justify the counter-intuitive view.

The belief in a God, creator, designer or supernatural cause is a self-evident truth. It is universal, untaught, natural and intuitive. In this light, the right question to ask is not: *Does God exist?* The right question should be: *Why do you reject God's existence?* This way you will have turned the tables and rightly so; atheism is unnatural. The onus of proof is on someone who challenges a self-evident truth. When someone claims that the past is an illusion or that other people do not have minds, he or she would have to shoulder the burden of proof. Atheists are no different. They have to justify their rejection of a cause or creator for the universe.

The innate disposition: *fitrah*

God as a self-evident truth relates to the Islamic theological concept concerning the *fitrah*. The word comes from the Arabic trilateral stem *fa ta ra* (ف ط ر), which relates to words such as *fatrun* and *fatarahu*, meaning a created or made thing. From a lexical point of view, the *fitrah* refers to something that has been created within us by God. Theologically, the *fitrah* is the natural state or the innate disposition of the human being that has been created by God with innate knowledge of Him and with the affinity to worship the Divine.[100] This is based on the authentic statement of the Prophet Muhammad ﷺ which states, "every child is born in a state of *fitrah*. Then his parents make him a Jew, a Christian or a Magian...."[101]

This Prophetic tradition teaches that every human being has this innate disposition, but external influences such as parenting and by extension society—change the human being into someone who adopts beliefs and practices that are not in line with the innate knowledge of God. There have been numerous scholarly discussions on the concept of the *fitrah*. For example, the 11th century theologian Al-Ghazali argues that the *fitrah* is a means that people use to acquire the truth of God's existence and that He is entitled to our worship. He also maintained that knowledge of God is something "every human being has in the depths of his consciousness".[102] Ibn Taymiyya, the 14th century scholar, describes the innate disposition as something God created within His creation that contains ingrained knowledge of God: "...the existence of a perfect Creator is known from the *fitra*, and this knowledge is ingrained, necessary, and obvious."[103]

In spite of the fact that the *fitrah* is a natural state, it can be 'veiled' or 'spoiled' by external influences. These influences, as indicated by the above Prophetic tradition, can include parenting, society and peer pressure. These influences can cloud the *fitrah* and prevent someone from acknowledging the truth. Ibn Taymiyya argues that when the natural state is clouded with other influences, the person may require other evidences for God's existence:

"Affirmation of a Creator and His perfection is innate and necessary with respect to one whose innate disposition remains intact, even though alongside such an affirmation it has many other evidences for it as well, and often when the innate disposition is altered... many people may be in need of such other evidences."[104]

These other evidences can include rational arguments. Ibn Taymiyya was not a strong advocate of rational arguments for God's existence. He maintained that the *fitrah* was the main way of affirming the Divine. However, he did not dismiss sound rational proofs for God's existence.[105] Nevertheless, these rational arguments must conform to Islamic theology and not adopt premises that contradict it.

From the perspective of Islamic epistemology, it is important to know that conviction in the existence of God is not solely inferred from some type of inductive, deductive, philosophical or scientific evidence. Instead, these evidences awaken and uncloud the *fitrah* so the human being can recognise the innate knowledge of God. The truth of God's existence and the fact that He is worthy of our worship is already known by the *fitrah*. However, the *fitrah* can be clouded by socialisation and other external influences. Therefore, the role of rational arguments is to 'remind' us of the truth that we already know. To illustrate this point imagine I am cleaning my mother's loft. As I move old bags around and throw away unwanted objects I find my favourite toy that I used to play with when I was 5 years old. I am reminded about something that I already have knowledge of. In my mind I think, "Oh yeah. I remember this toy. It was my favourite." The truth of believing in God and the fact that He is worthy of our worship is no different. Rational arguments serve as spiritual and intellectual awakenings to realise the knowledge that is contained in our *fitrah*.

Other ways the *fitrah* can be unclouded include introspection, spiritual experiences, reflection and pondering. The Qur'an promotes questioning and thinking deeply about things:

"Thus do We explain in detail the signs for who give thought."[106]

"Indeed in that is a sign for a people a people who give thought."[107]

"Or were they created by nothing? Or were they the creators [of themselves]? Or did they create the heavens and the Earth? Rather, they are not certain."[108]

Islamic epistemology views rational arguments as means and not ends. They serve as a way of awakening or unclouding the *fitrah*. This is why it is very important to note that guidance only comes from God, and no amount of rational evidence can convince one's heart to realise the truth of Islam. God makes this very clear: "Indeed, you do not guide whom you like, but God guides whom He wills. And He is most knowing of the [rightly] guided."[109] Guidance is a spiritual matter that is based on God's mercy, knowledge and wisdom. If God wills that someone is guided through rational arguments, then nothing will stop that person from accepting the truth. However, if God decides that someone does not deserve guidance—based on a Divine wisdom—then regardless of how many cogent arguments that are presented, that person will never accept the truth.

To conclude, the belief in God's existence is a self-evident truth. As with all self-evident truths, when someone challenges them, the onus of proof is on them. The only way the belief in God can be undermined is if there is any positive evidence for the non-existence of the Divine. However, as this book will show, the few arguments that atheists have against the existence of God are weak and philosophically shallow (*see Chapters 11 and 12*). The self-evident truth of God was addressed in the Qur'an over 1,400 years ago:

"Can there be doubt about God, Creator of the heavens and Earth?"[110]

To end this chapter, Islamic scholar Muhammad Salih Farfur aptly explains that God's existence is in line with our natural disposition:

"Indeed, the first sense in the depth of a person if he contemplates within himself and in the world around him is the sense of a higher power that reigns over the world with the command to dispose over life and death, creation and annihilation, motion and stillness and all the different types of meticulous changes that occur in it. Unequivocally, mankind senses this reality and believes in it deeply, regardless of whether one is able to produce evidence to verify the truth of this feeling or is unable. This is a natural instinct or the natural disposition of mankind, which is indeed a precise and exact evidence... In addition, we feel in ourselves the presence of compassion, love, hate, encouragement and dislike, though what is the proof that it exists, even while it flutters within us? Is one able to bring forth evidence more than that which he feels and senses, and yet it is real without doubt? One feels excitement and senses pain, yet is one unable to establish evidence to prove it exists with more than what he feels? Without doubt, this is the natural way [*fitrah*] or instinct on which mankind has been created, and these are the deep feelings that have been embedded within us. They are not within us for no reason or in vain, rather it is a natural truth that corresponds to the world."[111]

Chapter 5
A Universe from Nothing?
The Qur'an's Argument for God

Imagine you find yourself sitting in the corner of a room. The door that you entered through is now completely sealed and there is no way of entering or exiting. The walls, ceiling and floor are made up of stone. All you can do is stare into open, empty space, surrounded by cold, dark and stony walls. Due to immense boredom you fall asleep. A few hours pass by; you wake up. As you open your eyes, you are shocked to see that in the middle of the room is a desk with a computer on top of it. You approach the desk and notice some words on the computer screen: *this desk and computer came from nothing.*

Do you believe what you have read on the screen? Of course you do not. At first glance you rely on your intuition that it is impossible for the computer and the desk to have appeared from no prior activity or cause. Then you start to think about what could possibly have happened. After some thought you realise a limited number of reasonable explanations. The first is that they could have come from no causal conditions or prior activity—in other words, nothing. The second is that they could have caused or created themselves. The third is that they could have been created or placed there by some prior cause. Since your cognitive faculties are normal and in working order, you conclude that the third explanation is the most rational.

Although this form of reasoning is universal, a more robust variation of the argument can be found eloquently summarised in the Qur'an. The argument states that the possible explanations for a finite entity coming into being could be that it came from nothing, it created itself, it could have been created by something else created, or it was created by something uncreated. Before I break down the argument further, it must be noted that the Qur'an often presents rational intellectual arguments. The Qur'an is a persuasive and powerful text that seeks to engage its reader. Hence it positively imposes itself on our minds and hearts, and the way it achieves this is by asking profound questions and presenting powerful arguments. Associate Professor of Islamic Studies Rosalind Ward Gwynne comments on this aspect of the Qur'an: "The very fact that so much of the Qur'an is in the form of arguments shows to what extent human beings are perceived as needing reasons for their actions...."[112]

Gwynne also maintains that this feature of the Qur'an influenced Islamic scholarship:

> "Reasoning and argument are so integral to the content of the
> Qur'an and so inseparable from its structure that they in many ways
> shaped the very consciousness of Qur'anic scholars."[113]

This relationship between reason and revelation was understood even by early Islamic scholars. They understood that rational thinking was one of the ways to prove the intellectual foundations of Islam. The 14th century Islamic scholar Ibn Taymiyya writes that early Islamic scholarship "knew that both revelational and rational proofs were true and that they entailed one another. Whoever gave rational... proofs the complete enquiry due them, knew that they agreed with what the messengers informed them about and that they proved to them the necessity of believing the messengers in what they informed them about."[114]

The Qur'anic argument

The Qur'an provides a powerful argument for God's existence: "Or were they created by nothing? Or were they the creators [of themselves]? Or did they create the heavens and Earth? Rather, they are not certain."[115]

Although this argument refers to the human being, it can also be applied to anything that began to exist, or anything that emerged. The Qur'an uses the word *khuliqu*, which means created, made or originated.[116] So it can refer to anything that came into being.

Now let us break down the argument. The Qur'an mentions four possibilities to explain how something was created or came into being or existence:

- Created by nothing: "or were they created by nothing?"

- Self-created: "or were they the creators of themselves?"
- Created by something created: "or did they create the heavens and the Earth?", which implies a created thing being ultimately created by something else created.
- Created by something uncreated: "Rather, they are not certain", implying that the denial of God is baseless, and therefore the statement implies that there is an uncreated creator.[117]

This argument can also be turned into a universal formula that does not require reference to scripture:

1. The universe is finite.
2. Finite things could have come from nothing, created themselves, been ultimately created by something created, or been created by something uncreated.
3. They could not have come from nothing, created themselves, or have been ultimately created by something created.
4. Therefore, they were created by something uncreated.

The universe is finite

A range of philosophical arguments shows the finitude of the universe. The most cogent and simplest of these arguments involves demonstrating that an actual physical infinite cannot exist. The type of actual infinite that I am addressing here is a differentiated type of infinite, which is an infinite made up of discrete parts, like physical things or objects. These physical things can include atoms, quarks, buses, giraffes and quantum fields. The undifferentiated type of infinite, however, is an infinite that is not made of discrete parts. This infinite is coherent and can exist. For instance, the infinity of God is an undifferentiated infinite, as He is not made up of discrete physical parts. In Islamic theology He is uniquely one and transcendent.

The most persuasive and intuitive arguments to substantiate the impossibility of an actual infinite come in the form of thought experiments. Now the concern here is with the impossibility of the physical infinite being actualised. This is different from mathematical infinites. Although logically coherent, these exist in the mathematical realm, which is usually based on axioms and assumptions. Our concern is whether the infinite can be realised in the real physical world.

Take the following examples into consideration:

1. Bag of balls: Imagine you had an infinite number of balls in a bag. If you take two balls away, how many balls do you have left? Well, mathematically you still have an infinite number. However, practically, you should have two less than what is in the bag. What if you added another two balls instead of removing them? How many balls are there now? There should be two more than what was in the bag. You should be able to count how many balls are in the bag, but you cannot because the infinite is just an idea and does not exist in the real world. This clearly shows you cannot have an actualised infinite made up of discrete physical parts or things. In light of this fact the famous German mathematician David Hilbert said, "The infinite is nowhere to be found in reality. It neither exists in nature nor provides a legitimate basis for rational thought... the role that remains for the infinite to play is solely that of an idea."[118]

2. Stack of cubes with different sizes: Imagine you had a stack of cubes. Each cube is numbered. The first cube has a volume of $10cm^3$. The next cube on top of that has a volume of $5cm^3$ and the next cube is half of the previous cube. This goes on *ad infinitum* (again and again in the same way forever). Now go to the top of the stack and remove the cube at the top. You cannot. There is no cube to be found. Why? Because if there was a cube to be found at the top it would mean that the cubes did not reach infinity. However, since there is no cube at the top, it also shows—even though the mathematical infinite exists (with assumptions and axioms)—that you cannot have an actualised infinite in the real world. Since there is no end to the stack it shows the infinite—that is made up of discrete physical things (in this case the cubes)—cannot be physically realised.

Conceptually, the universe is no different to the bag of balls or the stack of cubes I have explained above. The universe is real. It is made up of discrete physical things. Since the differentiated infinite cannot exist in the real world, it follows that the universe cannot be infinite. This implies that the universe is finite, and since it is finite it must have had a beginning.

The scientific research that relates to the beginning of the universe has not been discussed here because the data is currently undetermined. Underdetermination is a "thesis explaining that for any scientifically based theory there will always be at least one rival theory that is also supported by the evidence given..."[119] There are around 17 competing models to explain the cosmological evidence. Some of these models conclude that the universe is finite and had a beginning and others argue that the universe is past eternal. The evidence is not conclusive, and the conclusions might change when new evidence is observed or new models are developed (*see Chapter 12*).

Now we are in a position to apply the four logical possibilities to explain the beginning of the universe and discuss each one.

Created from nothing?

Before I address this possibility, I need to define what is meant by 'nothing'. Nothing is defined as the absence of all things. To illustrate this better, imagine if everything, all matter, energy and potential, were to vanish; that state would be described as nothing. This is not to be confused with the quantum vacuum or field, a concept I will explain later. Nothing also refers to the absence of any causal condition. A causal condition is any type of cause that produces an effect. This cause can be material or non-material.

Asserting that things can come from nothing means that things can come into being from no potential, no matter or nothing at all. To assert such a thing defies our intuitions and stands against reason.

So could the universe have come into existence from nothing? The obvious answer is no, because from nothing, nothing comes. Nothingness cannot produce anything. Something cannot arise from no causal conditions whatsoever. Another way of looking at it is by way of simple math. What is $0 + 0 + 0$? It is not 3, it's 0.

One of the reasons that this is so intuitive is because it is based on a rational (or metaphysical) principle: being cannot come from nonbeing. To assert the opposite is what I would call counter discourse. Anyone could claim anything. If someone can claim that the entire universe can come from nothing, then the implications would be absurd. They could assert that anything could come into being without any causal conditions at all.

For something to arise from nothing it must have at least some type of potential or causal conditions. Since nothing is the absence of all things, including any type of causal condition, then something could not arise from nothing. Maintaining that something can arise from nothing is logically equivalent to the notion that things can vanish, decay, annihilate or disappear without any causal conditions whatsoever.

Individuals who argue that something can come from nothing must also maintain that something can vanish from no causal conditions at all. For example, if a building completely vanished, such individuals should not be surprised by the event because if things can come from no causal conditions at all, then it logically implies that things can vanish by means of no causal conditions as well. However, to argue that things can just vanish without reference to any causal condition would be rationally absurd.

A common contention is that the universe could come from nothing because in the quantum vacuum particles pop into existence. This argument assumes that the quantum vacuum is nothing. However, this is not true. The quantum vacuum is *something*; it is not an absolute void and it obeys the laws of physics. The quantum vacuum is a state of fleeting energy. So it is not nothing, it is something physical.[120]

Professor Lawrence Krauss's 'nothing'

Professor Lawrence Krauss's book, *A Universe from Nothing*, invigorated and popularised the debate on the Leibnizian question: "Why is there something rather than nothing?"[121] In his book, Krauss argues that it is plausible that the universe arose from 'nothing'. Absurd as this may sound, a few presuppositions and clarifications need to be brought to light to understand the context of his conclusions.

Krauss's 'nothing' is actually something. In his book he calls nothing "unstable"[122], and elsewhere he affirms that nothing is something physical, which he calls "empty but pre-existing space"[123]. This is an interesting linguistic deviation, as the definition of nothing in the English language refers to a universal negation, but it seems that Krauss's 'nothing' is a label for something. Although his research claims that 'nothing' is the absence of time, space and particles, he misleads the untrained reader and fails to confirm (explicitly) that there is still some physical stuff. Even if, as Krauss claims, there is no matter, there must be physical fields. This is because it is impossible to have a region where there are no fields because gravity cannot be blocked. In quantum theory, gravity at this level of reality does not require objects with mass but does require physical stuff. Therefore, Krauss's 'nothing' is actually something. Elsewhere in his book, he writes that everything came into being from quantum fluctuations, which explains a creation from 'nothing', but that implies a pre-existent quantum state in order for that to be a possibility.[124]

Professor David Albert, the author of *Quantum Mechanics and Experience*, wrote a review of Krauss's book, and similarly concludes:

"But that's just not right. Relativistic-quantum-field-theoretical vacuum states — no less than giraffes or refrigerators or solar systems — are particular arrangements of simple physical stuff. The true relativistic-quantum-field-theoretical equivalent to there not being any physical stuff at all isn't this or that particular arrangement of the fields —it is just the absence of the fields! The fact that some arrangements of fields happen to correspond to the existence of particles and some do not is not any more mysterious than the fact that some of the possible arrangements of my fingers happen to correspond to the existence of a fist and some do not. And the fact that particles can pop in and out of existence, over time, as those fields rearrange themselves, is not any more mysterious than the fact that fists can pop in and out of existence, over time, as my fingers rearrange themselves. And none of these poppings — if you look at them aright — amount to anything even remotely in the neighbourhood of a creation from nothing."[125]

Philosophical distinctions

Interestingly, Professor Krauss seems to have changed the definition of nothing in order to answer Leibniz's perennial question. This makes the whole discussion problematic as Krauss's definition blurs well-known philosophical distinctions. The term 'nothing' has always referred to non-being or the absence of something.[126] Therefore, the implications of Krauss's 'nothing' is that it could be reasonable for someone to assert the following:

"I had a wonderful dinner last night, and it was nothing."

"I met nobody in the hall and they showed me directions to this room."

"Nothing is tasty with salt and pepper."[127]

These statements are irrational statements and therefore amount to meaningless propositions, unless of course someone changes the definition of nothing. It is no wonder that Professor Krauss hints that his view of nothing does not refer to non-being. He writes: "One thing is certain, however. The metaphysical 'rule,' which is held as ironclad conviction by those with whom I have debated the issue of creation, namely that 'out of nothing, nothing comes,' has no foundation in science."[128]

This clearly means Krauss has changed the meaning of nothing to mean something, because science as a method focuses on things in the physical world. Science can only answer in terms of natural phenomena and natural processes. When we ask questions like, *what is the meaning of life? Does the soul exist? What is nothing?* the general expectation is to have metaphysical answers—and hence, outside the scope of any scientific explanation (*see Chapter 12*).

Science cannot address the idea of nothing or non-being, because science is restricted to problems that observations can solve. Philosopher of science Elliot Sober verifies this limitation. He writes in his essay *Empiricism* that "science is forced to restrict its attention to problems that observations can solve."[129] Therefore, Professor Krauss has changed the meaning of the word "nothing" in order for science to solve a problem that it could not originally solve. Perhaps this outcome should be accepted as a defeat as it is tantamount to someone not being able to answer a question, and instead of admitting defeat or referring the question to someone else, resorting to changing the meaning of the question.

It would have been intellectually more honest to just say that the concept of nothing is a metaphysical concept, and science only deals with what can be observed.

Inconclusive research and popularising linguistic gymnastics

Putting all of this aside, Professor Krauss admits that his 'nothingness' research is ambiguous and lacks conclusive evidence. He writes, "I stress the word *could* here, because we may never have enough empirical information to resolve this question unambiguously."[130] Elsewhere in his book he admits the inconclusive nature of his argument: "Because of the observational and related theoretical difficulties associated with working out the details, I expect we may never achieve more than plausibility in this regard."[131]

In light of this, Professor Krauss should have just said the universe came from something physical like a vacuum state, rather than redefining the word nothing. But Krauss seems to be adamant in popularising his linguistic gymnastics. During our debate, *Islam or Atheism: Which Makes More Sense?* I referred to his book to explain that his nothing is something, like some form of quantum haze. However, he reacted and said that his nothing is "No space, no time, no laws... there's no universe, nothing, zero, zip, nada."[132]

Krauss seemed to have deliberately omitted an important hidden premise: there is still some physical stuff in his nothing, something which he clearly admitted to in a public lecture. He said that something and nothing are "... physical quantities."[133]

In summary, Professor Krauss's nothing is something. The universe came from something physical which Krauss calls "nothing", and therefore failing to answer Leibniz's question: *Why is there something rather than nothing?* In reality, Krauss only answers the question: *How did something come from something?* That is a question that science can answer, and which does not require linguistic acrobatics.

God's existence is not undermined by Krauss's view on nothing. All that he has really presented to us is that the universe (time and space) came from something. Therefore, the universe still requires an explanation for its existence.

If you cannot have something from nothing, then how did God create from nothing?

This contention is false, as it implies that God is nothing. God is a unique agent with the potential to create and bring things into existence through His will and power. Therefore, it is not the case of something coming from nothing. God's will and power were the causal conditions to bring the universe into existence.

Something coming from nothing is impossible, because nothing implies non-being, no potential and no causal conditions. It is irrational to assert that something can emerge from an absolute void without any potential or prior causal activity. God provides that causal activity via His will and power. Even though the Islamic intellectual tradition refers to the God creating from nothing, this act of creation means that there was no material stuff. However, it does not assume that there were no causal conditions or potential. God's will and power form the causal conditions to bring the universe into existence.

Self-created?

Could the universe have created itself? The term 'created' refers to something that emerged, and therefore it was once not in existence. Another way of speaking about something being created is that it was brought into being. All of these words imply something being finite, as all things that were created are finite. Understanding the concept of creation leads us to conclude that self-creation is a logical and practical impossibility. This is due to the fact that that self-creation implies that something was in existence and not in existence at the same time, which is impossible. Something that emerged means that it once was not in existence; however, to say that it created itself implies that it was in existence before it existed!

Consider the following question: *Was it possible for your mother to give birth to herself?* To claim such a thing would suggest that she would have to be born before she was born. When something is created, it means it once did not exist, and therefore had no power to do anything. So to claim that it created itself is impossible, as it could not have any power before it was created in order to create itself. This applies to all finite things, and that includes the universe too. Islamic scholar Al-Khattabi aptly summarises the fallacy of this argument: "This is [an] even more fallacious argument, because if something does not exist, how can it be described as having power, and how could it create anything? How could it do anything? If these two arguments are refuted, then it is established that they have a creator, so let them believe in Him."[134]

Andrew Compson, the current chair of the British Humanist Association, once engaged in a public debate with me at the University of Birmingham. I presented the Qur'anic argument for God's existence. His response to my assertion that self-creation is impossible was that self-creation can be found in single-celled organisms, also known in biology as asexual reproduction.

Andrew's objection is false on a few grounds. Firstly, what he referred to in single-celled organisms is not self-creation but rather a mode of reproduction by which offspring arise from a single organism and inherit the genetic material of that parent only. Secondly, if we logically extend his example to the universe, it assumes that the universe always existed, because for asexual reproduction to occur you need a parent that existed prior to the offspring. Therefore, his objection actually proves the point I was making; the universe once never existed, so it could not bring itself into existence.

You may be thinking that this objection is absurd, and it was not necessary to discuss it. I agree. However, I included this to show how unreasonable some atheist counter-arguments can be.

Created by something else that was created?

For argument sake, let's answer "yes" to the following question: *Was the universe created by something else created?* Will that satisfy the questioner? Obviously not. The contentious person will undoubtedly ask, "Then, what created that thing?" If we were to answer, "Another created thing", what do you think he would say? Yes, you guessed right: "What created that thing?" If this ridiculous dialogue continued forever, then it would prove one thing: the need for an uncreated creator.

Why? Because we cannot have the case of a created thing, like the universe, being created by another created thing in an unlimited series going back forever (known as an infinite regress of causes). It simply does not make sense. Consider the following examples:

- Imagine that a sniper, who has acquired his designated target, radios through to HQ to get permission to shoot. HQ, however, tells the sniper to hold on while they seek permission from a higher-up. Subsequently, the higher-up seeks permission from the guy even higher up, and so on and so on. If this keeps going on forever, will the sniper ever get to shoot the target? Of course not! He will keep on waiting while someone else is waiting for a person higher up to give the order. There has to be a place or person from where the command is issued; a place where there is no one higher. Thus, our example illustrates the rational flaw in the idea of an infinite regress of causes. When we apply this to the universe we have to posit that it must have had an uncreated creator. The universe, which is a created thing, could not be created by another created thing, *ad infinitum*. If that were the case this universe would not exist. Since it exists, we can dismiss the idea of an infinite regress of causes as an irrational proposition.[135]

- Imagine if a stock trader at the stock exchange was not able to buy or sell his stocks or bonds before asking permission from the investor. Once the stock trader asked his investor, he also had to check with his investor. Imagine if this went on forever. Would the stock trader ever buy or sell his stocks or bonds? The answer is no. There must be an investor who gives the permission without requiring any permission himself. In similar light, if we apply this to the universe, we would have to posit a creator for the universe that is uncreated.

Once the above examples are applied to the universe directly, it will highlight the absurdity of the idea that the universe ultimately was created by something created. Consider if this universe, U1, was created by a prior cause, U2, and U2 was created by another cause, U3, and this went on forever. We wouldn't have universe U1 in the first place. Think about it this way, when does U1 come into being? Only after U2 has come into being. When does U2 come into being? Only after U3 has come into being. This same problem will continue even if we go on forever. If the ability of U1 to come into being was dependent on a forever chain of created universes, U1 would never exist.[136] As Islamic philosopher and scholar Dr.

Jaafar Idris writes: "There would be no series of actual causes, but only a series of non-existents... The fact, however, is that there are existents around us; therefore, their ultimate cause must be something other than temporal causes."[137]

Created by something uncreated?

So, what is the alternative? The alternative is a first cause. In other words, an uncaused cause or an uncreated creator. The 11th century theologian and philosopher Al-Ghazali summarised the existence of an uncaused cause or an uncreated creator in the following way: "The same can be said of the cause of the cause. Now this can either go on ad infinitum, which is absurd, or it will come to an end."[138]

What the above discussion is essentially saying is that something must have always existed. Now there are two obvious choices: God or the universe. Since the universe began and is dependent (*see Chapter 6*), it cannot have always existed. Therefore, something that always existed must be God. In the appendix to Professor Anthony Flew's book *There is a God*, the philosopher Abraham Varghese explains this conclusion in a simple yet forceful way. He writes: "Now, clearly, theists and atheists can agree on one thing: if anything at all exists, there must be something preceding it that always existed. How did this eternally existing reality come to be? The answer is that it never came to be. It always existed. Take your pick: God or universe. Something always existed."[139]

Thus, we can conclude that there exists an uncreated creator for everything that is created. The power of this argument is captured in the reaction of the companion of the Prophet Muhammad ﷺ Jubayr ibn Mut'im. When he heard the relevant verses of the Qur'an addressing this argument he said, "my heart almost began to soar."[140] The scholar Al-Khattabi said that the reason Jubayr was so moved by these verses was because of "the strong evidence contained therein touched his sensitive nature, and with his intelligence understood it."[141]

The 18th century scholar Shah Wali-Allah of Delhi summarises that God created from nothing and provides supporting evidence from the authentic traditions of the Prophet Muhammad ﷺ:

"Be informed that God has three attributes in relation to the bringing into being of the world, each presupposing the other. One of them is absolute origination which means bringing into being something from nothing, so that a thing comes out from the concealment of non-being without there being any matter. The Prophet of God, may the peace and blessing of God be upon him, was asked about the beginning of creation. He replied, 'There was God and there was nothing before Him.'"[142]

What has been established so far is that there must be an uncreated creator. This does not imply the traditional concept of God. However, if we think carefully about the uncreated creator, we can form conclusions that lead to the traditional understanding of God.

Eternal

Since this creator is uncreated, it means that it was always in existence. Something that did not begin has always existed, and something that has always existed is eternal. The Qur'an makes this very clear: "God, the Eternal Refuge. He neither begets nor is born."[143]

Who created God?

A typical response to the eternality of the Divine is the outdated atheist cliché: *Who created God?* This childish contention is a gross misrepresentation and misunderstanding of the argument I have been elucidating in this chapter. There are two main responses to this objection.

Firstly, the third possibility that we discussed concerning how the universe came into being was: *Could it be created by something created?* We discussed that this was ultimately not possible because of the absurdity of the infinite regress of causes. The conclusion was simple: there must have been an uncreated creator. Being uncreated means God was not created. I have already presented a few examples to highlight this fact.

Secondly, once we have concluded that the best explanation for the emergence of the universe is the concept of God, it would be illogical to maintain that someone created Him. God created the universe and is not bound by its laws; He is, by definition, an uncreated Being, and He never came into existence. Something that never began cannot be created.

Professor John Lennox explains these points in the following way:

"I can hear an Irish friend saying: 'Well, it proves one thing- if they had a better argument, they would use it.' If that is thought to be a rather strong reaction, just think of the question: Who made God? The very asking of it shows that the questioner has created God in mind. It is then scarcely surprising that one calls one's book The God Delusion. For that is precisely what a created god is, a delusion, virtually by definition—as Xenophanes pointed out centuries before Dawkins. A more informative title might have been: The Created-God Delusion. The book could then have been reduced to a pamphlet—but sales might just have suffered... For the God who created and upholds the universe was not created—He is eternal. He was not 'made' and therefore subject to the laws that science discovered; it was he who made the universe with its laws. Indeed, the fact constitutes the fundamental distinction between God and the universe. The universe came to be, God did not."[144]

Transcendent

This uncreated creator cannot be part of creation. A useful example to illustrate this is when a carpenter makes a chair. In the process of designing and creating the chair, he does not become the chair. He is distinct from the chair. This applies to the uncreated creator as well. He created the universe and therefore is distinct from what He created. The theologian and scholar Ibn Taymiyya argued that the term, "created", implied that something was distinct from God.[145]

If the creator was part of creation it would make Him contingent or dependent with limited physical qualities. This, in turn, would mean that He would require an explanation for His existence, which would imply He cannot be God (*see Chapter 6*).

The Qur'an affirms the transcendence of God. It says, "There is nothing like unto Him."[146]

Knowing

This uncreated creator must have knowledge because the universe that He created has established laws. These include the law of gravity, the weak and strong nuclear force, and the electromagnetic force (*see Chapter 8*). These laws imply there is a lawgiver, and a lawgiver implies knowledge. The Qur'an says, "Indeed God is, of all things, Knowing."[147]

Powerful

This uncreated creator must be powerful because He created the universe, and the universe has immense energy, both usable and potential. Take, for instance, the number of atoms in the observable universe, which is around 10^{80}.[148] If you were to take just one of these atoms and split it, it would release an immense amount of energy—known as nuclear fission. A created thing with usable and potential energy could not have acquired that from itself. Ultimately, it came from the Creator, who in turn must be powerful.

If the creator did not have power, it would mean that He is unable, incapable and weak. Since the universe was created, it is a simple proof that He must have ability and power. Now just imagine the immense power of the Creator by reflecting on the universe and all that it contains. The Qur'an asserts the power of God:

"God creates what He wills for verily God has power over all things."[149]

The omnipotence paradox

The Islamic position regarding God's ability is summed up in the following creedal statement found in *The Creed of Imam Al-Tahawi*. It states, "He is Omnipotent. Everything is dependent on Him, and every affair is effortless for Him."[150]

However, a common objection to God's power is the omnipotence paradox. This concerns the ability of an All-Powerful Being to limit its power. The question that is raised is: *If God is omnipotent, can He create a stone He cannot move?*

To answer this question, the meaning of 'omnipotence' needs to be clarified. What it implies is the ability to realise every possible affair. Omnipotence also includes the impossibility of failure. The questioner, however, is saying that since God is All-Powerful, He is capable of anything, including failure. This is irrational and absurd, as it is equivalent to saying "an All-Powerful Being cannot be an All-Powerful Being". Failure to achieve or do something is not a feature of omnipotence. From this perspective, the ability of God to "create a stone He cannot move" actually describes an event that is impossible and meaningless.

The question does not describe a possible affair, just as if we were to say "a white black crow" or "a circle triangle". Such statements describe nothing at all; they have no informative value and are meaningless. So why should we even answer a question that has no meaning? To put it bluntly, the question is not even a question.

In his discussion of the Qur'anic verse, "God has power over all things",[151] classical scholar Al-Qurtubi explains that God's power refers to every possible state of affairs: "This [verse] is general... it means that it is permitted to describe God with the attribute of power. The community agree that God has the name The-Powerful... God has power over every possibility whether it is brought into existence or remains non-existent."[152]

To conclude, God can create a stone that is heavier than anything we can imagine, but He will always be able to move the stone because failure is not a feature of omnipotence.[153]

Will

This uncreated creator must have a will for a number of reasons.

Firstly, since this creator is eternal and brought into existence a finite universe, it must have chosen the universe to come into existence. This creator must have chosen the universe to come into existence when the universe was non-existent and could have remained so. Something that has a choice obviously has a will.

Secondly, the universe contains beings that have a conscious will and volition. Therefore, the one who created the universe with living beings that have a will must also have a will. One cannot give something to a thing that one does not have (or give rise to something that one does not contain). Therefore, the Creator has a will.

Thirdly, there are two types of explanations we can apply to the creation of the universe. The first is a scientific explanation, and the second is a personal one. Let me explain this using tea. In order to make tea, I have to boil some water, place the tea bag in the cup and allow it to infuse. This process can be explained scientifically. The water must be 100 degrees

Celsius (212 degrees Fahrenheit) before it reaches boiling point, it has to travel across a semipermeable membrane (tea bag), and I have to use my glycogen stores to enable my muscles to contract to move my limbs to ensure all of this takes place. Obviously, a trained scientist could go into further detail, but I think you get the point. Conversely, the whole process can also be explained personally: the tea has been made because I wanted some tea. Now let's apply this to the universe. We do not have observations or empirical evidence on how the Creator created the universe; we can only rely on a personal explanation, which is that God chose for the universe to come into existence. Even if we had a scientific explanation, it would not negate a personal one, as shown in the tea example.[154]

The Qur'an affirms the fact that God has a will: "Your Lord carries out whatever He wills."[155]

Islamic scholar Al-Ghazali presents an eloquent summary of the implications of God having a will. He asserts that everything that happens is due to God's will and nothing can escape it:

"We attest that He is the Willer of all things that are, the ruler of all originated phenomena; there does not come into the visible or invisible world anything meager or plenteous, small or great, good or evil, or any advantage or disadvantage, belief or unbelief, knowledge or ignorance, success or failure, increase or decrease, obedience or disobedience, except by His will. What He wills is, and what He does not, will not; there is not a glance of the eye, nor a stray thought of the heart that is not subject to His will. He is the Creator, the Restorer, the Doer of whatsoever He wills. There is none that rescinds His command, none that supplements His decrees, none that dissuades a servant from disobeying Him, except by His help and mercy, and none has power to obey Him except by His will."[156]

Although there are some objections to the argument presented in this chapter, they do not qualify as defeaters. This means that even if these objections could not be responded to, the argument would still maintain its rational force. Nevertheless, there are some questions that challenge this argument, including: *If the Creator of the universe is eternal, why did the universe begin to exist when it did instead of existing from eternity? If God is maximally perfect and transcendent, what caused Him to create at all? Does God require creation in order to possess attributes of perfection?* These questions have been intelligently addressed in a paper entitled *The Kalam Cosmological Argument and the Problem of Divine Creative Agency and Purpose.*[157]

In this chapter we have seen that the Qur'an provides an intuitive and powerful argument for God's existence. Since the universe is finite, it had a beginning. If it began, then it can be explained as coming from nothing, creating itself, being ultimately created by something created or being created by something uncreated. The rational answer is that it the universe was brought into being by an uncreated creator who is transcendent, knowing, powerful and has a will. This creator must also be uniquely one, but that will be discussed in Chapter 10.

The argument of this chapter relies on the fact that the universe must be finite. However, the following argument shows that even if the universe did not have a beginning, it still necessitates God's existence.

Chapter 6
The Divine Link
The Argument from Dependency

Imagine you walk out of your house and on your street you find a row of dominoes that stretch far beyond what your eyes can see. You start to hear a noise that gets slightly louder as time passes. This noise is familiar to you, as you used to play with dominoes as a child; it is the sound of them falling. Eventually, you see this amazing display of falling dominoes approaching you. You greatly admire how the basic laws of physics can produce such a remarkable spectacle; however, you are also saddened because the last domino has now fallen a few inches away from your feet. Still excited about what has just happened, you decide to walk down the street to find the first domino, hoping to meet the person responsible for producing this wonderful experience.

Keeping the above scenario in mind, I want to ask you a few questions. As you walk down your street, will you eventually reach where the chain of dominoes began? Or will you keep on walking forever? The obvious response is that you will eventually find the first domino. However, I want you to ask *why*. The reason you know that you will find the first domino is because you understand that if the domino chain went on forever, the last domino that fell by your feet would never have fallen. An infinite number of dominoes would have to fall before the last domino could fall. Yet an infinite amount of falling dominoes would take an infinite amount of time to fall. In other words, the last domino would never fall. Putting this in simple terms, you know that in order for the last domino to fall, the domino behind must fall prior to it, and for that domino to fall, the domino behind it must fall prior to it. If this went on forever, the last domino would never fall.

Sticking with the analogy, I want to ask you another question. Let's say, walking down the street, you finally come across the first domino which led to the falling of the entire chain. What would your thoughts be about the first domino? Would you think this domino fell 'by itself'? In other words, do you think the falling of the first domino can somehow be explained without referring to anything external to it? Clearly not; that runs against the grain of our basic intuition about reality. Nothing really happens *on its own*. Everything requires an explanation of some sort. So the first domino's fall had to have been triggered by something else—a person, the wind or a thing hitting it, etc. Whatever this 'something else' is, it has to form a part of our explanation of falling dominoes.

So to sum up our reflections thus far: neither could the chain of dominoes contain an infinite number of items, nor could the first domino start falling for no reason whatsoever.

This above analogy is a summary of the argument from dependency. The universe is somewhat like a row of dominoes. The universe and everything within it is dependent. They cannot depend on something else, which in turn depends on something else, forever. The only plausible explanation is that the universe, and everything within it, has to depend on someone or something whose existence is in some ways independent from the universe (and anything else for that matter). Put differently, this thing must not be 'dependent' the way the universe is, because that would just add one more domino to the chain, which would then require an explanation. Therefore, there must be an independent and eternal Being that everything depends upon. Simple as this sounds, in order to understand this argument, I will have to define what I mean by 'dependent'.

What does it mean when we say something is dependent?

1. **Firstly, it is something that is not necessary.** The word 'necessary' has a specific, technical meaning in philosophy. Contrary to popular use, it does not indicate something you need. Rather, when philosophers say something is necessary, they mean that it was impossible, inconceivable for it to not have existed. I understand why this is may be a bit difficult concept to grasp. This is because nothing in our empirical experience is ever necessary. We can, however, get an adequate understanding of what 'being necessary' means by thinking about the opposite. A thing or object not being necessary implies that it does not have to exist. In other words, if it is conceivable that a thing could have not existed, it is

not necessary. The chair you are presumably sitting on is clearly not necessary—we can imagine a thousand different scenarios where it might not have existed. You may not have chosen to buy it, the manufacturer may not have chosen to make it, or the dealer may not have chosen to sell it. Clearly, your chair very easily could not have existed. Now this possibility of 'not-having-been-there' is a key feature of dependent things. Something that has this feature requires an explanation for its existence. This is because for something that might not have existed, you can easily ask: *Why does this thing exist?* That perfectly legitimate question calls for an explanation. It cannot be that the thing exists on its own, because there is nothing necessary about its existence. To say that the thing somehow explains itself would be to deny the property of dependence we just discussed. Thus, the explanation must be something external to it. An explanation in this context means an external set of factors that provide a reason for why something exists. Going back to our chair analogy, the collection of a number of factors—e.g., the manufacturer making it, the dealer selling it, and you buying it—form the explanation for the chair's existence. Therefore, if something requires an external set of factors, that means it is dependent on something other than itself. Consequently, its existence is dependent on something external. This is a basic, intuitive and rational form of reasoning. This is because questioning something that exists that could not have existed is the mark of a rational mind.

Think about what scientists do. They point to different features of reality and ask—why is this flower a certain way? Why does that bacteria cause this disease? Why is the universe expanding at the rate that it is? What gives these questions legitimacy is the fact that none of them are necessary; all of them might not have been the way that they are. To facilitate a greater understanding of this concept, consider the following example:

Waking up in the morning, you go down the stairs and walk into the kitchen. You open the fridge and on top of the egg box you find a pen. You obviously do not close the fridge door and conclude that the pen's existence is necessary. You do not think that the pen in the fridge got there by itself. You question why the pen is on top of the egg box. The reason you ask this question is because the pen's existence on the egg box is not necessary. It requires an explanation for its existence and for the way that it is. The explanations can vary, but the fact that an explanation is needed means that the pen is dependent. The pen requires an external set of factors to provide a reason for why it is placed in the fridge, and why it is the way that it is. For instance: the fact that the pen was made, and your son bought the pen from a stationary shop, and then put the pen in the fridge provides the external set of factors responsible for the pen. The pen is therefore dependent on these external factors, and these factors explain the pen's existence.

2. **Secondly, something is dependent if its components or basic building blocks could have been arranged in a different way.** This is because there must have been something external to that thing which determined its specific arrangement. Let me elaborate with an example:

You are driving home and you pass a roundabout. You see a bunch of flowers arranged in the following three words: 'I love you'. You can conclude that there is nothing necessary about the arrangement of the flowers. They could have been arranged in another way—for example, the words 'I adore you' instead of 'I love you' could have been used. Alternatively, the flowers could have not been arranged at all—they might have been randomly scattered. Since the flowers could have been set in a different way, some force external to them must have determined their arrangement. In this case, it could have been the local gardener or the result of a local government project. This point holds true for pretty much everything you observe. The components of everything, be it an atom or a laptop or an organism, are composed in a specific way. Furthermore, each basic building block does not exist necessarily. The basic components of something cannot explain themselves and therefore require an explanation (see the first definition above).

3. **Thirdly, a thing is dependent if it relies on something outside itself for its existence.** This is a common sense understanding of the word. Another way of explaining that something is dependent is by stating that it is not self-sustaining. An example includes a pet cat. The cat does not sustain itself; it requires external things to survive. These include food, water, oxygen and shelter.

4. **Finally, the defining features of a dependent thing are that it has limited physical qualities.** These can include shape, size, colour, temperature, charge, mass, etc. Why is this so? Well, if something has a limited physical feature, that feature must be limited by something external to itself, such as an external source or external set of factors. The following questions highlight this point: *Why does it have these limits? Why is it not twice the size, or a different shape or colour?* The thing did not give itself these limitations. For example, if I picked up a cupcake with its limited physical qualities of size, shape, colour and texture, and claimed that it existed necessarily, you would think I was foolish. You know that its size, colour and texture have been controlled by an external source: in this case, the baker.

It is reasonable to assert that all things with limited physical qualities are finite; there must have been something prior that was responsible for their qualities. This means that all limited physical objects at one point had a beginning, because it is inconceivable that limited physical objects are eternal. This is due to the fact that an external source or set of factors must have existed prior to any limited physical object, and caused its limitations.

Imagine if I picked up a plant and claimed that it was eternal. How would you respond? You would laugh at such an assertion. Even if you didn't witness the plant's beginning, you know it is finite because of its limited physical qualities. However, even if limited physical objects (including the universe) were eternal, it would not change the fact that they are dependent and do not exist necessarily. This argument works regardless of whether or not objects are eternal or have a beginning.

Applying the above comprehensive definition of what it means to be dependent leads us to conclude that the universe and everything within it is dependent. Reflect on anything that comes to mind—a pen, a tree, the sun, an electron, and even a quantum field. All of these things are dependent in some way. If this is true, then all that we perceive—including the universe—can be explained in one of the following ways:

1. The universe and all that we perceive are eternal, necessary and independent.
2. The existence of the universe and all that we perceive depends on something else which is also dependent.
3. The universe and all that we perceive derives its existence from something else that exists by its own nature and is *accordingly eternal* and *independent*.

I will take each explanation and discuss which one best explains the dependency of the universe and everything within it.

1. The universe and all that we perceive are eternal, necessary and independent.

Could everything that we perceive exist eternally and depend on itself? This is not a rational explanation. All the things that we perceive do not necessarily exist; they could have not existed. They also have limited physical qualities. Since they could not give rise to their own limitations, something external must have imposed these limitations on them. All the things we perceive do not explain themselves by virtue of their own existence, and their components could have been arranged in a different way. Therefore, they are dependent, and dependent things do not exist independently.

Even if the universe were eternal, it still stands that there must have been an external set of factors that gave rise to its limited physical qualities.

In addition, the universe's components or basic building blocks could been arranged in a different way, and the universe could have not existed. The universe cannot explain itself by virtue of its own existence. With these considerations, we can safely reject the view that the eternity of the universe in time somehow provides an explanation for its existence (this point is explained further below).

2. The existence of the universe and all we perceive depends on something else which is also dependent.

The existence of universe and all that we perceive could not depend on something else which is also dependent. Since the universe and all that we perceive do not explain themselves, then postulating another dependent thing to explain them does not explain anything at all. This is because the dependent thing that is supposed to explain the universe and everything that exists also requires an explanation. That dependent thing would also require an explanation for its existence. Therefore, the only way to explain things that are dependent is by referring to something that is not dependent and therefore necessary.

Despite this, someone may argue that the existence of all we perceive depends on something else, which in turn depends on another thing, *ad infinitum*. This is false. For instance: could this universe be explained by another universe, which in turn is explained by another universe, with the series of explanations continuing forever? This would not solve the problem of requiring an explanation. Even if there were an infinite number of universes all dependent on each other, we could still ask: *Why does this infinite chain of universes exist?* Whether or not the universe is eternal, it still requires an explanation for its existence.

Consider the following example. Imagine there are an infinite number of human beings. Each human being was produced by the biological activity of their parents, and each of these parents was in turn produced by the biological activity of their parents, *ad infinitum*. It would still be perfectly reasonable to ask: *Why are there any human beings at all?* Even if this chain of human beings had no beginning, the fact remains that this chain requires an explanation. Since each human being in the chain could have not existed and possesses limited physical qualities, they are dependent and not necessary. They still require an explanation. Just saying the chain of human beings is infinite does nothing to change the need for an explanation.[158]

This option also assumes that an infinite regress of dependencies is possible. However, this is inconceivable. To illustrate this point, imagine the existence of this universe was dependent on another universe, and the existence of that universe was also dependent on another universe, and so on. Would this universe ever come to be? The answer is no, because an infinite number of dependencies would need to be established before this universe could exist. Remember, an infinite number of things do not end; therefore, this universe could not exist if there were an infinite set of dependencies.

3. The universe and all that we perceive derives its existence from something else that exists by its own nature and is *accordingly eternal* and *independent*.

Since everything we perceive is dependent in some way, then the most rational explanation is that the existence of everything depends on something else that is independent, and therefore eternal. It has to be independent because if it were dependent, it would require an explanation. It also has to be eternal because if it was not eternal—in other words, finite—it would be dependent as finite things require an explanation for their existence. Therefore, we can conclude that the universe, and everything that we perceive, depends upon something that is eternal and independent. This is best explained by the existence of God.

The argument from dependency is supported by the Islamic intellectual tradition. The concept of an independent Being that is responsible for bringing everything into existence is highlighted in various places in the Qur'an. For example, God says:

"God is independent of all that exists (*al-ameen*)."[159]

"O mankind! It is you who stand in need of God, whereas He alone is self-sufficient, the One whom all praise is due."[160]

The classical exegete Ibn Kathir comments on the above verse: "They need Him in all that they do, but He has no need of them at all... He is unique in His being free of all needs, and has no partner or associate."[161]

Islam's intellectual tradition produced the like of Ibn Sina (known in the West as Avicenna), who articulated a similar argument. He maintained that God is *Waajib al-Wujood*, necessarily existent. Ibn Sina argued that God necessarily exists and He is responsible for the existence of everything. Everything other than God is dependent, which Ibn Sina described as *Mumkin al-Wujud*.[162] The argument from dependency has also been adopted—and adapted—by many other influential Islamic scholars, some of whom include Al-Razi, Al-Ghazali and Imam al-Haramayn al-Juwayni.

Al-Ghazali provides a concise summary of this argument:

"There is no denying existence itself. Something must exist and anyone who says nothing exists at all makes a mockery of sense and necessity. The proposition that there is no denying being itself, then, is a necessary premise. Now this Being which has been admitted in principle is either necessary or contingent... What this means is that a being must be self-sufficient or dependent... From here we argue: If the being the existence of which is conceded be necessary, then the existence of a necessary Being is established. If, on the other hand, its existence is contingent, every contingent being depends on a necessary Being; for the meaning of its contingency is that its existence and non-existence are equally possible. Whatever has such a characteristic cannot have its existence selected for without a determining or selecting agent. This too is necessary. So from these necessary premises the existence of a necessary Being is established."[163]

In summary, according to Islamic theology, God is:

- Independent
- The Being that everything depends on
- The One that sustains everything
- Everlasting
- Self-sufficient

- *Waajib al-Wujood* (necessarily existent)

I will now address some of the key objections against this argument.

The universe exists independently

A typical atheist contention is: *If we are saying that God is independent and necessary, why cannot we say the same thing for the universe?* This is a misplaced contention for the following reasons. Firstly, there is nothing necessary about the universe; it could have not existed. Secondly, the components of the universe could have been arranged in a different way. Whether one considers these components to be quarks or some type of quantum field, it still raises the question: *Why are they arranged the way that they are?* Since a different arrangement of quarks or fields could have existed instead of the collection that does exist, it follows that the universe is dependent.[164] Everything we perceive within the universe has limited physical qualities; this includes the galaxies, stars, trees, animals, and electrons. They have a specific shape, size and physical form. As such, these things that we perceive around us—the things that make up the entire universe—are finite and dependent.

The universe is just a brute fact

Another contention suggests that we should not ask any questions about the universe. During his famous radio debate with Father Copleston, the philosopher Bertrand Russell said, "I should say that the universe is just there, and that's all"[165]. This position is frankly an intellectual cop-out. Consider the following hovering green ball analogy:[166]

Imagine you were walking in your local park and you saw a hovering green ball in the middle of the children's playground. How would you react? Would you walk by and accept it as a necessary part of the playground? Of course not; you would question why it exists and how it is the way that it is. Now, extend the ball to the size of a universe. The question still remains: *Why does the ball exist and why is it the way that it is?* Hence, the validity of questioning why the universe is the way that it is.

Furthermore, this contention is absurd because it undermines science itself. Within the scientific community is a field of study dedicated to trying to explain the existence and basic features of the universe. This field is called cosmology. This is a perfectly legitimate field of scientific enquiry, and to label the universe as a 'brute fact' does a disservice to an established scientific practice.

Science will eventually find an answer!

This objection argues that what has been presented in this chapter is a form of the 'God of the gaps' fallacy. It argues that our ignorance of scientific phenomena should not be taken as proof of God's existence or of Divine activity because science will eventually provide an explanation. This is a misplaced objection because the argument from dependency does not aim to address a scientific question. Its concern is with metaphysics; it seeks to understand the nature and implications of dependent things. This argument can be applied to all scientific explanations and phenomena. For example, even if we were to theorise many universes as an explanation for natural phenomena, they would still be dependent. *Why?* Because the components of these explanations could be arranged in a different way and cannot be explained by virtue of their own existence, or they require something else outside of themselves to exist and have limited physical qualities. Therefore, they are dependent, and—as discussed in this chapter—you cannot explain a dependent thing with another dependent thing. If members of the scientific community claim to have found something that is independent and eternal, and in turn explained the existence of the universe, I would ask for proof. Interestingly, the minute they provide some empirical proof would be the moment they contradict themselves, because things that can be sensed have limited physical qualities, therefore qualifying as dependent.

Science cannot ever discover anything independent and eternal, not only because it would be empirical, but also because science only works on observable dependent things. Therefore, it makes no sense to say that science would discover an unscientific object! Let's take a moment and think about what science is. Science, as a discipline, is in the business of providing answers and explanations (*see Chapter 12*). Only dependent things can have external explanations. With this in mind, we realise the scope of science is restricted to the realm of dependent objects, objects about which we can ask: *Why does it exist? Why is it the way that it is?* Therefore, science can only provide an answer that would relate to another dependent object. However, as we have explained, you cannot explain a dependent object with another dependent object, because that dependent object would also require an explanation (and if you recall, we have already discussed that there cannot be a thing that depends on something else to exist, which in turn depends on still another thing, *ad infinitum*). Since the explanation is something that is independent and eternal, science can never enter into the discussion because it has a limited scope of empirical, dependent things.

Ending on a spiritual note

This understanding of God is not just an intellectual exercise; rather, it should instil a deep sense of yearning and love for God. In this chapter, we have concluded that God necessarily exists and everything can only exist because of Him. In this sense we as human beings are not only dependent on God in the philosophical sense, but also in the normal use of the word; we couldn't be here without Him, and everything that we have is ultimately due to Him alone.

The following marvellous short story teaches us that, since we are ultimately dependent on God and our success in this life and the hereafter lies with His boundless mercy, we should submit to God and accomplish His will:

"One day I set out to tend my fields, accompanied by my little dog, sworn enemy of the monkeys which ravaged the plantations. It was the season of great heat. My dog and I were so hot that we could scarcely breathe. I began to think that one or other of us would soon fall in a faint. Then, thank God, I saw a Tiayki tree, the branches of which presented a vault of refreshing greenery. My dog gave little cries of joy and turned towards this blessed shade.

When he had reached the shade, instead of staying where he was, he came back to me, his tongue out. Seeing how his flanks were palpitating, I realised how completely exhausted he was. I walked towards the shade. My dog was full of joy. Then, for a moment, I pretended to continue on my way. The poor beast groaned plaintively, but followed me none the less, his tail between his legs.

He was obviously in despair, but determined to follow me, whatever might come of it. This fidelity moved me profoundly. How could one fully appreciate the readiness of this animal to follow me, even to death, although he was under no constraint to do so? He is devoted to me, I said to myself, because he regards me as his master and so risks his life simply to stay beside me. 'Oh my Lord,' I cried, 'Heal my troubled soul! Make my fidelity like that of this being whom I call, contemptuously, a dog. Give me, as You have given to him, the strength to master my life so that I may accomplish Your will and follow—without asking, Where am I going?—the path upon which You guide me! I am not the creator of this dog, yet he follows me in docility, at the cost of a thousand sufferings. It is You, Lord, who has gifted him with this virtue. Give, O Lord, to all who ask it of You—as I do—the virtue of Love and the courage of Charity!' Then I retraced my steps and took refuge in the shade. Full of joy, my little companion lay down facing me so that his eyes were turned to mine, as though he wished to speak seriously to me."[167]

Chapter 7
Denying God, Denying You
The Argument from Consciousness

My father loves going for walks. He ponders the profound questions that plague the thinking man. On one of these walks, he decided to visit the famous Speakers Corner in London. It is known for its loud and heated discussions about man, life and the universe, including politics and all sorts of conspiracies. It is a place for unfettered free speech, where anyone and everyone can say almost what they want in any way they want. The corner usually witnesses theological and philosophical debates centred on God's existence. The day my father visited the corner he was listening to a discussion about whether or not we have good reasons to believe in the Divine. My father interrupted the discussion and told them, "If you reject God, you deny yourself." When my father told me this story, I didn't really understand the implications of what he said. However, fast-forward a few decades, I would like to expand on his profound wisdom in this chapter.

My father was trying to tell the crowd that since we have an awareness of who we are (and what we feel), it is a sign that God exists. In a broad sense, what my father was referring to was phenomenal consciousness; in simple terms, the fact that we have inner subjective experiences. Phenomenal consciousness relates to our ability to have an inner subjective awareness of what it is like to experience a particular conscious state. For example, when I eat my favourite chocolate or when I listen to a recitation of the Qur'an, I am aware of that internal experience, and I can appreciate what it is like to be in that conscious state. However, no one else can access what it is like for me to have those subjective experiences. Of course, other people will have their own perspectives of chocolate and the recitation of the Qur'an, but they will never truly experience or comprehend what I feel during those experiences.

Even if you were to know everything about my physical brain, you would not be able to find out what it is like for me to have a particular experience, whether drinking orange juice, staring at a beautiful sunset or falling in love. The main reason for this is that neuroscience is mostly a science of correlations. Neuroscientists observe brain activity and correlate that activity with what the participants report they are conscious of. However, these correlations can never tell us anything about what it is like for participants to be in a given state of consciousness; it can only tell us when it occurs. You may argue that a participant may provide neuroscientists with first-person data by describing his or her subjective experience, thereby answering the question. Nonetheless, this is not an answer, because even if someone uses words like 'cold', 'painful', 'sweet', 'beautiful' and 'sad', they can never tell us what it is like to have those experiences and feelings. Words are vehicles for meaning and experience, but we must go beyond words to fully understand the conscious experience of another. Another elusive aspect of internal conscious experiences is why subjective experiences arise from non-conscious biological and physical processes. Why does a unique internal experience arise from non-conscious matter? This is another important question in the philosophy of the mind and neuroscience.

The issues I have introduced so far form what academics call *the hard problem of consciousness*. This has remained unresolved, despite having sparked many heated debates on the nature of who we are and our conscious experiences. Research fellow Daniel Bor states the problem in the following way:

> "There are a lot of hard problems in the world, but only one gets to call itself 'the hard problem'. That is the problem of consciousness—how 1300 grams or so of nerve cells conjures up the seamless kaleidoscope of sensations, thoughts, memories and emotions that occupy every waking moment... The hard problem remains unresolved."[168]

The very fact that we have internal subjective conscious experiences can only be explained by the existence of an All-Aware Being. This Being created the physical universe with conscious creatures, and gave them the ability to be aware of their internal subjective experiences. Other explanations fail from the onset—for instance, a cold, materialistic view on the universe offers no hope for a solution to the problem. Imagine in the beginning of the universe all you had were simple arrangements of matter, and after a long period of time, they rearranged themselves into human beings to form consciousness. This sounds like magic, because matter is cold, blind and non-conscious, so how can it be responsible for such a phenomenon? It cannot. For example, I cannot give you £10 if I do not have it. Likewise, matter cannot give rise to consciousness if it does not contain it or have the potential to give rise to it. You may argue that I can earn the money and then give it to someone; likewise, matter can somehow 'earn' consciousness via some complex process. This is false, because an individual non-conscious process plus another individual non-complex process still equal two non-conscious processes. It is like trying to turn a piece of iron into wood: no matter how you manipulate the iron, it will never turn into wood, even if you add more iron.

The scope of this chapter is to deconstruct the popular explanations for the hard problem of consciousness and explain how a theistic approach, and by extension God's existence, provides a far better explanation. I will also bring to light that this is not an issue for which 'science will eventually give us the answers', because even if we were to know everything about the brain and insist on referring solely to biological, materialist (or even non-theistic philosophical) explanations, we will still not answer the hard problem of consciousness.

More about the hard problem

By their own admission, the issue of consciousness has caused many academics unsolvable problems, especially those who are excessively dogmatic in their materialistic approach. In his book *Consciousness: Confessions of a Romantic Reductionist* Professor Christof Koch openly admits:

> "How the brain converts bioelectrical activity into subjective states, how photons reflected off water are magically transformed into the percept of an iridescent aquamarine mountain tarn is a puzzle. The nature of the relationship between the nervous system and consciousness remains elusive and the subject of heated and interminable debates... Explaining how a highly organized piece of

matter can possess an interior perspective has daunted the scientific method, which in so many other areas has proved immensely fruitful."[169]

These unresolved problems do not concern the physical makeup of the brain and how we can correlate some conscious states with brain activity. If I am experiencing pain, some sort of activity in my brain indicates that I am experiencing pain. No one is denying that the physical brain and consciousness are related, but I must stress here, it is *just* a relationship. The brain and consciousness are not the same thing. Take the following analogy into consideration: the brain is the car, and consciousness is the driver. The car will not move without the driver, and the driver will not be able to start the car—or use it properly—if it is damaged or broken. However, they are both different and independent in some way.

What are the problems that specialists in the field are trying to address, and why are the brain and consciousness not the same thing? The answer to these questions lies in what is known as the *hard problem* of consciousness. The hard problem of consciousness concerns the fact that we have internal subjective experiences. In other words, the problem is that we cannot explain *what it is like* for a particular organism to have a subjective conscious experience in terms of the third-person language of science. Professor David Chalmers, who popularised the phrase *the hard problem of consciousness*, explains:

"The really hard problem of consciousness is the problem of *experience*. When we think and perceive, there is a whir of information processing, but there is also a subjective aspect... This subjective aspect is experience. When we see, for example, we *experience* visual sensations: the felt quality of redness, the experience of dark and light, the quality of depth in a physical field. Other experiences go along with perception in different modalities: the sound of a clarinet, the smell of mothballs. Then there are bodily sensations from pains to orgasms; mental images that are conjured up internally; the felt quality of emotion; and the experience of a stream of conscious thought. What unites all these states is that there is something it is like to be in them. All of them are states of experience... If any problem qualifies as *the* problem of consciousness, it is this one. In this central sense of 'consciousness', an organism, and a mental state is conscious if there is something it is like to be in that state."[170]

Professor Torin Alter adds another dimension to the definition of the hard problem of consciousness by focusing on the inability to answer why physical brain processes produce conscious experience:

"As I type these words, cognitive systems in my brain engage in visual and auditory information processing. This processing is accompanied by states of phenomenal consciousness, such as the auditory experience of hearing the tap-tap-tap of the keyboard and the visual experience of seeing the letters appear on the screen. How does my brain's activity generate those experiences? Why those and not others? Indeed, why is any physical event accompanied by conscious experience? The set of such problems is known as the hard problem of consciousness... Even after all the associated functions and abilities are explained, one might reasonably wonder why there is something it is like to see letters appear on a computer screen."[171]

Let me simplify the above definitions with an example. Say you were to eat a strawberry. Scientists and philosophers would be able to find correlations in the brain that indicate that you are eating something, maybe even the fact that you are eating a piece of fruit, and whether or not you find it tasty or sweet by asking you to describe your conscious experience. Nevertheless, they could never find out or examine *what it is like* for you to eat a strawberry, or what tastiness or sweetness mean and feel for you, and why you have had that particular subjective experience of eating a strawberry arising from physical processes.

Addressing the failed approaches

A range of competing approaches attempt to explain the phenomenon of consciousness and its hard problem. These approaches include biological, materialist, and non-materialist explanations. I will attempt to discuss why they do not address the hard problem of consciousness, and why a theistic approach provides the best explanation. In other words, God's existence provides a rational basis to answer the questions philosophers and neuroscientists have been unable to answer.

Biological approaches

Let us first address why biological explanations have failed. Some of these attempts include Francis Crick and Christof Koch's *Toward a Neurobiological Theory of Consciousness*, Bernard Baars's *Global Workplace* theory, Gerald Elderman's and Giulio Tononi's *The Dynamic Core* theory, Rodolfo Llinas's *Thalamocortical Binding* theory, Victor Lamme's *Recurrent Processing* theory, Semir Zeki's *Microconsciousness* theory and Antonio Damasio's *The Feeling of What Happens* theory. Although it is not the purpose of this chapter to discuss the technicalities and shortcomings of these empirical theories (because they all have philosophical implications, which are addressed below), none of them comprehensively addresses the hard problem of consciousness. Professor David Chalmers explains the failure of the biological approaches in addressing the hard problem of consciousness. In his book *The Character of Consciousness* he mentions five perilous strategies that have been adopted[172]:

1. The first strategy is to explain something else. Researchers simply admit the problem of experience is too difficult for now. Koch openly admits this failed strategy. In a published interview, he confessed: "Well, let's first forget about the real difficult aspects, like subjective feelings, because they may not have a scientific solution. The subjective state of play, of pain, of pleasure, of seeing blue, of smelling a rose—there seems to be a huge jump between the materialistic level, of explaining molecules and neurons, and the subjective level."[173]

2. The second strategy is to deny the hard problem of consciousness. It is to decide that we are zombies, with only an illusion of free will. This strategy describes the human reality as a biological machine with no subjective experience. In other words, it ignores the problem and redefines what it means to be human.

3. The third strategy claims that subjective experience is explained by understanding the physical processes in our brain. However, this sounds like magic. Conscious experience somehow emerges without any explanation. The question, *how do these processes give rise to an inner subjective experience?* is never answered. Furthermore, understanding physical processes tells us nothing about what it is like for a person to have a particular internal conscious experience.

4. The fourth strategy is to explain the structure of experience. This strategy tells us nothing of why experience exists in the first place, and just by explaining the structure of experience, it provides us with no answers to what it is like for a person to have unique experiences.

5. The fifth strategy is to isolate the substrate (*the underlying basis or layer*) of experience. This strategy aims to isolate the neural basis for experience by understanding certain processes. However, this strategy does not explain what it is like to have an internal conscious experience, why it emerges from these processes and how.

Enter the philosophy of mind

Now we are in a position to address how philosophers of the mind explain consciousness in a way that attempts to address the hard problem. An important note to add here is that scientific theories have implied philosophical assumptions. Therefore, addressing the philosophical theories will also address the empirical theories. Professor Antti Revonsuo makes this point clear:

> "However, it is useful also for empirical scientists to be aware of the different philosophical alternatives, because every empirical theory also necessarily involves some sort of implicit philosophical commitments... The overall empirical approach that a scientist takes to consciousness is guided by his prior philosophical commitments or intuitions about the nature of science and the nature of consciousness, whether he is aware of such commitments or not."[174]

Professors Ricardo Manzotti and Paolo Moderato also highlight that the neurosciences are "not metaphysically innocent"[175] and that "empirical data needs to be interpreted from the perspective of some premise."[176]

None of the various philosophical attempts to explain consciousness are comprehensive enough to challenge the theistic alternative. These attempts can be broadly categorised as materialist or physicalist, and non-materialist. Below is a brief account of these attempts and an explanation of why they have failed.

Materialistic approaches

Echoing other researchers and academics, the terms physicalism and materialism will be used interchangeably.[177] [178] Although they have separate histories and some conceptual differences[179], these do not pose a problem to the concepts dealt with in this chapter. The two terms mean that consciousness can be explained by the physical sciences, but do not always imply that conscious states must be equated to bits of matter.

Physical facts are not all the facts!

Before I get into all the materialist approaches, I would like to explain how physicalism and materialism in general are undermined by Frank Jackson's powerful Mary argument. Here is a summary of it:

Mary has lived in a black and white room all her life and acquires information about the world via black and white computers and televisions. In her room, Mary has access to all of the scientific objective information about what happens when humans see physical phenomena. She knows everything about the science related to perceiving objects with the human eye. Yet, she is unaware of what it is like to see colours. One day she is allowed to leave the room. The moment she opens the door she looks at a red rose, and experiences the colour red for the first time. She only appreciates the colour red the moment she sees it.[180] Her knowledge about all the physical facts concerning visual perception and colours did nothing to prepare her for the new experience of seeing red. She did not know what it is like to see a red rose by learning the physical facts, she only knew what that experience was like the moment it occurred.

Chalmers provides the following premises to show that the Mary argument renders materialism unable to solve the hard problem of consciousness:

1. Mary knows all the physical facts.
2. Mary does not know all the facts.
3. The physical facts do not exhaust all the facts.[181]

Chalmers's argument here shows that knowledge of the physical world will not lead to knowledge of subjective conscious reality—for example, what it is like to see red. This seems to undermine materialism. Chalmers generalises the argument in the following way:

1. There are truths about consciousness that are not deducible from physical truths.
2. If there are truths about consciousness that are not deducible from physical truths, then materialism is false.
3. Materialism is false.[182]

Physicalism and materialism do not explain subjective consciousness because knowledge of the physical brain does not lead to an understanding of a subjective experience, and why that experience emerges from brain activity. Materialism is inadequate, because there are facts about consciousness that cannot be deduced from physical facts.

The Mary argument has generated interesting objections. One objection argues that it is not possible to identify what Mary would know if she acquired all of the physical facts. This objection misunderstands the Mary argument. It assumes that the Mary argument is focused on what it is like to know all the physical facts. However, the argument is focused on Mary's inability to know what it is like to see red if she never had the experience of seeing red. Therefore, any objection to the Mary argument must focus on what Mary gains by seeing red and not what she would know if she had all the physical facts.

Another objection is the Ability Hypothesis. This hypothesis asserts that Mary does not gain any new knowledge, but only acquires new abilities. For example, when someone learns how to ride a bike they are not learning new things about the bike, they simply acquire the ability to ride it. This objection is considered inadequate. If Mary can gain new abilities when she leaves the room, then it is also possible that she gains new facts that she did not have prior to leaving the room. When someone learns how to ride a bike they do not only acquire the ability to do so, they also gain new facts. For example, if someone is riding downhill fast, they will eventually learn not to constantly use the brakes as this will cause the rims to overheat. For a controlled descent, the brakes must be gently squeezed with around two second pulses.

Professor Brian Loar's objection provides a strong challenge to the Mary argument. Loar argues that Mary does not acquire new knowledge about red, only a new way of conceptualising what she already knew about the colour. This strategy declares that there is only one property that can give rise to distinct concepts of that property. These concepts are physical-functional concepts and phenomenal concepts (concepts that refer to subjective experience). So when Mary saw red for the first time she was not experiencing a new property and learning new facts about it. She was experiencing a different way of conceptualising what she already knew. Prior to leaving the room, she recognised the property of red in physical-functional terms. However, when she left the room she acquired a new way of recognising the physical property of red in phenomenal terms. Mary can only acquire phenomenal concepts when she sees red because these concepts come about only by seeing the colour red. The main problem with Loar's strategy is that it is based on the assumption that we can acquire phenomenal concepts from observing physical properties. However, this begs the question: *How can a brain state observing a physical-functional property acquire a phenomenal concept?* Loar does not provide any adequate answer. The non-physicalist will then state that the Mary argument holds its ground because it provides an answer to that fundamental question: we gain phenomenal concepts because things contain physical and phenomenal properties. In summary, to claim that phenomenal concepts can arise from a physical property is inadequate to explain the knowledge one gains from experiencing a subjective conscious experience.[183]

I appreciate that the above responses to the objections are succinct summaries. For a detailed defence of the Mary argument, please refer to Brie Gertler's essay, *A Defense of the Knowledge Argument*[184]; Jeff McConnell's essay, which shares the same title[185]; and David Chalmers's essay, *Phenomenal Concepts and the Explanatory Gap*[186].

'Let's ignore the problem': Eliminative materialism

Eliminative materialists assume everything can be explained via physical processes, and do not accept that subjective conscious states exist. They argue that the brain is made up of neurons undergoing physical and chemical processes; therefore, explaining these complex processes will somehow explain consciousness.[187] Eliminative materialists assert that the ideas of 'folk psychology' we have developed to describe subjective consciousness (due to the current lack of solutions provided by the physical sciences) will be made redundant when neuroscience has "matured"[188]. This is when neuroscience will replace subjective consciousness with "neural activity in specialized anatomical areas".[189] In summary, science will one day explain what we call subjective consciousness; therefore, the hard problem will be solved.

Echoing the eliminative materialist approach, the analytical philosopher Patricia Churchland asserts that the apparent question of subjective consciousness will be demystified when we improve our scientific knowledge. Churchland argues the hard problem of consciousness should not be distinguished from other problems in neuroscience. The reason, according to Churchland, is that researchers have an array of problems that are unaddressed, and to argue that they will never be solved seems unreasonable. Just because the hard problem is described as mysterious or a difficult challenge to physicalism does not mean that it will never have a scientific solution. Churchland refers to the history of science in support of her arguments. History shows that science has solved many 'hard problems', indicating that the hard problem of consciousness will also be solved.[190]

However, physical and chemical processes tell us nothing about what it is like for a particular conscious being to have an internal subjective experience. This implies that, for the eliminative materialist, inner subjective experiences are just an illusion. In other words, proponents of this view do not really accept the hard problem of consciousness because they claim that matter and physical processes are all that is required to explain anything. Nevertheless, matter and physical processes cannot tell us anything about what it is like to have an inner subjective conscious experience. Furthermore, matter cannot explain the emergence of subjective conscious experience because matter is cold, blind and non-conscious. Something cannot give rise to anything unless it contains that thing in the first place or has the ability to give rise to it. Matter and physical processes are non-conscious and therefore cannot give rise to subjective conscious experience as they do not contain it.

In light of this, eliminative materialism is not an adequate explanation of the hard problem of consciousness as it ignores what requires explaining in the first place. The conclusions of Eliminative materialism can be reduced to the following absurdity: we do not have inner subjectivity. However, our ability to have inner subjective experiences is a first-person fact; it is ludicrous to deny it.

Eliminative materialism became popular with the philosopher Daniel Dennet when he published his book, *Consciousness Explained*. In this heavily criticised book, he redefined consciousness by ignoring what requires explaining: our subjective conscious states. According to Dennet, we have no real personal subjective experiences; we are simply biological robots. In other words, we are zombies with the illusion of subjective experience. Criticism of Dennet's approach, also known as *Multiple Drafts* theory, has been summarised by Professor Antti Revonsuo in his book, *Consciousness: The Science of Subjectivity*:

"Dennet's theory has been heavily criticized because it seems to redefine 'consciousness' in such a way that the term comes to mean something very different from what we originally set out to explain. Dennet's famous 1991 book is titled 'Consciousness Explained', but many felt it should have been called 'Consciousness *Explained Away*'. What most people wanted to find an explanation for is phenomenal consciousness, qualia and subjectivity, but Dennet dismisses them as mere illusions."[191]

'Subjectivity exists, but it's just matter': Reductive materialism

Reductive materialism asserts that there is a knowledge-gap between physical processes and subjective conscious experiences. However, they maintain that the gap can be explained within a materialistic philosophy. Proponents of this view assert that subjective conscious experience exists but is not distinct from physical processes. The basis for their arguments is that there is a link between certain activities in the brain and certain experiences of consciousness; therefore, consciousness can be reduced to physical processes.

Reductive materialism, unlike eliminative materialism, accepts that subjective consciousness exists but can be reduced to physical happenings in our brains. In this way, subjective consciousness is identical with neurochemical activity.[192] Although there is currently is no way of reducing all subjective conscious states to physical phenomena, reductive materialism is based on the expectation that neuroscience will follow the other sciences in that old terms, such as 'heat', will have been replaced with 'the science of mean kinetic energy of molecules'. Similarly, neuroscience may replace words like 'love' with a neurochemical equivalent. In essence, "consciousness is nothing over and above a complex set of neural activities going on in our brain".[193]

This view is not an adequate explanation for subjective conscious states because it is based on the assumption that subjective experiences are real but will be explained in the future by developments in neuroscience. Essentially, reductive materialism argues that subjective conscious states will be reduced to physical brain states. This does not solve the hard problem of consciousness. It is impossible to know what it is like for a particular organism to experience a subjective state simply by observing a bunch of neurons firing. Just like the eliminative materialists, reductive materialists cannot solve the hard problem. The inner subjective realities of the human being are once again being ignored. Professor Revonsuo explains:

> "Still, it seems clear that to talk about neural firings, activations and deactivations in different brain areas or oscillatory synchrony in neural assemblies is not at all the same thing as talking about

feelings of pain, sensations of colour, passionate emotions or inner thoughts—and never will be. What is being left out is, first and foremost, the subjective aspect of the conscious mental events."[194]

The difference between eliminative materialism and reductive materialism is quite subtle. Eliminative materialism argues that subjective consciousness is an illusion and does not exist. According to this approach, the illusion of subjective consciousness is nothing more than neurons firing. Reductive materialism accepts that subjective consciousness exists but maintains that it is nothing more than physical activity in the brain. Both fail to address the first-person fact of subjective consciousness.

'It's what you do': Behaviourism

Another approach that shares the conclusions of eliminative materialism is behaviourism. Behaviourism postulates that consciousness is defined in behavioural terms. Behaviourists assert that a person only has a certain conscious state if it can be verified by that person's behaviour (for example, Susan is in pain if, after being struck with something, she cries 'ouch!'). Behaviourism denies subjective conscious experience, and defines consciousness as the way we act rather than the way we are. This approach denies the hard problem of consciousness because it fails to acknowledge that humans can have mental states without displaying any behaviour. As the philosopher David Lund argues, we cannot dismiss the fact that we do experience inner subjective states that are not always revealed via our behaviours.[195]

Behaviourism makes a conscious state identical to a physical state. The problem with this approach is that it ignores the fact that it is the conscious state that causes the behaviour. For example, it is the pain that provokes Susan to say 'ouch!', so pain and saying 'ouch!' are not identical to each other.

'Just a bunch of inputs, mental states and outputs': Functionalism

Functionalists postulate that consciousness is defined as the functions or roles it plays, emerging from a set of relations within an organism or system, just like a computer. A function is defined as a relation of inputs, mental states and outputs. For example, if I see my bus arriving (input), I experience the mental state of worrying that I may be late due to the possibility of missing my bus (mental state); I then run towards the bus stop (output). Functionalists assert that consciousness is similar to a computer program, which arises from complex patterns within the brain.[196] Functionalism has faced a number of objections.[197] One of these is that functionalism is unable to consider subjective conscious states because they cannot be understood functionally.[198] It does not follow that just by knowing all of the inputs, mental states and outputs we will somehow know what it is like for a particular organism to experience a mental state. I can understand that when someone sees a dangerous dog running towards them (input), they will experience fear (mental state), then they will run for safety (output). However, by knowing the relations between the input, mental state and output, I am no closer to understanding what it is like for that person to be in a particular mental state. Referring back to the above example, I cannot know what it is like for someone else to experience the feeling of being threatened by a dangerous animal. Understanding how mental states relate to inputs and outputs does not give rise to knowing what it is like to be in that mental state. Many academics maintain that despite its popularity functionalism does not carry much weight as a solution to the hard problem of consciousness.[199]

'It's in the complexity': Emergent materialism

This idea is based on the concept of emergence. Emergence occurs when things become arranged in such a way that they transform into complex entities and have complicated causal relationships from which new phenomena appear.[200] There are two types of emergent materialism: the strong and the weak.

The weak form asserts that we will eventually understand subjective consciousness once all of the complex physical processes are understood. The weak form may explain how consciousness emerges from physical processes, but it does not follow that it will lead to knowledge of what is like for a conscious organism to have an inner subjective experience. Will the mystery of subjective consciousness disappear once we have understood how it emerges from all of the complex physical processes? If it does, then it seems to be denying what requires explaining in the first place. If subjective consciousness remains, then emergent materialism suffers from the same problems as reductive materialism; subjective consciousness may have a physical basis without telling us anything about what it is like to have these subjective conscious experiences.[201]

A variant of weak emergent materialism maintains that we will never understand all of the physical processes that underpin subjective consciousness. However, theoretically speaking, if we were ever to have a perfect understanding of how the brain works we could understand subjective consciousness. This form of weak emergent materialism does not explain anything at all. In the context of the argument presented in this chapter, accepting an explanation that actually explains the hard problem of consciousness is more rational then accepting an approach that does not.

The strong form of emergent materialism argues that subjective consciousness is a natural phenomenon; however, any physicalist theory that attempts to address its reality is beyond the capacity of the human intellect. This form of emergence argues that we can get a new phenomenon X from Y, without knowing how X emerges from Y. Strong emergent materialism maintains that we can get something new from the complex physical processes, but the gap in our understanding of how this new thing emerges will never be closed. This approach does not explain the hard problem of consciousness, as it admits that it cannot be explained. In my view this is no different to saying, "It just happens. It is so complex that no one knows." Revonsuo argues that strong emergent materialism will never be able to address subjective consciousness, and even if we were to be given the correct theory, it "would equal what hamsters could make of Charles Darwin's *Origins of Species* if a copy was placed in their cage."[202] Since we are trying to explain the hard problem of consciousness, then dismissing subjective consciousness as a mystery does nothing to prevent a rational person from accepting an approach that actually does coherently explain it.

Will science eventually explain subjective consciousness?

As seen from the above materialist approaches, the main argument is that a scientific explanation will someday close the current gap in our knowledge. This approach, however, does not provide an adequate explanation of consciousness, as I believe it is a form of the 'science of the gaps' fallacy.

If we examine the scientific method and the philosophy of science, we will understand that subjective consciousness is beyond the reach of science. The previous successes of science stemmed from the fact that they were able to observe new phenomena or provide new theoretical models that explained existing observable data. The likeness of a particular conscious organism cannot be understood by science. Scientists are limited to the observations they have, because science is "forced to restrict its attention to problems that observations can solve".[203] Since it is impossible to observe subjective consciousness (first-person perspective) from the perspective of the third person, science cannot address subjective consciousness.

As mentioned before, even if we were to know everything about the brain we would still not be able to address the hard problem of consciousness. Brain activity only indicates that something is happening, not what it is like for that something to happen. Even if all of the neurochemical activity were mapped out in someone's brain and correlated with first-person accounts of his or her subjective experience, science would be unable to determine that particular person's experience or why it results from physical processes.

Even if, ten years from now, a new scientific theory or biological explanation for consciousness is developed, it would still not be able to determine what it is like for a person to have a subjective experience, or why that particular subjective experience emerges from physical processes. Subjective conscious experience is outside of the scope of a scientific explanation. In light of the above, materialistic attempts to explain consciousness fail comprehensively. The neurophysiologist John C. Eccles aptly summarises this failure: "I maintain that the human mystery is incredibly demeaned by scientific reductionism, with its claim in promissory materialism...."[204]

Non-materialistic approaches

These approaches admit that there is more to reality than matter. This is a view that Islam, and theism in general, recognises. We are more than matter and energy; there is a spiritual component to our existence. However, several of these strategies aim to explain consciousness without admitting, or invoking, the existence of God. I will criticise these and explain how theism provides the most rational way of explaining consciousness.

'They're different, but we do not know how': Substance Dualism

Substance dualism is the view that there are two different substances: one is physical and the other is non-physical. These substances are fundamentally distinct and exist independently of each other. In the context of our discussion, substance dualism maintains that consciousness and the brain are different and are not from the same substance; one is material and the other immaterial, yet they interact with each other. This account of consciousness is very intuitive, making sense of our everyday experiences. For instance, we experience that conscious states can cause physical states, and vice versa. If I have the subjective conscious experience of sadness, it can cause the physical state of frowning or crying. On the converse side, if I bump my head on an object, I will feel the inner subjective experience of pain.

A key objection to substance dualism is that since conscious states and the brain are radically different, then knowing how they interact is impossible. This is known as the interactionist problem; there is—according to some philosophers—no coherent account of how and why the material brain and the immaterial consciousness interact.[205] However, this objection is based on the false assumption that if we do not know how X causes Y, then we are not justified to believe that X causes Y. There are many cases of causal interactions in which we know one thing causes another without knowing how.

Although substance dualism is a strong contender to the theistic alternative, if substance dualism is adopted within a non-theistic paradigm, it does not address some fundamental questions: *Where did the immaterial substance come from? How does it exist in the physical universe?* Moreover, a theistic explanation provides a more coherent account of how the physical brain and non-physical consciousness interact. This is why a theistic type of dualism is the most coherent approach (see *God Is the Best Explanation* section below).

'It's a lucky accident': Epiphenomenalism

With this theory, conscious states are distinct from physical states, and physical states cause conscious states, but not the other way around. In this way, conscious states are causally impotent. Popular rejections of epiphenomenalism include that, if true, a sensation of pain in my hand (conscious experience) due to a hot flame plays no causal role in my hand moving away (physical state). Another example includes that if you were to have the unfortunate experience of being chased by a drunkard hell-bent on throwing a broken bottle at you, the sight of the bottle moving towards you might create the conscious experience of fear, but the feeling of fear would not cause you to duck and protect yourself; your defensive move would occur due to some random accident. This contradicts our basic understanding of the human reality. We know that we have physical reactions due to subjective conscious states, and we also experience subjective feelings and experiences due to physical causes. If epiphenomenalism were true, human psychology would be in ruin. Just imagine a patient with depression telling his psychotherapist that his internal feelings of depression cause his anxiety attacks, only to be told that it has nothing to do with it.

'Everything is conscious': Panpsychism

Panpsychism is somewhat similar to property dualism, which asserts that one substance exists (physical substance) but contains two properties (physical and non-physical or subjective conscious properties). Panpsychism asserts that matter contains a form of subjective consciousness. From this perspective it argues that consciousness is an intrinsic property of the universe and it plays a causal role. Advocates of panpsychism include professors David Chalmers and Thomas Nagel. Since each component of matter contains consciousness, the brain's consciousness is just an accumulation of these components of consciousness. One form of panpsychism states that all matter is conscious in the same way humans are. The other form of panpsychism asserts that consciousness contained in matter is in a basic state, also known as protoconsciousness.

There are a number of problems with panpsychism. Firstly, there is an absence of evidence for the claim that matter contains subjective consciousness. Protons, electrons, quarks and atoms do not exhibit any signs of having subjective consciousness.[206] Secondly, this approach fails to provide an adequate metaphysical or physical explanation of how matter contains consciousness. Where did the property of consciousness come from? How does matter contain this subjective conscious property? The panpsychist's failure to answer these questions undermines any metaphysical and physical explanation. Thirdly, there are no examples of consciousness existing outside of the subjective experience of a living entity. For instance, what does pain mean without a self or an 'I'? What does being conscious of a thought mean without someone who is thinking? These questions strongly suggest that consciousness only makes sense with a unified conscious being experiencing an array of subjective states. Thirdly, how can a unified conscious experience emerge from many pieces of matter that all contain a form of consciousness? How do individual pieces of matter that contain subjective consciousness manage to add up to a meaningful, unified experience? If our conscious experiences were just a result of many conscious elements contained in the physical parts that make up the brain, our experience would be incoherent, or less unified. Professor Edward Feser comments on the unified meaning of a single conscious experience. He explains that our experiences are not just a summation of many different conscious elements; our experiences have a unified feel. He presents his case using the conscious experience of reading a book:

"The experience has a coherent significance or meaning, and significance or meaning for a single subject of experience. You are not only aware of the shape, texture, colors, etc. as separate elements, but are aware of them as a book; and it is you who are aware of them, rather than myriad neural events somehow each being 'aware' of one particular aspect of the book."[207]

There is a lot of academic discussion around the approaches I have summarised above. However, the main intention was to briefly introduce these approaches and bring to light some criticisms which undermine their ability to explain subjective consciousness as sufficiently as theism does.

God is the best explanation

How do we explain consciousness in light of the failed attempts to comprehensively explain our subjective personal experiences? A theistic approach is the most adequate explanation. It is far more reasonable to postulate that an All-Aware, conscious agent with volition and purpose is the author of all consciousness. Here are three main reasons why God is the best explanation:

Firstly, it answers a question that none of the existing views have answered: *Where did consciousness come from?* Professor J. P. Moreland explains how it could not have been via natural physical processes: "Our knowledge of the natural world would give us positive reasons for not believing that irreducible consciousness would appear in it, e.g., the geometrical rearrangement of inert physical entities into different spatial structures hardly seems sufficient to explain the appearance of consciousness."[208]

If matter and consciousness are distinct, it follows that consciousness could not have emerged from matter. However, if matter contains conscious properties, then how did these properties arise? In order to explain the fact that subjective conscious experiences exist, God must have created consciousness. It is far more coherent to postulate an All-Aware conscious agent to explain consciousness. From this point of view, theism offers a far richer explanation. Moreland argues that physicalist and materialist accounts of consciousness have "...no plausible way to explain the appearance of irreducible, genuine mental properties/events in the cosmos... when compared to the rich explanatory resources for theism...."[209]

Secondly, theism answers how consciousness could have entered the physical world. It often surprises people how non-physical entities like the soul can interact, and in fact control, physical aspects like the bodies of humans and animals, but theism explains this very naturally. God's comprehensive will and Divine activity ensure a world where the physical and non-physical interact. Charles Taliaferro explains:

"But in a theistic view of consciousness, there is no parlor trick or discrete miraculous act of God behind the emergence of consciousness. Consciousness emerges from the physical cosmos through an abiding comprehensive will of God that there be a world of physical and non-physical objects, properties, and relations. The relation between matter, energy, consciousness, the laws of space-time, *tout court*, all stem from an overwhelming, divine, activity."[210]

According to a non-theistic approach to consciousness, consciousness seems to have miraculously popped into existence without any adequate physical explanation. However, theism does not face this problem, as the emergence of consciousness is viewed as part of reality. Since God is conscious, Ever-Living and All-Aware, it is plausible that the world He created contains beings with a conscious awareness of themselves. Taliaferro similarly concludes:

"From the vantage point of a fundamentally materialist cosmology, the emergence of consciousness seems strange; it is likened to claiming 'then a miracle happens.' But from the vantage point of theism, the emergence of consciousness may be seen as something deeply rooted in the very nature of reality. The creation of animal and human consciousness is not some isolated miracle, but a reflection of the underlying structure of reality."[211]

Theism explains the interaction between nonphysical mental and physical brain states. God's will and power have enabled such interaction to take place, as this interaction is part and parcel of the reality that God has created. Simply, if, in the beginning of the cosmos, only matter existed, then consciousness would not. However, if in the beginning a type of consciousness created the physical world, then the interaction between nonphysical mental states and physical brain states makes sense.

Thirdly, theism explains our ability to have subjective conscious states and the fact that we have an awareness of what it is to be like ourselves, experiencing tastes, sounds and textures. Since the universe was created by an Ever-Living, Alive, All-Aware Being, it follows that we have been given

130 | *The Divine Reality*

this capacity to be aware of our inner subjective states:

"God, there is no god except Him, the Ever Living."[212]

"And He is the All-subtle, the All-aware."[213]

A theistic explanation for the emergence of consciousness has greater explanatory power than competing explanations. I must stress here, however, that I am not denying the usefulness of biological explanations in unearthing neuro-correlations. Neuroscience can be conducted just as vigorously and fruitfully in a theistic context. What I am advocating is adding theism as a philosophical basis to fully explain what non-theistic explanations cannot: the hard problem of consciousness. In this sense, my approach is a form of dualism, which can be called theistic-dualism. In theistic-dualism, neuroscience is not undermined and all the research projects can continue to provide their amazing insights and conclusions on the topic. However, theistic-dualism is a metaphysical thesis that provides a comprehensive explanation. Professor Taliaferro advocates a similar position:

"I do not see why the brain sciences cannot continue with its study of psycho-physical interaction. The failure to identify metaphysically consciousness with brain states does not for a nanosecond impede the study of correlation. Moreover one may be a dualist and treat consciousness and brain states, the person and body, as functional units without supposing that there is only one kind of thing metaphysically that is in play. Mind-body (or, as I prefer to call it, integrative) dualism is a thesis in metaphysics... integrative dualism is not a scientific hypothesis that competes with any scientific claims."[214]

God's existence is required to explain subjective conscious experience. In addition, the hard problem of consciousness and the existence of inner subjective experiences clearly point to an All-Aware Being that created the universe and the ability for you and I to have an awareness of our subjective conscious states.

We are not meant to know much about the soul

Muslim readers will rightly ask if this argument is compatible with normative Islamic theology. The common objection usually includes the fact that the Qur'an explicitly states that the *rooh* (meaning soul, spirit, consciousness or the thing that animates the body) is the affair or command of God, and humanity has been given very little knowledge about it. Therefore, we should keep silent on the matter:

> "And they ask you, [O Muhammad], about the soul. Say, 'The soul is of the affair of my Lord. And mankind have not been given of knowledge except a little.'"[215]

To reconcile this apparent theological conflict, it must be understood that this verse concerns the essence of consciousness or the soul, not its existence. The verse affirms that an immaterial substance animates the body—in other words, a soul or consciousness. This is exactly what the argument in this chapter has presented: that the existence of consciousness can only be explained by a non-materialist worldview. The chapter is not discussing anything beyond what is already implied by Islamic source texts. For instance, the Qur'an affirms that the *rooh* is different from our material universe, that it animates the body, that it is a unified 'I', and that it was created by God. Therefore, nothing here contradicts core orthodox Islamic principles.

To conclude, I think we must consider the fact that God tells us to ponder within ourselves, and by doing so we may conclude that if there is no God, then we could not have any subjective conscious experience—in other words, by denying God, we deny ourselves!

> "Do they not reflect within themselves?"[216]

Chapter 8
Divine Precision
The Designed Universe

Imagine you woke up one morning and walked to the kitchen to prepare your breakfast. As you approached the kitchen table, you found two pieces of toast with your favourite chocolate spread all over them. However, the spread has been arranged into the words 'I love you'. You are surprised, but why? Do you think that the pieces of bread somehow managed to toast themselves, and the chocolate spread was able to arrange itself in such a way—all by chance? Or do you assume that your loved one decided to wake up a little early and prepare the toast in advance? Every rational human being on this planet will deny that it happened without any intention or cause; blind chance does not suffice as an explanation.

The universe is no different. It has an orderly and precise cosmic architecture that points towards purposeful design. The universe has the right set of laws to permit the existence of life, and it is ordered in a particular way to allow humans to flourish. If the laws were different or the universe did not contain a life-sensitive arrangement of stars, planets, and other physical things of varying sizes, you would not be here reading this book. In fact, there would be no human life at all.

Consider another analogy.[217] Imagine you are an astronaut working for NASA. The year is 2070, and you will be the first human being to visit an Earth-like planet in another galaxy. Your mission is to search for life. You finally land, and as you get out of your spaceship, you see nothing but rocks. However, as you continue your travels you eventually find something that looks like a huge greenhouse. Inside, you can see human-like creatures walking around, eating, playing, working and living normal productive lives. You also notice plants, trees, and other vegetation. As you approach the structure, friendly ambassadors receive you and invite you in. During your initial meeting with these friendly 'aliens', they tell you that the structure has the right levels of oxygen. It also has adequate amounts of water and chemical compounds to facilitate the production of food and life-supporting vegetation. Amazed by what you hear, you ask them how they managed to create a fully functioning ecological system that sustains life. One of the ambassadors responds, "It happened by chance".

Immediately your mind starts to comprehend the implications of such a ludicrous statement. The only possible explanation for the structure is that it was designed by an intelligent being, not some random physical process.

As these thoughts run through your mind, another ambassador interrupts and says, "He is only joking." Everybody laughs.

If a small ecological structure on a rocky planet evokes the conclusion that it must have been designed, then imagine what we should conclude about the whole universe. The universe and everything within it obeys physical laws. If these laws were different there would be no complex conscious life. The universe contains billions of stars and galaxies. Among the countless galaxies occur innumerable planets. One of these planets is our home, Earth. Our planet contains trillions of conscious creatures. Imagine the conclusion we must reach if the reason these conscious beings exist is due to a sensitive arrangement of celestial bodies and physical laws.

The inevitable conclusion is simple, yet profound: this was not a result of chance.

The Islamic basis

This argument has an Islamic foundation. The Qur'an refers to celestial objects, the alternation of night and day, vegetation, animals and other physical phenomena. God created all of these things with a Divine precision: "The sun and the moon [move] by precise calculation. And the stars and trees prostrate. And the heaven He raised and imposed the *meezaan*."[218]

The Arabic word *meezan* has a few meanings. These include balance and Divine precision. This word indicates that the cosmos was created with precision, balance and harmony. Many other references in the Qur'an indicate this cosmic precision, order and harmony in the universe:

"Indeed, in the creation of the heavens and the Earth and the alternation of the night and the day are signs for those of understanding."[219]

"The sun and the moon [move] by precise calculation."[220]

"And He has subjected for you the night and day and the sun and moon, and the stars are subjected by His command. Indeed in that are signs for a people who reason."[221]

Islamic scholarship has referred to the design of the cosmos to evoke the need for a designer and maker. They have even used it in public debates. For example, Al-Ghazali writes: "How can even the lowest mind, if he reflects at all the marvels of this earth and sky, the brilliant fashioning of plants and animals, remain blind to the fact that this wonderful world with its settled order must have a maker to design, determine and direct it?"[222]

Abu Hanifa, one of the great scholars of Islam, once engaged in a discussion with an atheist. It was reported that the scholar successfully used a variant of design argument:

"'Before we enter into a discussion on this question, tell me what you think of a boat in the Euphrates which goes to shore, loads itself with food and other things, then returns, anchors and unloads all by itself without anyone sailing or controlling it?'

They said, 'That is impossible; it could never happen.' Thereupon he said to them, 'If it is impossible with respect to a ship, how is it possible for this whole world, with all its vastness, to move by itself?'"[223]

These Qur'anic verses and Islamic scholarship echo the discoveries in physics in the past decade, which have shown that the universe has physical laws that seem to be precisely set for life, and that the universe has a particular order that facilitates human existence. This precision has also been referred to as 'fine-tuning' by myriad physicists, theologians and philosophers.

Fine-tuning

The fine-tuning of the universe consists of various aspects. Firstly, if the laws of the universe were to not exist, life, especially complex conscious life, would not be possible. Secondly, the universe displays a fascinating order; the way celestial and other physical objects have been arranged facilitates life on Earth. All of the data associated with these different aspects of fine-tuning provide a strong cumulative case for the universe being designed to harbour complex, sentient life.

Physical laws

There must have been exactly the right set of laws for life to exist. If these laws were even slightly changed, the result would be a universe without complex life:

- **The law of gravity**: Gravity is the force of attraction between two masses. Without gravity, there would be no force to aggregate things. Therefore, there would be no stars (and no planets). Without any stars there would not be any sustainable source of energy to facilitate life.[224] The universe would be a dark, empty vacuum.

- **The electromagnetic force**: This unique force affects everything within the universe. The electromagnetic force is responsible for giving things strength, shape and hardness. Without it, atoms would not exist, because nothing would keep the electrons in orbit. If there were no atoms, there could not be any life. The electromagnetic force also causes chemical bonding by attracting charges. In absence of any chemical bonding, life could not exist.[225]

An interesting aspect of the electromagnetic force is that it has one-force strength, yet it satisfies a range of requirements. In his book, *Infinite Minds: A Philosophical Cosmology*, Professor John Leslie writes:

"Electromagnetism has one-force strength, which enables multiple key processes to take place: it allows stars to burn steadily for billions of years; it enables carbon synthesis in stars; it ensures that leptons do not replace quarks, which would have made atoms impossible; it is responsible for protons not decaying too fast or repelling each other too strongly, which would have made chemistry impossible. How is it possible for the same one-force strength to satisfy so many different requirements, when it seems that different strengths would be required for each of these processes?"[226]

Maybe a satisfactory answer to Leslie's question is that this force is precisely calibrated to satisfy all of these requirements.

- **The strong nuclear force**: Since the nucleus is made up of positively charged protons, it should just fly apart, because like charges repel each other. However, the nucleus remains intact because of the strong nuclear force. If this were changed, "the universe would most likely consist of a giant black hole."[227]

- **The weak nuclear force**: The weak nuclear force is stronger than the force of gravity, but its strength is only effectual at extremely small distances. It is responsible for fuelling stars and the formation of elements. It is also responsible for radioactive decay. The sun would not be able to burn without this force, as it plays an important role in nuclear fusion. If this force were slightly stronger or weaker, stars would not form.

In light of the above examples of the fine-tuning of physical laws, any rational person would ask some serious questions: *Where did these laws of physics come from? Why do we observe these laws rather than a different set? How do these laws drive non-conscious, non-rational, blind and random physical processes to facilitate human life?* It is a sign of a rational mind to conclude that a lawmaker, a 'grand' mathematician, or cosmic 'mind' created these laws to facilitate conscious life.

Cosmic order

The orderly display we observe in the universe, and its celestial harmony, has not only evoked awe in the average thinker, but also mesmerised the greatest minds. Albert Einstein once said:

"I'm not an atheist, and I do not think I can call myself a pantheist. We are in the position of a little child entering a huge library filled with books in many languages. The child knows someone must have written those books. It does not know how. It does not understand the languages in which they are written. The child dimly suspects a mysterious order in the arrangement of the books but does not know what it is. That, it seems to me, is the attitude of even the most intelligent human being toward God. We see the universe marvellously arranged and obeying certain laws but only dimly understand these laws. Our limited minds grasp the mysterious force that moves the constellations."[228]

Even the outspoken atheist Richard Dawkins has commented on the order in the universe. Although he dismisses the design hypothesis and provides his own naturalistic explanation, he still highlights what mesmerised the likes of Einstein:

"But what I see as I write is that I am lucky to be alive and so are you. We live on a planet that is all but perfect for our kind of life: not too warm and not too cold, basking in kindly sunshine, softly watered; a gently spinning, green and gold harvest fe gravitational pull 'sucks' up asteroids stival of a planet... what are the odds that a planet picked at random would have these complaisant properties?"[229]

The universe is indeed "marvellously arranged" and it displays intricate order. If this order were different, it would be highly unlikely that human life could flourish. Here are some selected examples to reflect upon:

- **The position of our planet**: One of the life-supporting features of our planet is its distance from the Sun. Earth is located in an area known as the habitable zone. This zone is defined as the "region where heating from the central star provides a planetary surface temperature at which a water ocean neither freezes over nor exceeds boiling point."[230] If our planet were slightly closer to the Sun, it would be too hot to host life. If it were farther away, it would be too cold to facilitate complex life, such as our own.

- **Jupiter's gravitational pull**: The absence of the gas giant Jupiter in our solar system would have severe implications for life. Professor of Geological Sciences Peter Ward maintains, "Without Jupiter, there is a strong likelihood that animal life would not exist on Earth today."[231] Jupiter acts as a cosmic shield; it prevents comets and asteroids from bombarding our planet because its gravitational pull 'sucks' up asteroids. Without our friendly gas giant, the development of advanced life might not have been possible.

  Rebecca Martin, a NASA Sagan Fellow who studied the influence of Jupiter, states, "Our study shows that only a tiny fraction of planetary systems observed to date seem to have giant planets in the right location to produce an asteroid belt of the appropriate size, offering the potential for life on a nearby rocky planet... Our study suggests that our solar system may be rather special."[232]

  Without the presence of Jupiter, life on our planet would have been extremely difficult to sustain, due to the large number of collisions by asteroids and comets.[233] [234]

- **Lunar tides**: The relatively large size of Earth's moon is responsible for tides, due to its gravitational pull. After the Moon's formation, it was closer to the Earth than it is now, but this proximity was short-lived. If the Moon had not receded (due to angular momentum), there would have been serious effects on our planet. These include heating the Earth's surface, which would have prevented complex life from emerging. Professor Ward explains that a closer Moon would have flexed the Earth's crust and produced frictional heating, possibly melting its surface: "The ocean tides (and land tides) from a nearby Moon would have been enormous, and the flexing of the Earth's crust, along with the frictional heating, may have actually melted the rocky surface."[235]

- **Stabilizing the tilt of the Earth's spin axis**: The Moon has also been responsible for stabilizing the tilt of the Earth's axis. Professor Ward explains that even though "the direction of the tilt varies over periods of tens of thousands of years as the planet wobbles, much like precession of a spinning top, the angle of the tilt relative to the orbit plane remains almost fixed."[236]

This angle has held steady for hundreds of millions of years due to the gravitational pull of the moon. If the moon were smaller, or had a different location in relation to the Sun and Jupiter, it would not provide "long-term stability of the Earth's temperature".[237] Therefore, if the Earth did not have a moon, the climate of our planet would be dynamic, severe and ever changing. Only small organisms would have emerged, and complex life would not be possible.

In light of the above, what best explains the laws of physics and the orderly display of our solar system? There are a few options: chance, physical necessity, the multiverse or design.

Chance

For this fine-tuning to have arisen by chance indicates that the laws of physics and the display of our solar system occurred without any intention or purpose. They were a result of accidental, random and haphazard causes. This is an irrational assertion. Consider this painting of Bruce Lee[238].

If I told you that it was a result of chance—that some ink fell on the canvas and produced this picture—you would dismiss the idea immediately. That's because your experiences and background information tell you it is impossible. Similarly, if I argued that the Statue of Liberty was a result of blind chance, you would think I was deluded.

The chance hypothesis is not only irrational, it is counter-discourse. What I mean by this is that if someone were to claim chance, it would be equivalent to making any type of irrational claim. For instance, I could tell an atheist that I believe that my mother is not really the woman who I call my mother, but rather a large pink elephant that was born on Pluto and flew here on a giant feather. My atheist friend would call me crazy, but I would reply, "There's still a chance." Adopting the chance hypothesis renders all claims possible, and the role of reason would be made redundant in our academic and everyday discussions. I could assert that Islam is truth because there is a chance that it is, and I would be within my epistemic rights to make such a claim because the minute someone adopts the chance hypothesis as an argument, it opens the door to anyone claiming anything they want to claim.

An atheist who accepts the chance hypothesis as a valid explanation for the fine-tuning of the physical laws must be accused of intellectual double standards. In their everyday decisions, chance is not factored in as a reasonable justification for extremely improbable things. Consider an atheist telling her son not to eat any cookies before he goes to bed, only to find him sleeping on the floor with crumbs all over his face and the cookie jar open right next to him. What do you think she will conclude? Do you think the chance hypothesis would even enter her mind? Of course not. Imagine such reasoning being applied to our financial transactions, or in courts of law and politics. Day-to-day life, world affairs and our economy would be chaotic.

Many atheists raise the epistemic bar when it comes to God, yet for their day-to-day lives use a different standard. The reason is because their insistence in denying the obvious has an emotional—and some would argue, spiritual—cause. For some atheists, the so-called rational arguments serve as a veil to hide a greater issue: the arrogance of not wanting to worship God (*see Chapter 15*).

But there's still a chance!

Some atheists still argue that there is still—no matter how unreasonable—a possibility that cosmic order is not the result of any intention or purpose. They claim that our life-permitting universe exists due to a remarkably lucky accident.

To answer this objection, take the likelihood principle into consideration. A rational mind would agree that whenever a set of data is unlikely under one hypothesis, then that data counts as evidence in support of a hypothesis that is more likely. Let me illustrate this principle with an example.[239] Imagine a paternity test for baby George had to be done on Paul Y and John X. The mother argues that Paul Y is most likely to be the biological father. Nevertheless, she is unsure and wants a paternity test to be performed on them both. John X, however, believes he is the father and is determined to prove it.

The DNA results report that Paul Y's DNA matches baby George's DNA, and John X's DNA does not. In light of the evidence, the mother's hypothesis is far more likely. John X's hypothesis is not supported by the data at all. According to this principle, both DNA results support the mother's hypothesis. Because for her hypothesis to be true, John X's DNA must not match with baby George's, and Paul Y's DNA must provide a match. Therefore, the data supports the mother's hypothesis over John X's.

The data of the fine-tuning of the universe are best explained by design rather than chance, because fine-tuning supports the fact that there was some type of intelligent 'pre-planning' involved, rather than an accidental, random and haphazard set of causes. Applying this principle to the argument I have presented so far, we can see that the data does not make sense under the chance hypothesis and favours the design hypothesis.

Physical necessity?

With the concept of physical necessity, the cosmic order has to be the way that it is. This is false for two main reasons. Firstly, we would have to believe that a universe that could not permit our existence would be impossible. This, however, is not the case. Another universe with a different set of laws could have been created.[240] The physicist Paul Davies explains that "the physical universe does not have to be the way it is: it could have been otherwise."[241]

Secondly, those who state that the universe had to permit life are making a claim that has no evidence. Referring back to the toast analogy, it is like looking at your toast and the chocolate spread and saying that it had to occur. This is obviously false, because the bread could have not been toasted and the chocolate spread could have been replaced with butter.

Multiverse?

Some argue that the fine-tuning can be explained by postulating the existence of many universes. One of these is our universe. If the number of universes was a very high number, then the likelihood of having a universe that permits life would be reasonable. Referring back to our example of the painting, the multiverse essentially suggests that spilling ink multiple times might result in the image of Bruce Lee. There are a few variations of the multiverse theory, and this is not the space to address every one. However, a few fundamental points can be made to dismiss the multiverse theory in general.

Firstly, the multiverse theory is superfluous. It unnecessarily multiplies entities beyond necessity. Professor Richard Swinburne asserts, "It is crazy to postulate a trillion (causally connected) universes to explain the features of one universe when postulating one entity (God) will do the job."[242]

Secondly, there is no evidence to support the multiverse theory. Professor Anthony Flew writes, "...the fact that it is logically possible that there are multiple universes with their own laws of nature does not show that such universes do exist. There is currently no evidence in support of a multiverse. It remains a speculative idea."[243]

Not only does the multiverse have no evidence, it is unscientific. Luke A. Barnes, a postdoctoral researcher at the Sydney Institute for Astronomy, explains that the multiverse theory is beyond the reach of observation:

"The history of science has repeatedly taught us that experimental testing is not an optional extra. The hypothesis that a multiverse actually exists will always be untestable. The most optimistic scenario is where a physical theory, which has been well-tested in our universe, predicts a universe-generating mechanism. Even then, there would still be questions beyond the reach of observation, such as whether the necessary initial conditions for the generator hold in the metaspace... Moreover, the process by which a new universe is spawned almost certainly cannot be observed."[244]

The most popular version of the multiverse, as advocated by many leading cosmologists and theoretical physicists, is the idea that universes are generated by a physical process or set of laws. Essentially, they argue that the laws of physics had to exist for the universe, and all the other universes, to emerge. The problem with this version of the multiverse theory is that it takes more faith to believe in some physical process producing universes than God, because we would have to believe that the physical processes magically manifested themselves without any explanation. Furthermore, it would be within our epistemic rights to ask where these physical laws or processes came from. Significantly, the physical processes themselves would need to be 'well designed' to produce a single universe to permit our existence.[245] So it seems to me that advocates of this version of the multiverse are just pushing fine-tuning and order up a level and not explaining anything at all. Either way, if the multiverse were true it would not provide a challenge to God's existence (*see Chapter 6*).

It must have been designed!
The physical laws and the remarkable order in the universe cannot be explained by chance, necessity or the multiverse, and therefore the best explanation is that it is a result of design. Postulating purposeful 'pre-planning' and intelligence behind the cosmos is a more coherent and rational explanation than the alternatives. The simplicity and force of this argument is evident in the example of someone coming across a garden with a neatly arranged bed of flowers forming the words 'I love you', and concluding they were designed by a gardener.

However, there are a few objections that need to be addressed.[246]

Who designed the designer?
The 'who designed the designer' objection can be found in Richard Dawkins's book, *The God Delusion:* "...because the designer hypothesis immediately raises the larger problem of who designed the designer."[247] This contention claims that if a designer exists, then surely the designer also

requires a designer.

Firstly, a basic principle in the philosophy of science dictates that when an explanation is understood to be the best possible account for a particular phenomenon, the explanation itself does not require a further explanation. The following example illustrates this point:

Imagine 5000 years from now, a group of archaeologists start digging in London's Hyde Park and find parts of a car and a bus. They would be justified in concluding that these finds were not the result of any biological process but the products of an unidentified civilization. However, if some sceptics argued that we cannot make such inferences because we do not know anything about this civilization, how they lived and who created them, would the archaeologists' conclusions be deemed untrue? Of course not.

Secondly, if we take this contention seriously, it could undermine the very foundations of science and philosophy themselves. If we require an explanation for the basic assumptions of science—for example, that the external world exists—where do you think our level of scientific progress would be? Additionally, if we were to apply this type of question to every attempted explanation, we would end up with an infinite regression of explanations, and an infinite regression of explanations would defeat the whole purpose of science in the first place—which is to provide an explanation.[248]

The designer must be more complex

Another objection argues that since an explanation must be as simple as possible—and not create more questions than it answers—postulating God's existence to explain the design fails. God must be more 'complex' than the universe; therefore, maintaining that God designed the universe just moves the problem up a level.

This objection misrepresents the Islamic conception of God. In Islamic theology, God is simply and uniquely one. Consider the eloquent summary of God in the Qur'an: "Say, 'He is God the One, God the eternal. He begot no one nor was He begotten. No One is comparable to Him.'"[249]

Professor Anthony Flew comments on the simplicity of the concept of God, stating that the idea of God is "an idea so simple that it is understood by all the adherents of the three great monotheistic religions"[250].

Is God physically complex?

Another problem with this contention is that it assumes God is made of many physical parts. The reason that this assumption is implied is due to the fact that entities with complex abilities must also be physically complex. If God can answer billions of prayers, maintain the vast universe and know everything that happens within it, then He must have a complex physical makeup. This, however, is a false assumption. Complex ability does not imply complex makeup. Consider a straight razor and an electric shaver as an example. An electric shaver can shave hair and a straight razor can also shave hair. They both have the same ability, but the electric shaver is far more complex than the straight razor. Yet the straight razor can have more abilities than the physically complex electric shaver. It can cut fruit and materials such as cardboard; it can even carve and make holes.

I believe this objection can be easily dismissed by the following illustration: I know that humans are far more complex than cars. However, just because a human is more complex than a car does not mean that a human did not design it. This simple consideration is enough to take the wind out of the prior false objection.

'God of the gaps'?
The 'god of the gaps' objection is an overused atheist cliché. In popular atheist discourse it is used as an almost indiscriminate weapon in their 'intellectual' armoury. The assumption of this objection is that science will eventually explain the need for God by providing explanations for the currently unexplained phenomena. In the context of the design argument, the 'god of the gaps' objection carries little weight. Here are three reasons why:

1. When an atheist puts forward this objection, he or she is essentially claiming that given the scientific data we have accumulated thus far, God is actually the best explanation for the universe's design, but there's still some hope that in some unspecified future, scientific progress will refute the design argument. This is nothing short of blind faith in science, as it is tantamount to saying, "Science cannot address this issue, but we have hope."

2. The atheist's predicament gets worse once we consider that a key premise of the 'god of the gaps' objection is false. It holds that science will eventually close the gap in our knowledge. However, science does not always close the gaps; it sometimes widens them. A hundred years ago we believed that cells were just blobs of protoplasm. However, since the 1950s we have become aware of the vast information-coding system in all cells. This discovery, instead of answering our questions, widened the gap in our understanding of how the first cells emerged.

3. Finally, I would like to ask the atheist to consider what questions science has actually answered. Science has shown mechanisms within the universe, how everything works and the physical laws involved. However, science has failed to provide answers that have deep existential significance. Science has not explained fine-tuning, the beginning of the universe (*see Chapter 5*), the origins of life, nor the nature and emergence of consciousness (*see Chapter 7*). Science does not have a good track record of answering questions that have profound metaphysical implications (*see Chapter 12*).

There is no likelihood!

Some contend that the argument presented in this chapter does not make sense because terms like 'probability' and 'likelihood' cannot be applied to the fine-tuning and cosmic order in the universe. This contention holds that mathematical probability cannot be assumed, because we only have one universe to observe. To have a mathematical probability we need to have a probability distribution. A mathematical probability is the number of ways an event can occur divided by the total number of possible outcomes. Since there are no other universes that we can observe, there are no other possible outcomes. Therefore, mathematical probability cannot be applied, and it renders the design hypothesis redundant.

This contention is misplaced. It mistakenly assumes that the argument refers to a mathematical probability; it does not. The type of probability that it takes into consideration is epistemic.[251] This type of probability is not based on any number of possible outcomes; rather, it addresses the rational acceptability of a particular event considering the data we have at our disposal. Generally speaking, epistemic probability involves a hypothesis (H) and evidence (E). The greater the E for a particular H, the more likely that H is true. A good example is a crime scene:

Imagine there is a dead man with a knife next to him and blood all over the floor and on his body. The detective believes that his wife is guilty of his murder. He discovers the following vital pieces of data: the wife has no alibi, and he has detected her fingerprints and DNA on the knife. The detective concludes that it is highly likely that the deceased's wife is responsible for his murder. The evidence provides support for the detective's hypothesis. This is a clear example of epistemic probability.

None of the above examples of the fine-tuning of the physical laws and the cosmic order involve mathematical probability. All that has been said is that if the laws were different, the existence of a life-permitting universe would be unlikely, and given our background knowledge of designed things, the order of the cosmos supports the fact that this universe is designed for human existence.

Most of the universe is uninhabitable! So where is this so-called design?

This objection posits that if the universe was supposed to be designed by a cosmic designer, then why does the universe permit life only in an extremely small section of the universe? This objection is based on a flawed assumption that the whole universe is supposed to exist for human habitation. According to Islamic theology, this assumption is false. The Islamic texts are explicitly clear that the size of our life-permitting planet is insignificant compared to the rest of the universe.

Why did God design an imperfect universe?

This objection follows from the previous one. The disputants maintain that if God designed the universe, why would He design one that exhibits 'bad design'? In other words, why is the universe designed in a way that facilitates life only in a very small section?

This objection does not deny the fact that the universe is designed. However, it addresses the ability of the designer. A key assumption behind this objection is that if the designer is God, a perfect Being, then what He creates must exhibit a better design to facilitate human habitation. This is a false assumption because this is not the purpose of the entire cosmos. Rather, part of its purpose is to contain human beings in a small section of the universe. This is the Islamic view of human habitation. It holds that every corner of the universe is not supposed to be fit for life, and is not supposed to last forever. (This, however, does not dismiss the idea that life can exist on other planets. The point is that life is not meant to exist in every part of the universe.) From this perspective the design of the universe perfectly fits its purpose. Therefore, this contention is incorrect.

The Weak Anthropic Principle objection

The weak anthropic principle argues that we should not be surprised that there is fine-tuning of the physical laws and cosmic order in the universe, because if the universe was not finely tuned for life, our existence would not be possible. However, we do exist. Therefore, we should not be surprised that the universe permits our existence. This is why, according to this objection, the fine-tuning of the universe needs no explanation.

This contention can be summarised in the following way:

1. If we exist, the universe must have features that would permit our existence.
2. We exist.
3. Therefore, the universe has features that permit our existence.

The conclusion is indisputable. However, once again we have a misplaced contention. The fine-tuning does not assert that we need to explain the fact that our existence fits with the universe's features. It seeks an explanation for the way our existence seems to fit with the universe's features. In other words, it seeks an explanation for the improbability of these features permitting our existence. The laws of the universe and the cosmic order could have been different to permit our existence.

The following story clarifies why the anthropic principle objection is misplaced.[252] Imagine one day, while driving home, you accidentally take a wrong turn and end up in a secluded industrial area. Your car stops working, so you decide to take a walk to see if you can find anyone to help you. Suddenly a group of armed people dressed in nuclear-type suits handcuff you, put a bag over your head and push you into the back of a car.

After a few hours you are forced out of the car and walk towards a building. Eventually the armed group take the bag off your head, and place you in a chair. You look around the room, and all you can see are white walls and bright lights. However, right in front of you is a huge machine that looks like a giant futuristic washing machine. Everything turns silent and you hear a voice ordering you to climb the stairs and get inside the machine. You are told you are the first participant to try the newly invented time machine. You have no choice in the matter. You enter the machine and within minutes you feel lots of heat and hear lots of noise, and your surroundings become blurry. You lose consciousness. After a while, you wake up and find yourself in 1625. You are tied up against a tree and you can see 100 Native Americans, approximately 10 yards away, pointing their arrows at you. These Native Americans have never missed when shooting an arrow, and they all have the ability to kill a fly while riding on a horse, blindfolded. You hear someone count down from 10, and then someone screams, 'Fire'. Every single one of these American Indians is aiming for your heart. However, you open your eyes and realize every single one of them has missed their intended target: you. Now, there are two points I want to bring to your attention. Firstly, you should not be surprised that you are still alive because they missed; if you were not alive you wouldn't be able to know. Secondly, you should be extremely surprised that the reason you are alive is based on the improbability of them missing. The anthropic principle argues the first point, while the argument presented in this chapter makes a case for the second. We should not be surprised that we are alive in a universe that has features to permit our existence. However, we should be surprised of the improbability of these features permitting our existence. Hence, the anthropic principle misses the point.

You are assuming life is special

An interesting objection to the fine-tuning argument is that it is 'anthropocentric'. In other words, it assumes that there is something special about human life that requires fine-tuning. If there was no sentient life, we could still say that the universe was finely tuned for stars and planets. If there were no celestial objects, we could say that the universe was finely tuned for sub-atomic particles. This implies that the fine-tuning argument can be applied to anything in the universe; therefore, it is not a good argument at all.

This objection can be responded to in two ways:

1. Even if the universe was not fine-tuned for human existence, the argument could still be made for the existence of the universe itself. The universe contains complex celestial objects, along with the intricate chemical processes that are responsible for—and make up—these cosmic objects. This complexity requires an explanation. If such a universe did not exist, and there was just an empty universe with random particles, there wouldn't be much for the universe to fine-tune for. However, there is a complex cosmic order that the universe seems to be fine-tuned for, therefore it is deserving of an explanation.

2. Life, especially human life, is extremely complex. Therefore, it is the mark of a rational mind to search for an explanation for the existence of such complexity, given the fact that this complexity is based on the physical laws and cosmic order being fine-tuned.

Other-forms-of-life objection

Another common objection to the fine-tuning argument is that it is based on the assumption that the only life that could exist is carbon-based life. If the laws of physics were different, carbon-based life might have been impossible. However, other non-carbon forms of life could have existed if the laws of physics were different. Therefore, intelligent life could exist under a different cosmic order. The fine-tuning argument, however, is not based on this hypothesis. It is based on two reasonable assumptions. The first is that conscious intelligent life requires an energy source, whether that life is carbon-based or not. For instance, without gravity there would be no stars, and without stars there would be no energy source for life. The second is that conscious life requires some form of complexity. For example, if the strong nuclear force were slightly changed no atoms would exist apart from hydrogen. It is inconceivable that complex conscious life could be derived from hydrogen alone. If the physical laws were different, any form of stable and complex life could not exist. These are rational and coherent assumptions to make.[253]

The fine-tuning or design argument is one of the most intuitive. Its power and simplicity are difficult to challenge, just as it would be difficult to prove that your toast toasted itself and managed to spell out 'I love you', using your favourite chocolate spread, all by chance. It is clear that there must have been some purposeful design. However, the universe is far more complex and displays far more precision than three words on a piece of toast. It stands to reason that the only conclusion is that there is a cosmic designer who established order and precision in the universe to facilitate conscious life.

Chapter 9
Know God, Know Good
God and Objective Morality

Imagine you have come back from a busy day and you switch on the television. You skim through some of the channels. Shocked by a headline, you stop at a popular international news channel. Sure enough, the headline is truly appalling: *Man Beheads Five-Year-Old Boy*.

Now let me ask you a question. Was what this man did morally wrong? You, like the majority of decent human beings, say yes. Now answer *this* question: is it *objectively* morally wrong? Again, like most, you say yes.

However, here's a final question: *Why is it objective?*

This is where it gets tricky.

Defining 'objective'

In order to answer this question, the best place to start is with the word 'objective'. A basic definition of the term refers to considering or representing facts without being influenced by personal feelings or opinions. In the case of morals, objective means that morality is not dependent or based on one's mind or personal feelings. In this sense, it is 'outside' of one's personal limited faculties. Mathematical truths (1+1=2) or scientific truths, like the Earth going around the Sun, are true regardless of what we feel about them. Therefore, if these morals are 'outside' ourselves, they have to be grounded. In other words, they need a foundation. If objective morals do not depend on our limited faculties, then answers to the following questions are required: *Where did they come from? What are their nature?* In order to answer these questions a rational foundation is required. This will explain their objective nature and provide a rationale of where they came from. These questions refer to an area in philosophy known as moral ontology.

Another way of describing objective moral truths is that they transcend human subjectivity. For instance, the fact that killing a five-year-old is morally wrong will always be true, even if the whole world were to agree that killing a young child is morally right. Not only do we recognise that some morals are objective, they also provide us with a sense of moral obligation or duty. In other words, there are some things that we ought to do and other things that we ought not to do. We have moral duties and obligations, and these seem to come from outside the limited self. Professor Ian Markham explains that our moral language denotes something above and beyond ourselves: "Embedded in the word 'ought' is the sense of a moral fact transcending our life and world... The underlying character of moral language implies something universal and external."[254]

Back to the question

Coming back to the tricky question I raised earlier, let us try to answer it: *Why is it objective?* The answer is simple. The morals that we consider to be objective are so because God exists.[255] Before I explain this further, I want to ensure that this has nothing to do with the beliefs that someone has. I am not saying "you cannot be an atheist and display moral or good behaviour" or "you have to believe in God to have moral traits such as defending the innocent or feeding the poor" or "just by being a believer you will behave well." What I am saying is that if God does not exist, then there are no objective moral truths. Sure, we can act as if moral truths are objective, and many atheists throughout history have demonstrated admirable moral fortitude without believing morality requires a Divine basis. However, what I'm arguing is that, with God out of the picture, these moral values are nothing more than social conventions. Therefore, moral truths such as "murdering innocent people for entertainment is wrong" and "defending the innocent is good", for example, are merely social conventions without God, just like saying it is wrong to pass wind in public. This conclusion is based on the fact that God is the only rational foundation for objective morals. No other concept adequately provides such a foundation.

God provides this foundation because He is external to the universe and transcends human subjectivity. Professor Ian Markham similarly explains, "God explains the mysterious ought pressing down our lives; and God explains the universal nature of the moral claim. As God is outside the world, God the creator can be both external and make universal commands."[256]

In Islam, God is believed to be a Being of maximal perfection. He is maximally knowledgeable, powerful and good. Perfect goodness is God's essential nature. When God makes a moral command, it is a derivative of His will, and His will does not contradict His nature. Therefore, what God commands is good because He is good, and He defines what good is:

"Say, 'Indeed, God does not order immorality.'"[257]

Interestingly, some atheists, believing that God cannot exist under any circumstance, have understood that in absence of the Divine, there are no objective morals. In *Ethics: Inventing Right and Wrong*, the influential atheist philosopher J. L. Mackie reflects this position: "There are no objective values... The claim that values are not objective... is meant to include not only moral goodness, which might be most naturally equated with moral value, but also other things that could be more loosely called moral values or disvalues—rightness and wrongness, duty, obligation, an action's being rotten and contemptible, and so on."[258] Aside from being counter-intuitive, and not representing a mainstream atheist position, Mackie seems to have understood the implications of adopting an atheist worldview. If there is no God, there is no objective good.

Euthyphro's dilemma

Many atheists respond to the above argument from morality by citing Plato's dilemma or Euthyphro's dilemma. It goes like this: *Is something morally good because God commands it, or does God command it because it is morally good?*

This dilemma poses a problem for theists who believe in an All-Powerful God because it requires them to believe in one of two things: either morality is defined by God's commands or morality is external to His commands. If morality is based on God's commands, what is considered good or evil is arbitrary. If this is the case, there is nothing we as humans should necessarily recognise as objectively evil. This would imply that there is nothing intrinsically wrong with, say, killing innocent children—just that God puts the 'evil' label on it arbitrarily. The other horn of the dilemma implies that some sort of a moral standard is completely outside and independent of God's essence and nature, and even God is obligated to live by this standard. However, that would be clearly undesirable for the theist, since it would make him admit that God is not All-Powerful or independent after all; rather, He has to rely on a standard external to Himself.

This intuitively sounds like a valid contention. However, a little reflection exposes it as a false dilemma. The reason is due to a third possibility: God is good. In his book, *The Qur'an and the Secular Mind*, professor of Philosophy Shabbir Akhtar explains:

> "There is a third alternative: a morally stable God of the kind found in scripture, a supreme being who would not arbitrarily change his mind about the goodness of compassion and the evil of sexual misconduct. Such a God always commands good because his character and nature are good."[259]

What Professor Akhtar is saying is that there is indeed a moral standard, but unlike what the second horn of the dilemma suggests, it is not external to God. Rather, it follows necessarily from God's nature. As previously discussed, Muslims, and theists in general, believe that God is necessarily and perfectly good. As such, His nature contains within it the perfect, non-arbitrary, moral standard. This means that an individual's actions—for example, the killing of innocents—is not arbitrarily bad, because it follows from an objective, necessary, moral standard. On the other hand, it does not mean God is somehow subservient to this standard because it is contained in His essence. It defines His nature; it is not in any way external to Him.

An atheist's natural response would be: "You must know what good is to define God as good, and therefore you haven't solved the problem". The simple reply would be that God defines what good is. He is the only Being worthy of worship because He is the most perfect and moral Being. The Qur'an affirms these points:

> "And your god is one God. There is no deity [worthy of worship] except Him, the Entirely Merciful, the Especially Merciful."[260]

> "He is God, other than whom there is no deity, Knower of the

unseen and the witnessed. He is the Entirely Merciful, the Especially Merciful. He is God, other than whom there is no deity, the Sovereign, the Pure, the Perfection, the Bestower of Faith, the Overseer, the Exalted in Might, the Compeller, the Superior. Exalted is God above whatever they associate with Him. He is God, the Creator, the Inventor, the Fashioner; to Him belong the best names. Whatever is in the heavens and Earth is exalting Him. And He is the Exalted in Might, the Wise."[261]

In summary, moral truths are ultimately derivatives of God's will expressed via His commands, and His commands do not contradict His nature, which is perfectly good, wise, pure and perfect.

Are there any alternative foundations for objective morals?

Many atheists argue that there are alternative explanations to answer why some morals are objective. Some of the most popular alternatives include biology, social pressure, and moral realism.

Biology

Can biology explain our sense of objective morality? The simple answer is no. Charles Darwin provides us with an interesting 'extreme example' of what happens when biology or natural selection forms the foundation of morality. He argues that if we were the result of a different set of biological conditions, then what we consider morally objective could be totally different: "If men were reared under precisely the same conditions as hive-bees, there can hardly be a doubt that our un-married females would, like the worker-bees, think it a sacred duty to kill their brothers, and mothers would strive to kill their fertile daughters, and no one would think of interfering."[262]

In other words, if morals are contingent on biological changes, it would render morals subject to these changes; therefore, they cannot be objective. Extending Darwin's example, if we happened to be reared under the same conditions as the nurse shark, we would think it acceptable to rape our partner, as the nurse shark wrestles with its mate.[263] Some respond by asserting that it is specifically natural selection that forms the basis for our sense of objective morality. Again, this is false. Conceptually, all that natural selection can do is give us the ability to formulate moral rules to help us survive and reproduce. As the moral philosopher Philip Kitcher writes, "All that natural selection may have done for us is to equip us with the capacity for various social arrangements and the capacity to formulate ethical rules."[264]

Maintaining that biology provides a basis for morality removes any meaning we attach to morals. Morals become meaningless, as they are just a result of non-rational and non-conscious biological changes. However, the fact that morality comes from Divine commands gives morals meaning, because being moral would be responding to these commands. In other words, we have moral duties, and these are owed to God. You cannot owe anything to a collection of molecules.

Social pressure

The second alternative is social pressure or consensus. This, I believe, is where a lot of atheists and humanists face some difficulty, philosophically speaking. If social pressure really forms the basis of objective morals, then the proponents of this assertion face a huge issue. Firstly, it makes morals relative, as they are subject to inevitable social changes. Secondly, it leads to moral absurdities. If someone accepts consensus as a basis for morals, then how can we justify our moral position towards what the Nazis did in 1940s Germany? How can we claim that what they did was objectively morally wrong? Well, we cannot. Even if you claim that some people in Germany fought against the Nazis, the point is that there was a strong consensus supporting the evil. There are many other examples in history to highlight this point.

Moral realism

The final alternative is moral realism. Moral realism, also referred to as moral objectivism, is the view that morals are objective and they are external and independent of our minds and emotions. However, the difference between moral realism and what this chapter has been advocating is that moral realists do not assert that they require any foundation. So moral truths such as compassion, justice and tolerance just exist objectively.

There are a few problems with this position. Firstly, what does it mean to say that justice just exists? Or that objective moral values just exist? This position is counterintuitive and meaningless. We simply do not know what 'justice' is, existing on its own. Significantly, one has to understand that if morals are objective (in that they are outside of an individual's personal opinion), then they require a rational explanation. Otherwise, the question *How are they objective?* is unanswered. Secondly, morality is not limited to recognizing the truth of compassion or justice. Morality entails a sense of duty or obligation; we are obligated to be compassionate and just. Under moral realism such obligations are impossible, because recognising that a certain moral truth is objective does nothing to ensure that we are obligated to implement that moral truth. A moral obligation does not follow from just acknowledging that it is objective. Following through with one's moral obligations would make sense if they are owed, or if there is a sense of duty. Moral realism does not provide any reason why someone must be obliged to be moral. However, if these moral truths are Divine commands, then not only do they make these morals objective, but they establish the basis for being obligated to be moral—because we have a duty to obey the commands of God.

In light of the above discussion, it is obvious that objective morality necessitates God's existence, as He is external to the universe and can make the universal moral claim via His commands.

What if they reject objective morality?

As a last resort some atheists try to avoid intellectual embarrassment by replying to the above conclusion by denying that morality is objective. Fair enough. I agree. If someone does not accept the axiom that morals are objective, then the argument does not work. But that is a double-edged sword. The minute the atheist denies the objectivity of any moral claim, he has no right to point the finger at religion, or more specifically Islam, in any objective way. He cannot even point the finger at the KKK, ISIS or even the dictatorship of North Korea! The irony here is that this is exactly what many atheists do. They make moral judgments that have an objective flavour to them. They should put a caveat to all of their moral judgments and simply say, "This is my subjective view." Doing that renders their moral disagreements or outrage pointless. However, deep down inside, most sane human beings do not deny the objectivity of some basic morals, such as murder, theft and abuse.

Misunderstanding the argument

Some atheists, and even some academics, misunderstand the argument by conflating moral *epistemology* with moral *ontology*. The argument I have presented so far is not concerned with how we get to know what is good, which refers to moral epistemology—it directs its attention to where morals come from and their nature, which refers to moral ontology. God's commands provide the ontological foundation for morals to be objective. How we get to know what these morals are is a matter of moral epistemology.

The argument presented in this chapter does not concern moral *epistemology*. This argument is about moral *ontology*, which refers to the foundations and nature of morality. The argument in its simplest form goes something like this: if something is good, is it objectively good? If it is objectively good, then it necessitates God's existence, as He is the only foundation for objective good. The argument does not ask how we know when something is good.

Absolute vs. objective

A valid concern that can be raised by the keen and aspiring theologian is that within Islamic theological discourse (and virtually all of the justice systems in the world), certain situations exist where killing (such as defending one's self and family) becomes morally permissible. Therefore, nothing is objectively evil. This is an interesting reflection, but it conflates absolute morality with objective morality; they are very different. Absolute morality entails that a moral act is good or bad regardless of the given situation. For example, someone who believes killing is absolutely wrong would believe killing is wrong even in self-defence. Objective morality, however, readily acknowledges the context-sensitivity of some moral facts. An objective moral fact might be *killing human beings without appropriate justification is wrong*. The context-sensitive nature of this moral claim includes an important caveat that the killing must also be unjustified. For instance, killing another human being might be seen as morally justified, if the person who was killed had been indiscriminately shooting children at a local school. The argument I have presented does not involve absolute notions of morality.

A note on ethical relativism

An ethical relativist, who maintains that morality is relative to cultural norms, would argue that the discussion on absolute and objective morality proves that morals are not objective, and that they are relative. Those who maintain that morals are objective would argue that what people believe or feel or do is irrelevant, and does not take away from objective moral truths (and that is precisely the definition of objectivity). Ethical relativism is bankrupt from this perspective because it points to cultural practices to refute what is objectively true. This is doomed to failure because the definition of objective morality states that morals are independent of feelings, beliefs and cultural practices, so to use them as a means to deny the objectivity of morals is meaningless.

This chapter has some striking implications for the atheist. If atheists consider some morals to be objective, they must either admit that God exists—as He is the only rational foundation for the existence of objective morality—or provide a compelling alternative. If they cannot, they have to ignore their innate disposition that recognises objective good and evil, and reject the notion of objective morals altogether. Once they do that, all their finger-pointing and moral judgements against Islam will be diminished to the level of personal subjectivity. The argument from the stance of morality truly makes sense of the Islamic conception of the Divine. God is perfectly good and wise, and His commands do not contradict His perfect nature. Therefore, His commands are perfectly good. Knowing this about God gives us a foundation for objective morals. In other words, knowing God is knowing good.

Chapter 10
Divine Singularity
The Oneness of God

Imagine you are an explorer who took a spaceship to another planet to visit human-like creatures. Once you land on the planet, you meet your guide. He tells you that your spaceship landed on Sphinga, the planet's borderless country. You are confused and ask your guide if there are any other countries on the planet. He laughs and replies, "Yes, there are two." You retort, "Well, how do you know when you're in another country if there is nothing to differentiate them?" Your guide sighs and says, "Yeah, we have the same problem. There are no borders and the features of one country are the same as the other." You finally end the discussion by saying, "You should have just made them into one country then, because that is what it looks like to me."

You both continue your journey to meet a group of officials for lunch. During the meal one of the officials praises the kings of the country. Upon hearing this, you politely ask, "You mean, there is more than one king?" The official replies, "Yes, we have two kings." You seem perplexed and ask how the country can function with two kings. "How do you have harmony in your laws, and order in your society?" The official replies, "Well, they always agree. Their wills are one." You cannot hold yourself back and you respond, "Well, you do not really have two kings, then. Because they are acting in accordance with one will."

This story contains three of the five arguments I will present for the fact that there can only be one God. The first part of the story summarises an argument that I call 'conceptual differentiation'. It postulates that in order for multiplicity to exist, there must be some concepts that differentiate one thing from another. For example, if I said that there are two bananas on the table, you would be able to verify that statement by observing them. The reason you can see two bananas is because there are concepts that differentiate them; for example, their size, shape, and location on the table. However, if there was nothing to differentiate them you could not distinguish between them. Similarly, since this book so far has argued that there is a necessary uncreated creator who is powerful, knowing, All-Aware and transcendent, then to claim that there are two would require a concept that differentiates them. But in order for the Creator to be a creator, He must have these attributes, so saying there are two without one being different from another is basically saying that there is only one creator. If whatever is true of one creator is true of another, then we have just defined one creator and not two.

The second part of the story summarises both the argument from exclusion and the argument from definition. The argument from exclusion maintains that there can only be one Divine will. If there were two creators and one wanted to create a tree, only three options would be possible. The first is that they both cancel each other out; this is not a rational possibility since creation exists, and if they cancelled each other out, there would be no creation at all. The second is that one creator overpowers the other by ensuring his tree is created. The third option is that they both agree to create the same tree in the same way. The second and third options imply that there is only one will, and one will in the context of our discussions indicates one creator.

The argument from definition asserts that there cannot be more than one creator. If there was more than one creator, the cosmos would not display the harmony that it does. As well as presenting arguments for a creator, this book warrants the traditional conception of God. Since the traditional conception refers to God as having an imposing will that cannot be limited by anything external to Him, then it logically follows there cannot be two unlimited Divine wills.

This chapter will elaborate on these arguments and present another two to show that this creator must be one:

- The argument from exclusion
- Conceptual differentiation
- Occam's razor
- The argument from definition
- The argument from revelation

Argument from exclusion

This argument maintains that the existence of multiple creators is impossible because there can only be one will. I have already discussed that the Creator must have a will (*see Chapter 5*), so questioning how many wills can exist leads us nicely to discuss this argument in detail.

For the sake of argument, let's say there were two creators. Creator A wanted to move a rock, and creator B also wanted to move the same rock. There are three possible scenarios that can arise:

1. One of the creators overpowers the other by moving the rock in a different direction from the other.
2. They both cancel each other out, and the rock does not move.
3. They both move the rock in the same direction.

The first scenario implies only one will manifests itself. The second scenario means that there is no will in action. This is not possible because there must be a will acted upon, as we have creation in existence. The third scenario ultimately describes only one will. Therefore, it is more rational to conclude that there is only one creator because there is only one will.

If someone argues that you can have more than one entity and still have one will, I would respond by asking: *How do you know there is more than one entity?* It sounds like an argument from ignorance, because there is no evidence whatsoever for such a claim. This leads us to the next argument.

Conceptual differentiation

For two creators to exist, they must be different in some way. For example, if you have two trees, they will differ in size, shape, colour and age. Even if they had identical physical attributes, there would be at least one thing that allows us to distinguish that they are in fact two trees. This can include their placement or position. You can also apply this to twins; we know there are two people because something makes them different. This could even be the mere fact that they cannot occupy the same place at the same time.

If there were more than one creator, then there must be something to differentiate between them. However, if they are the same in every possible aspect, then how can we say there are two? If something is identical to another, then what is true of one is also true for the other. Say we had two things, A and B. If they are the same in every way, and nothing allows us to differentiate between them, then they are the same thing. We can turn this into a hypothetical proposition: If whatever is true of A is true of B, then A is identical to B.

Now let us apply this to the Creator. Imagine that two creators exist, called creator X and creator Y, and that whatever is true of creator X is also true of creator Y. For instance, creator X is All-Powerful and All-Wise; so, creator Y is All-Powerful and All-Wise. How many creators are there in reality? Only one, due to the fact that there is nothing to differentiate between them. If someone were to argue that they are different, then they would not be describing another creator but something that is created, as it would not have the same attributes befitting the Creator.

If someone is adamant in claiming that there can be two creators and they are different from each other, then I simply ask, "How are they different?" If they attempt to answer the question, they enter the realm of arguing from ignorance, because they will have to make up evidence to justify their false conclusion.

Occam's razor

In light of the above, we might find a few irrational and stubborn people who still posit a plurality of creators or causes. In light of Occam's razor, this is not a sound argument. Occam's razor is a philosophical principle attributed to the 14th century logician and Franciscan friar, William of Occam. This principle enjoins: 'Pluralitas non est ponenda sine necessitate'; in English: 'Plurality should not be posited without necessity.' In other words, the simplest and most comprehensive explanation is the best one.

In this case, we have no evidence that the Creator of the universe is actually a combination of two, three or even one thousand creators, so the simplest explanation is that the Creator is one. Postulating a plurality of creators does not add to the comprehensiveness of the argument either. In other words, to add more creators would not enhance the argument's explanatory power or scope. To claim that an All-Powerful creator created the universe is just as comprehensive as claiming that two All-Powerful creators created it. One creator is all that is required, simply because it is All-Powerful. I would argue that postulating multiple creators actually has reduced explanatory power and scope; this is because it raises far more problems than it solves. For example, the following questions expose the irrationality of this form of polytheism: *How do many external beings co-exist? What about the potential of any conflicting wills? How do they interact?*

A popular objection to this argument is that if we were to apply this principle to the pyramids in Egypt, we would absurdly adopt the view that they were made by one person, because it seems to be the simplest explanation. This is a misapplication of the principle, because it ignores the point about comprehensiveness. Taking the view that the pyramids were built by one person is not the simplest and most comprehensive explanation, as it raises far more questions than it answers. For instance, how could one man have built the pyramids? It is far more comprehensive to postulate that it was built by many men. In light of this, someone can say that the universe is so complex that it would be absurd to postulate that only one creator created it. This contention, although valid, is misplaced. A powerful Being creating the whole universe is a far more coherent and simple explanation than a plurality of creators, because a plurality of creators raises the unanswerable questions stated in the previous paragraph. Nevertheless, the critic may continue to argue that it wasn't one person that created the Pyramids, but an All-Powerful creator. The problem with this is that nothing within the universe is an All-Powerful Being, and since the Pyramids are buildings, and buildings are built by an efficient cause (a person or persons that act), then the Pyramids must have been created by the same type of cause. This leads us back to the original point, that more than one of these causes was required to build the Pyramids.

The argument from definition

Reason necessitates that if there were more than one creator, the universe would be in chaos. There would also not be the level of order we find in the cosmos. The Qur'an has a similar argument: "Had there been within the heavens and Earth gods besides God, they both would have been ruined."[265]

The classical commentary known as *Tafsir al-Jalalayn* states: "Heaven and the Earth would have lost their normal orderedness since there would have inevitably been internal discord, as is normal when there are several rulers: they oppose one another in things and do not agree with one another."[266]

However, one might point out that since more than one person made your car—one person fitted the wheels, someone else installed the engine and another person installed the computer system—maybe the universe was created in the same way. This example indicates that a complex object can be created by more than one creator.

In order to respond to this contention, what has to be understood is that the most rational explanation for the origins of the universe, as discussed in the previous chapters, is the concept of God and not just a 'creator'. There may be an abstract conceptual possibility of multiple creators, as highlighted by the car example, but there cannot be more than one God. This is because God, by definition, is the Being that has an imposing will that cannot be limited by anything external to Him. If there were two or more Gods, they would have a competition of wills, which would result in chaos and disorder. The universe we observe is governed by mathematical laws and order; therefore, it makes sense that it is the result of one imposing will. Interestingly, the objection above actually supports Divine oneness. In order for the car to work, the different people who were responsible for making it had to conform to the overall 'will' of the designer. The design limited the wills of those responsible for making the car. Since God, by definition, cannot have His will limited by anything outside of Himself, it follows that there cannot be more than one Divine will.

However, one may argue that multiple Gods can agree to have the same will or they can each have their own domain. This would mean that their wills are limited and passive, which would require that they are not Gods any more, by definition.

The 12th century Muslim thinker and philosopher Ibn Rushd, also known as Averroes in the western tradition, summarises this argument:

"The meaning of the... verse is implanted in the instincts [of man] by nature. It is self-evident that if there are two kings, the actions of each one being the same as those of the other, it would not be possible [for them] to manage the same city, for there cannot result from two agents of the same kind one and the same action. It follows necessarily that if they acted together, the city would be ruined, unless one of them acted while the other remained inactive;

and this is incompatible with the attribute of Divinity. When two actions of the same kind converge on one substratum, that substratum is corrupted necessarily."[267]

The argument from revelation

A simpler way of providing evidence for God's oneness is to refer to revelation. This argument postulates that if God has announced himself to humanity, and this revelation can be proven to be from Him, then what He says about Himself is true. However, a sceptic may question some of the assumptions behind this argument. These include that God has announced Himself to humankind and that the revelation is in the form of a book.

Let's first tackle the last assumption. If God has announced Himself to humankind, there are only two possible ways to find out: internally and externally. What I mean by 'internally' is that you can find out who God is solely by introspection and internalisation, and what I mean by 'externally' is that you can find out who God is via communication from outside of yourself; in other words, it is instantiated in the real world. Finding out about God internally is implausible for the following reasons:

1. Human beings are different; they have what psychologists call 'individual differences'. These include DNA, experiences, social contexts, intellectual and emotional capacities, gender differences, and many more. These differences play a role in our ability to internalise via introspection or intuition. Therefore, the results of thinking will differ. If these processes were solely used to find out about God, inevitably differences in our conception of Him would arise. This is true from a historical point of view. From the ancient world of 6000 BCE to the present, there are records of approximately 3,700 different names and concepts for God.

2. Since the method used to conclude that God does exist is a 'commonsense' method (referred to by philosophers as 'rational thought' and by Muslim theologians as 'innate thinking'), then trying to find out who God is, rather than just affirming His existence, would be fallacious. There are limits to our reasoning. Abstract thinking and reflections on the physical world can only

lead us to the conclusion that a creator exists, and He is powerful, knowing, etc. To go beyond those conclusions would be speculative. The Qur'an aptly asks, "Do you say about God that which you do not know?"[268] Trying to find out who God is via introspection would be like a mouse trying to conceptualise a galaxy. The human being is not eternal, unique and powerful. Therefore, the human being cannot conceptualise who God is. God would have to tell you via external revelation.

Take the following example into consideration. Your knowledge that God exists is like the knocking of the door; you safely assume that something is there, but do you know who it is? You weren't expecting anyone, so the only way to find who is behind the door is if the person tells you. Therefore, you can conclude that if God has said or announced anything, it must be external to the human being. Anything else would be mere speculation.

From an Islamic perspective this external communication is the Qur'an (*see Chapter 13*), as it is the only text to claim to have come from God that fits the criteria for a Divine text. These criteria include:

1. It must be consistent with the rational and intuitive conclusion of God existence. For example, if a book says God is an elephant with 40 legs, you could safely assume that this book is not from God, as God must be external to the universe and independent. An elephant, regardless of form, is a dependent being. This is because it has limited physical qualities, such as size, shape and colour. All things with limited physical qualities are dependent because there are external factors that gave rise to their limitations. God is not 'physical' and is independent. Therefore, nothing with limited physical qualities can be God (*see Chapter 6*).

2. It must be internally and externally consistent. In other words, if it says on page 20 that God is one and then on page 340 its says God is three, that would be an internal, irreconcilable inconsistency. Additionally, if the book says that the universe is only 6,000 years

old, then that would be an external inconsistency as reality affirms that the universe is older than that (however, our understanding of reality can change; see Chapter 12).

3. It must have signposts to the transcendent. The revelation must contain material that indicates it is from the Divine and that it cannot be adequately explained naturalistically. In simple terms, it must have evidence to show that it is from God.

The Qur'an has signposts that indicate it is a Divine text. The book cannot be explained naturalistically; therefore, supernatural explanations are the best explanation. Some of these signposts include:

1. The Qur'an's linguistic and literary inimitability (*see Chapter 13*).
2. Some of the historical accounts in the Qur'an could not have been known to man at the time of revelation.
3. Its unique arrangement and structure.[269]

To conclude, since the only way to know what God has announced to humankind is via external revelation, and this revelation can be proven to be the Qur'an—then what it says about God is true. The Qur'an is explicitly clear concerning His oneness: "And do not argue with the people of the Scripture except in a way that is best, except for those who commit injustice among them, and say, 'We believe in that which has been revealed to us and revealed to you. And our God and your God is one; and we are Muslims [in submission] to Him.'"[270]

These are some of the arguments that can be used to show that God is one; however, this topic—once truly understood—will have some profound effects on the human conscience. If one God has created us, it follows that we must see everything via His oneness and not our abstracted perspectives of disunity and division. We are a human family, and if we see ourselves this way, it can have profound effects on our society. If we love and believe in God, then we should show compassion and mercy to what He has created. Just like what the Prophet Muhammad ﷺ said:

"Those who are merciful will be shown mercy by the Most Merciful. Be merciful to those on the Earth and the One in the heavens will have mercy upon you."[271]

Chapter 11
Is God Merciful?
Islam's Response to Evil and Suffering

When I was a child, my parents would always chide me for trying to drink my grandfather's whisky. You can imagine, an active and inquisitive young child observing his grandfather sip this thick, gold, smooth liquid. I wanted some! However, every time I attempted to secretly drink the enticing beverage, I would get into big trouble. I never understood why, thus negative thoughts about my parents would race through my mind. Fast-forward many years, I now realise why they didn't allow me to drink my grandfather's whisky; it could have poisoned me. A 40 percent volume alcoholic drink would not have been pleasant on my young stomach or liver. However, when I was younger, I did not have access to the wisdom that formed the basis of my parents' decision, yet I thought I was justified in my negativity towards them.

This sums up the atheist attitude towards God when trying to understand evil and suffering in the world. The above story is not intended to belittle the suffering and pain that people experience. As human beings we must feel empathy and find ways of alleviating people's hardships. However, the example is meant to raise a conceptual point. Due to a valid and genuine concern for human and other sentient beings, many atheists argue that the existence of a powerful and merciful[272] God is incompatible with the existence of evil and suffering in the world. If He is The-Merciful, He should want the evil and suffering to stop, and if He is All-Powerful, He should be able to stop it. However, since there is evil and suffering, it means that either He is not powerful, or He lacks mercy, or both.

The evil and suffering argument is a very weak one because it is based on two major false assumptions. The first concerns the nature of God. It implies that God is only The-Merciful and All-Powerful, thereby isolating two attributes and ignoring others that the Qur'an has revealed about God. The second assumption is that God has provided us with no reasons for why He has allowed evil and suffering to exist.[273] This is not true. Islamic revelation provides us with many reasons for why God has allowed evil and suffering to exist. Both assumptions will be addressed below.

Is God only The-Merciful and All-Powerful?

According to the Qur'an, God is *Al-Qadeer*, meaning the All-Powerful, and *Ar-Rahmaan*, meaning The-Merciful, which also implies compassion. Islam requires that mankind know and believe in a God of power, mercy and goodness. However, the atheist grossly misrepresents the comprehensive Islamic conception of God. God is not only The-Merciful and All-Powerful; rather, He has many names and attributes. These are understood holistically via God's oneness (*see Chapter 15*). For instance, one of His names is *Al-Hakeem*, meaning the The-Wise. Since the very nature of God is wisdom, it follows that whatever He wills is in line with Divine wisdom. When something is explained by an underlying wisdom, it implies a reason for its occurrence. In this light, the atheist reduces God to two attributes and by doing so builds a straw man, thereby engaging in an irrelevant monologue.

The writer Alom Shaha, who wrote *The Young Atheist's Handbook*, responds to the assertion that Divine wisdom is an explanation for evil and suffering by describing it as an intellectual cop-out:

> "The problem of evil genuinely stumps most ordinary believers. In my experience, they usually respond with an answer along the lines of, 'God moves in mysterious ways.' Sometimes they'll say, 'Suffering is God's way of testing us,' to which the obvious response is, 'Why does he have to test us in such evil ways' To which the response is, 'God moves in mysterious ways.' You get the idea."[274]

Alom, like many other atheists, commits the fallacy of *argumentum ad ignoratium*, arguing from ignorance. Just because he cannot access Divine wisdom does not mean it does not exist. This reasoning is typical of toddlers. Many children are scolded by their parents for something they want to do, such as eating too many sweets. The toddlers usually cry or have a tantrum because they think how bad mummy and daddy are, but the child does not realise the wisdom underlying their objection (in this case, too many sweets are bad for their teeth). Furthermore, this contention misunderstands the definition and nature of God. Since God is transcendent, knowing and wise, then it logically follows that limited human beings cannot fully comprehend the Divine will. To even suggest that we can appreciate the totality of God's wisdom would imply that we are like God, which denies the fact of His transcendence, or suggests that God is limited like a human. This argument has no traction with any believer, because no Muslim believes in a created, limited God. It is not an intellectual cop-out to refer to Divine wisdom, because it is not referring to some mysterious unknown. Rather, it truly understands the nature of God and makes the necessary logical conclusions. As I have pointed out before, God has the picture, and we have just a pixel.

As mentioned in Chapter 1, the problem of the evil and suffering argument exposes a cognitive bias known as 'egocentrism'. Such a person cannot see any perspective on a particular issue apart from their own. Some atheists suffer from this cognitive bias. They assume that since they cannot possibly fathom any good reasons to justify the evil and suffering in the world, everyone else—including God—must also have the same problem. Thus they deny God, because they assume that God cannot be justified for permitting the evil and suffering in the world. If God has no justification, then the mercy and power of God are illusions. Thus, the traditional concept of God is nullified. However, all atheists have done is superimposed their perspective on God. This is like arguing that God must think how a human thinks. This is impossible because human beings and God cannot be compared, as God is transcendent and has the totality of wisdom and knowledge.

At this point, the atheist might respond by describing the above as an intelligent way of evading the problem: If the theist can refer to God's wisdom as so great that it cannot be understood, then we can explain anything 'mysterious' in reference to a Divine wisdom. I somewhat empathise with this reply; however, in the context of the problem of evil and suffering, it is a false argument. It is the atheist that refers to God's attributes to begin with; His power and mercy. Atheists should refer to God as who He is, not as an agent with only two attributes. If they were to include other attributes such as wisdom, their argument would not be valid. If they were to include the attribute of wisdom, they would have to show

how Divine wisdom is incompatible with a world full of suffering or evil. This would be impossible to prove because there are so many examples in our intellectual and practical lives where we admit our intellectual inferiority—in other words, there are cases where we submit to a wisdom we cannot understand. We rationally submit to realities that we cannot understand on a regular basis. For example, when we visit the doctor we assume that the doctor is an authority. We trust the doctor's diagnosis on this basis. We even take the medicine the doctor prescribes without any second thought. This and many other similar examples clearly show that referring to God's wisdom is not evading the problem. Rather, it is accurately presenting who God is and not making out that God has only two attributes. Since He is The-Wise, and His names and attributes are maximally perfect, it follows that there is wisdom behind everything that He does—even if we do not know or understand that wisdom. Many of us do not understand how diseases work, but just because we do not understand something does not negate its existence.

The Qur'an uses profound stories and narratives to instil this understanding. Take, for instance, the story of Moses and a man he encountered on his travels, known as Khidr. Moses observed him do things that seemed unjust and evil, but at the end of their journey, the wisdom that Moses did not have access to was brought to light:

"So the two turned back, retraced their footsteps, and found one of Our servants— a man to whom We had granted Our mercy and whom We had given knowledge of Our own. Moses said to him, 'May I follow you so that you can teach me some of the right guidance you have been taught?' The man said, 'You will not be able to bear with me patiently. How could you be patient in matters beyond your knowledge?' Moses said, 'God willing, you will find me patient. I will not disobey you in any way.' The man said, 'If you follow me then, do not query anything I do before I mention it to you myself.' They travelled on. Later, when they got into a boat, and the man made a hole in it, Moses said, 'How could you make a hole in it? Do you want to drown its passengers? What a strange thing to do!' He replied, 'Did I not tell you that you would never be able to bear with me patiently?' Moses said, 'Forgive me for forgetting. Do not make it too hard for me to follow you.' And so they travelled on. Then, when they met a young boy and the man killed him, Moses said, 'How could you kill an innocent person? He has not killed anyone! What a terrible thing to do!' He replied, 'Did I not tell you that you would never be able to bear with me patiently?' Moses said, 'From now on, if I query anything you do, banish me from your company— you have put up with enough from me.' And so they travelled on. Then, when they came to a town and asked the inhabitants for food but were refused hospitality, they saw a wall there that was on the point of falling down and the man repaired it. Moses said, 'But if you had wished you could have taken payment for doing that.' He said, 'This is where you and I part company. I will tell you the meaning of the things you could not bear with patiently: the boat belonged to some needy people who made their living from the sea and I damaged it because I knew that coming after them was a king who was seizing every [serviceable] boat by force. The young boy had parents who were people of faith, and so, fearing he would trouble them through wickedness and disbelief, we wished that their Lord should give them another child—purer and more compassionate—in his place. [275] The wall belonged to two young orphans in the town and there was buried treasure beneath it belonging to them. Their father had been a righteous man, so your Lord intended them to reach maturity and then dig up their treasure as a mercy from your Lord. I did not do [these things] of my own accord: these are the explanations for those things you could not bear with patience.'"[276]

In addition to contrasting our limited wisdom with God's, this story also provides key lessons and spiritual insights. The first lesson is that in order to understand God's will, one has to be humble. Moses approached Khidr, and knew that he had some Divinely inspired knowledge that God had not given to Moses. Moses humbly asked to learn from him, yet Khidr responded by questioning his ability to be patient; nevertheless, Moses insisted and wanted to learn. (The spiritual status of Moses is very high according to the Islamic tradition. He was a prophet and messenger, yet he approached the man with humility.) The second lesson is that patience is required to emotionally and psychologically deal with the suffering and evil in the world. Khidr knew that Moses would not be able to be patient with him, as he was going to do things that Moses thought were evil. Moses tried to be patient but always questioned the man's actions and expressed his anger at the perceived evil. However, at the end of the story, Khidr explained the Divine wisdom behind his actions after exclaiming that Moses was not able to be patient. What we learn from this story is that to be able to deal with evil and suffering in the world, including our inability to understand it, we must be humble and patient.

Commenting on the above verses, the classical scholar Ibn Kathir explained that Khidr was the one to whom God had given knowledge of the reality behind the perceived evil and suffering, and He had not given it to Moses. With reference to the meaning of the statement, "You will not be able to bear with me patiently", Ibn Kathir wrote: "You will not be able to accompany with me when you see me doing things that go against your law, because I have knowledge from God that He has not taught you, and you have knowledge from God that He has not taught me."[277]

In essence, God's wisdom is unbounded and complete, whereas we have limited wisdom and knowledge. Another way of putting it is that God has the totality of wisdom and knowledge; we just have its particulars. We see things from the perspective of our fragmentary viewpoint. To fall for the trap of egocentrism is like believing you know the entire puzzle after seeing only one piece. Hence Ibn Kathir explains that the verse, "How could you be patient in matters beyond your knowledge?" means that there is a Divine wisdom that we cannot access: "For I know that you will denounce me justifiably, but I have knowledge of God's wisdom and the hidden interests which I can see but you cannot."[278]

The view that everything that happens is in line with a Divine wisdom is empowering and positive. This is because God's wisdom does not contradict other aspects of His nature, such as His perfection and goodness. Therefore, evil and suffering are ultimately part of a Divine purpose. Among many other classical scholars, the 14th century scholar Ibn Taymiyya summarises this point well: "God does not create pure evil. Rather, in everything that He creates is a wise purpose by virtue of what is good. However, there may be some evil in it for some people, and this is partial, relative evil. As for total evil or absolute evil, the Lord is exonerated of that."[279]

This does not negate the concept of objective moral truths mentioned in the previous chapter. Even if everything is in line with ultimate goodness, and evil is 'partial', it does not undermine the concept of objective evil. As discussed, objective evil is not absolute, but rather it is evil based on a particular context or set of variables. So something can be objectively evil due to certain variables or context, and at the same time it can be included with an ultimate Divine purpose that is good and wise.

This evokes positive psychological responses from believers because all the evil and all the suffering that occur are for a Divine purpose. Ibn Taymiyya summarises this point as well: "If God—exalted is He—is Creator of everything, He creates good and evil on account of the wise purpose that He has in that by virtue of which His action is good and perfect."[280]

Henri Laoust, in his *Essay sur les doctrines sociales et politiques de Taki-d-Din Ahmad b. Taimiya*, also explains this position: "God is essentially providence. Evil is without real existence in the world. All that God has willed can only conform to a sovereign justice and an infinite goodness, provided, however, that it is envisaged from the point of view of the totality and not from that of the fragmentary and imperfect knowledge that His creatures have of reality...."[281]

Does God give us reasons for why He has allowed evil and suffering to exist?

A sufficient response to the second assumption is to provide a strong argument that God has communicated some reasons to us about why He has allowed evil and suffering in the world. The intellectual richness of Islamic thought provides us with many reasons.

Our purpose is worship

The primary purpose of the human being is not to enjoy a transitory sense of happiness; rather, it is to achieve a deep internal peace through knowing and worshipping God (*see Chapter 15*). This fulfilment of the Divine purpose will result in everlasting bliss and true happiness. So, if this is our primary purpose, other aspects of human experience are secondary. The Qur'an states, "I did not create either *jinn* [spirit world] or man except to worship Me."[282]

Consider someone who has never experienced any suffering or pain, but experiences pleasure all the time. This person, by virtue of his state of ease, has forgotten God and therefore failed to do what he was created to do. Compare this person with someone whose experiences of hardship and pain have led him to God, and fulfilled his purpose in life. From the perspective of the Islamic spiritual tradition, the one whose suffering has led him to God is better than the one who has never suffered and whose pleasures have led him away from God.

Life is a test

God also created us for a test, and part of this test is to experience trials with suffering and evil. Passing the test facilitates our permanent abode of eternal bliss in paradise. The Qur'an explains that God created death and life, "so that He may put you to test, to find out which of you is best in deeds: He is the The-Almighty, The-Forgiving."[283]

On a basic level, the atheist misunderstands the purpose of our existence on Earth. The world is supposed to be an arena of trials and tribulations in order to test our conduct and for us to cultivate virtue. For example, how can we cultivate patience if we do not experience things that test our patience? How can we become courageous if there are no dangers to be confronted? How can we be compassionate if no one is in need of it? Life being a test answers these questions. We need challenges to ensure our moral and spiritual growth. We are not here to party; that is the purpose of paradise.

So why is life a test? Since God is perfectly good, He wants every single one of us to believe and, as a result, experience eternal bliss with Him in paradise. God makes it clear that He prefers belief for us all: "And He does not approve for His servants' disbelief."[284]

This clearly shows that God does not want anyone to go to hell. However, if He were to send everyone to paradise, then a gross violation of justice would take place; God would be treating Moses and the Pharaoh and Hitler and Jesus as the same. A mechanism is needed to ensure that people who enter paradise do so based on merit. This explains why life is a test. Life is just a mechanism to see who among us are truly deserving of eternal happiness. As such, life is filled with obstacles, which act as tests of our conduct.

In this regard, Islam is extremely empowering because it sees suffering, evil, harm, pain and problems as a test. We can have fun, but we have been created with a purpose and that purpose is to worship God. The empowering Islamic view is that tests are seen as sign of God's love. The Prophet Muhammad ﷺ said, "When God loves a servant, He tests him."[285]

The reason God tests those whom He loves is because it is an avenue to achieve the eternal bliss of paradise—and entering paradise is a result of Divine love and mercy. God points this out clearly in the Qur'an: "Do you suppose that you will enter the Garden without first having suffered like those before you? They were afflicted by misfortune and hardship, and they were so shaken that even [their] messenger and the believers with him cried, 'When will God's help arrive?' Truly, God's help is near."[286]

The beauty of the Islamic tradition is that God, who knows us better than we know ourselves, has already empowered us and tells us that we have what it takes to overcome these trials. "God does not burden any soul with more than it can bear."[287]

However, if we cannot overcome these trials after having tried our best, God's mercy and justice will ensure that we are recompensed in some way, either in this life or the eternal life that awaits us.

Knowing God

Hardship and suffering enables us to realise and know God's attributes, such as The-Protector and The-Healer. For example, without the pain of illness we would not appreciate God's attributes as The-Healer, or the one who gives us health. Knowing God in the Islamic spiritual tradition is a greater good, and worth the experience of suffering or pain, as it will ensure the fulfilment of our primary purpose, which ultimately leads to paradise.

Greater good

Suffering and evil allow a greater good, also known as second-order good. First-order good is physical pleasure and happiness, and first-order evil is physical pain and sadness. Some examples of second-order goodness include courage, humility and patience. However, in order to have a second-order good (like courage) there must be a first-order evil (like cowardice). According to the Qur'an, elevated good such as courage and humility do not have the same value as evil: "Say Prophet, bad cannot be likened to good, though you may be dazzled by how abundant the bad is. Be mindful of God, people of understanding, so that you may prosper."[288]

Free will

God has given us free will, and free will includes the ability to choose to commit evil acts. This explains personal evil, which is evil or suffering committed by a human being. One can ask: *Why has God given us free will at all?* In order for the tests in life to be meaningful, there must be free will. An exam is pointless if the student is obligated or forced to answer correctly on each question. Similarly, in the exam of life, human beings must be given adequate freedom to do as they please.

Good and evil lose their meaning if God were to always ensure we chose good. Take the following example into consideration: someone points a loaded gun to your head and asks you to give to charity. You give the money, but does it have any moral value? It does not, for it only has value if a free agent chooses to do so.

Detachment from the world

According to the Islamic tradition, God has created us so that we may worship and draw near to Him. A fundamental principle concerning this is that we must detach ourselves from the ephemeral nature of the world. Known as *dunya*, meaning low or lowly, the ephemeral world is the place of limitations, suffering, loss, desires, ego, excessiveness and evil. Suffering shows us how truly low the *dunya* is, thereby facilitating our detachment from it. Thus we are able to draw closer to God.

The Prophet Muhammad ﷺ was reported to have said, "Love of the *dunya* is the root of all evil."[289] The greatest evil, according to Islam, is denying and associating partners with God; therefore, detachment from the *dunya* is necessary to reach the ultimate spiritual goal of nearness to God, and subsequently paradise.

The Qur'an makes it very clear that the *dunya* is ephemeral and a deceiving enjoyment: "Know that the life of this *dunya* is but amusement and diversion and adornment and boasting to one another and competition in increase of wealth and children—like the example of a rain whose [resulting] plant growth pleases the tillers; then it dries and you see it turned yellow; then it becomes [scattered] debris."[290]

The concept of the *dunya* should not be confused with the positive aspects of creation, known in Arabic as *'alam* and *khlaq*. These concepts relate to the beauty and wonder of what God has created. They are intended to encourage people to reflect and understand, which serve as a means to conclude that there is a Divine power, mercy and wisdom behind them.

Suffering of innocent people is temporary

Even if there is a lot of greater good to be actualised, one may observe that some people still suffer without experiencing any relief. This is why in Islam, God not only provides justifications for evil and suffering in this world but also recompenses them. At the end, all believers who suffered and were innocent will be granted eternal bliss, and all the suffering they had— even if they suffered all of their lives—will be forgotten forever. The Prophet Muhammad ﷺ said:

> "...the person who had suffered the most affliction in the world of those destined for Paradise will be brought forth and merely dipped into Paradise for a moment. Then he will be asked 'O son of Adam, have you ever seen suffering? Have you ever experienced hardship in your life?' He will reply 'No my Lord, by God. I have never undergone suffering. I have never seen hardship.'"[291]

Spiritual perspectives

Under atheism, evil has no purpose. It is one of the blind forces in the world that indiscriminately chooses its prey. Those who are victims of suffering and evil have no emotional and rational perspectives to help alleviate their suffering or put their experiences into context. Someone could have suffered all their life and just ended up in the grave. All of their suffering, sacrifice and pain would have absolutely no meaning whatsoever. Evil is viewed to occur due to prior physical processes, and those who experience evil have no recourse. They cannot attribute any type of will to it, whether human or Divine, because everything is just reduced to blind, random and non-rational physical occurrences. Thus, the logical implications of atheism are quite depressing.

The Islamic tradition has a fountain of concepts, principles and ideas that facilitate the believer's journey in life. The Prophet Muhammad ﷺ empowered the believers with hope and patience. All of the suffering that we face is a means of spiritual purification, thereby facilitating paradise in which we will forget every suffering that we ever experienced:

"No calamity befalls a Muslim but that God expiates some of his sins because of it, even though it were the prick he receives from a thorn."[292]

"Amazing is the affair of the believer, verily all of his affair is good, and this is for no one except the believer. If something of good/happiness befalls him he is grateful and that is good for him. If something of harm befalls him he is patient and that is good for him."[293]

Even natural disasters and fatal illnesses are seen through the eyes of hope, mercy and forgiveness. The Islamic perspective on illness is that it is a form of purification, which facilitates eternal bliss in paradise for the sick. The Prophet Muhammad ﷺ encouraged visiting the sick: "Feed the hungry, visit the sick, and free the captives."[294] Those who take care of the sick are rewarded with mercy and forgiveness, and ultimately paradise. There are many Prophetic traditions that elaborate on these points. For example, the Prophet Muhammad ﷺ said that if a believer dies of the plague or a stomach illness, they are considered a martyr, and all martyrs[295] go to paradise.[296] There are inspiring traditions of mercy, reward and blessings for those who visit and care for the sick; the Prophet Muhammad ﷺ said that whoever visits a sick person "is plunging into mercy until he sits down, and when he sits down he is submerged in it."[297] A moving and powerful narration from the Prophet Muhammad ﷺ teaches us that those who visit the sick will find God with them:

"Verily, God, the Exalted and Glorious, will say on the Day of Judgement: 'O Son of Adam! I fell ill, but you did not visit Me.' The human will ask, 'O my Sustainer! How could I visit You when You are the Sustainer of the Worlds? And how can You fall sick?' He, the Almighty, will say, 'Did you not know that such and such a servant of Mine was sick. But you did not visit him. Did you not know that, had you visited him, you would have found Me by his side?'"[298]

Even in the case of natural disasters like tsunamis, the believing victims would be considered people of paradise because death by drowning is considered martyrdom in the Islamic tradition. The Prophet Muhammad ﷺ said in this regard, "Anyone who drowns is a martyr."[299] Islamic scholars conclude that if a believer died as a result of being crushed by a building during an earthquake (some even extend this to a plane or a car crash), then they are considered people of paradise. The Prophet Muhammad ﷺ said that one of the martyrs includes "the one who died in a collapsed (building)".[300]

But God could create a world without suffering

Notwithstanding the discussion so far, a key objection that usually follows is "but God could create a world without suffering". This contention is just a repackaging of the original argument; in other words: *Why has God allowed evil and suffering to exist?* Therefore, the same answer applies; Divine wisdom. The one who makes this objection does so because they cannot understand why there is evil and suffering in the first place, and they believe that a merciful and powerful God should prevent every evil and suffering. Nevertheless, this has already been addressed in this chapter.

The 'problem' of evil and suffering is not a problem for the believer, as evil and suffering are understood as functions of God's profound wisdom, perfection and goodness. The spiritual teachings of Islam create a sense of hope, patience and tranquillity. The logical implication of atheism is that one is plunged into a hopeless state and does not have any answers to why evil and suffering exist. This ignorance is mostly due to an egocentrism that causes atheists to fail in their ability to see things from another perspective, just as I was when I thought my parents were malicious when they prevented me from drinking my grandfather's whisky.

Chapter 12
Has Science Disproved God?
Deconstructing False Atheist Assumptions

Imagine you entered an amazing palace. As you walk through the hallway, you are struck by the size of the building and decide to explore by opening the nearest door. As you enter the room, you see hundreds of chairs and tables arranged like a classroom. Suddenly you lose any motivation to explore the other rooms. You decide to leave the palace and head off to meet your friend at a local coffee shop. As you drink coffee with your friend he asks you, "So what did you see in the palace?" You reply, "Just a room full of tables and chairs arranged like a classroom". Your friend then asks, "Why didn't you see the other rooms?" You reply by saying, "There's no point, there was nothing to see. If this room was full of chairs and tables, then the other rooms will have nothing in them."

Is your reply rational? Does it logically follow that just because there is something in one room, there will be nothing in the other rooms? Of course it does not. Atheists who claim that science has disproved God follow a similar logic.

Science focuses its attention on only what observations can solve. However, God, by definition, is a Being who is outside the physical universe. Therefore, any direct observation of Him is impossible. However, an atheist may argue that indirect observation may support or negate God's existence. This is not true. Any form of indirect observation could never negate God's existence, because it is like saying an observed phenomenon can negate an unobserved phenomenon. This follows the same logic as the above example in the palace.

The fact that science does not lead to atheism is attested by the majority of the philosophers of science. For example, Hugh Gauch rightly concludes that to "insist that... science supports atheism is to get high marks for enthusiasm but low marks for logic."[301] Gauch makes perfect sense because the method of thinking that relies on observation cannot deny what cannot

186 | *The Divine Reality*

be observed. What science can do, however, is stay silent on that matter or suggest evidence that someone can use to infer that God exists.

Why do some atheists believe science can deny God?

Science has changed the world. From medicine to telecommunications, science has improved our lives and well-being in ways that no other field of study has. Science continually improves our lives, and aids our understanding of the world and the universe. However, science's successes have led many atheists to adopt incoherent and false assumptions. Below is a summary of these assumptions.

- First, some atheists perceive that science is the only yardstick for truth and that science has the answers for all of our questions. This motivates the atheist to believe that God is no longer required as a reason for things we do not understand. This is a false assumption because science has many limitations, and there are many things that it cannot answer. In addition, there are other sources of knowledge that science cannot justify, yet they are indispensable and fundamental sources of knowledge. This implies that science is not the only way to establish truths about the world and reality.

- The second assumption is that since science is so successful, scientific conclusions must be true. This exposes a common ignorance concerning the philosophy of science. Simply put, just because something works does not mean it is true. This is a basic idea in the philosophy of science. Unfortunately, even some highly acclaimed atheists take the incoherent view that the successful practical application of a scientific theory proves it to be true in an absolute sense. I once met Richard Dawkins at the World Atheist Convention in 2010, held in Dublin, Ireland. I spoke to him briefly and asked him why he told one questioner not to study the philosophy of science and "just do the science". He didn't give me much of a reply. Surveying his public work, it is now becoming clear that one of his main reasons is that science "works, b*tches"[302]. Although intuitive, it is false. It does not, in any way, show that just because something works, it is true.

- The third assumption is that science leads to certainty. When something is labelled as a 'scientific fact' we must dismiss Divine revelation if it opposes it in some way. This is not true. When scientists call something a fact, they are not saying it is absolute and that it will never change. It means it is the best description of a particular phenomenon, based on our limited observations. However, there can always be a new observation—or way of seeing things—that is at odds with previous observations. This is the beauty of science; it is not set in stone. Therefore, if religious scripture and science seem to conflict, it is not a huge problem. Why? Because science can change. All that we can say is our current understanding of an observed phenomenon—based on our limited observations—is at odds with what a particular scripture says, but it may change. This is a huge difference from using science as a baseball bat to smash the claims of religious scripture. Some self-evident facts are unlikely to change in science, but most of the arguments that are used to bash religious discourse are based on more complex theories, such as Darwinian evolution. If the content of Divinely revealed text seems to be at odds with scientific facts, you must not reject revelation to accept the science. In addition, you must not reject the science to accept the revelation. It is within your epistemic right to accept both! The correct approach, therefore, is to accept the science as the best that we have without making massive epistemic leaps of faith and concluding that it is absolute; at the same time, you can accept the revealed text because you have good reasons to do so (*see Chapter 13*).

- The final assumption forms the lens by which many atheists see the world. This lens, as discussed in various chapters of this book, is naturalism. There are two types of naturalism: philosophical and methodological. Philosophical naturalism is the philosophy that all phenomena in the universe can be explained via physical processes, and that there is no supernatural. Methodological naturalism is the view that if anything is deemed scientific, it can never refer to God's Divine activity or power.

The rest of this chapter will address these assumptions, and the best way to do that is to go back to basics: understand what science is, explore its limitations and unravel some of the discussions that exist in the philosophy of science.

What is science?

The word science comes from the Latin word *scientia,* meaning knowledge. Science is the human endeavour to understand how the physical world works. Mathematician and philosopher of science Bertrand Russell nicely explains that science is "the attempt to discover, by means of observation and reasoning based upon it... particular facts about the world, and the laws connecting facts with one another."[303]

In light of Russell's definition, let's further break down the scientific method.

Science has a particular scope. It focuses on the physical world, and can only address natural processes and phenomena. From this perspective, questions such as, *what is the soul? What is meaning?* are questions outside the scientific process.

Science aims to explain the physical world. As a collective institution, it aims to produce accurate explanations of how the natural world works. The way science aims to produce explanations is that it comes up with testable hypotheses. For a hypothesis to be testable, it must logically generate specific expectations. Consider the following hypothesis: "Coffee improves the performance of Olympic wrestlers." This hypothesis is testable because it generates the following specific expectations:

- coffee improves performance
- coffee impairs performance
- there is no change in performance

One of the beautiful aspects of science is that it does not just examine true hypotheses; rather, it necessitates experimentation and testing. This is why, ultimately, scientific ideas must not only be testable; they must actually be tested. A single set of results is not the preferred option; true science involves that different scientists repeat the experiment as many times as possible.

There is obviously more to science than what we have discussed so far, but these observations are sufficient to understand the basic elements of the scientific method. This leads us to respond to the key assumptions about science that some atheists use to falsely conclude that science leads to atheism.

Assumption #1: Science is the only way to establish the truth about reality, and it can answer all questions.
This assertion, known as scientism, claims that a statement is not true if it cannot be scientifically proven. In various conversations I have had with atheists and humanists, I have found that they constantly presume this assertion. Science is not the only way to acquire truth about the world. The limitations of the scientific method demonstrate that science cannot answer all questions. Some of its main limitations include that it:

- is limited to observation
- is morally neutral
- cannot delve into the personal
- cannot answer why things happen
- cannot address some metaphysical questions
- cannot prove necessary truths

However, before we discuss these limitations, it is important to note that scientism is self-defeating. Scientism claims that a proposition is not true if it cannot be scientifically proven. Yet the above statement itself cannot be scientifically proven. It is like saying, "There are no sentences in the English language longer than three words", which is self-defeating because that sentence *is* longer than three words.[304]

Limited to observation

This may sound like an obvious limitation, but it is not entirely understood. Scientists are always limited to their observations. For example, if a scientist wants to find out the effect of caffeine on baby mice, they will be restricted to the number and type of mice they have and all the variables in place during their experiment. Philosopher of science Elliot Sober makes this point in his essay, *Empiricism*: "At any moment scientists are limited by the observations they have at hand... the limitation is that science is forced to restrict its attention to problems that observations can solve."[305]

Not only are scientists restricted to observations, but they are also limited by the fact that a future observation may form new conclusions that in turn can go against what was previously observed (see the section below, 'The Problem of Induction'). Another limitation involves the fact that what is considered to be non-observable today could be perceived by our senses in the future, either due to improved technology or persistent investigation. The discovery and use of the microscope and the electron microscope are good examples of scientific progress. Therefore, we can never be certain about our current understanding of the physical world, because it can change with improved observations.

Morally neutral

Science is morally neutral. Now this does not mean that scientists do not have morals. What it means is that science cannot provide a foundation for morality (*see Chapter 9*). For instance, science cannot be a basis for the meaningfulness and objectivity of morals, and it cannot tell us what is right or wrong. This does not mean that it cannot be part of a multidisciplinary approach that informs some ethical and moral decisions. However, science on its own fails to provide a basis for what we consider good or bad.

Science essentially tells us what *is* and not what *ought* to be. The statement, "you cannot get an *ought* from an *is*", has become a philosophical cliché; however, it has some truth in it. Science can tell us what happens when a knife penetrates someone's skin, including all of the processes involved, but it cannot tell us whether it is immoral. The blood, pain and physical damage could be due to important life-saving surgery or the result of a murder. The point is that understanding all the processes involved in cutting and penetrating the human flesh does not lead us to a moral decision.

As mentioned in Chapter 9, Charles Darwin considered morals and science (specifically biology), and came up with an extreme example of the possible implications of our morality stemming from a biological process. He suggested that if we were reared under a different set of biological conditions, then what we would consider moral could be very different from our current views.[306] What Darwin may have been telling us is that if what human beings consider to be moral was just a result of previous biological conditioning, then having a different set of conditions would result in different moral standards. This has immense implications for the foundations and meaningfulness of morality. Firstly, establishing biology or a set of physical conditions as a basis for morality renders morals subjective—because they are (and were) subject to inevitable changes in our physical make up. However, this contradicts the innate and undeniable fact that some morals are objective (*see Chapter 9*). Secondly, if our sense of morality was based on biological conditions, then what meaning do our morals have? Since our morals could have been different if we were 'reared' differently, then our morals lose their meaning. This is because there is nothing necessary about our moral outlook, as it is simply a result of chance and physical processes.

In his book, *The Moral Landscape*, the outspoken atheist and neuroscientist Sam Harris has attempted to justify our sense of objective morality by explaining how science can determine our moral values. Fellow atheists have commended his efforts, but he has also faced tremendous criticism from both theists and his comrades in arms. Harris presents us with his landscape of morality. On the peaks is moral goodness and in the troughs is moral evil. How does he know what is good and evil? Well, the peaks represent well-being and the troughs represent suffering. This may sound like a crude summary of his discussion, but in fairness it boils down to Harris equating evil with suffering and goodness with well-being. This is where Harris fails. If it can be shown that people can increase their own well-being by harming others, his moral landscape is demolished. Consider, for instance, incest with the use of contraception. Both parties have increased well-being (as they freely decide to act upon their desires), and there is no chance of harm or suffering—such as conceiving a child with genetic defects—due to the use of contraception. I even raised the issue of incest to Professor Krauss during our debate, and he wasn't entirely sure about his position (he argued that it was not clear to him that it was wrong and he could not morally condemn it[307]). Some things that can promote our well-being are morally abhorrent. Even if you disagree with this example, there are many other examples to choose from to make this point.

In his book, *Rational Morality*, fellow atheist and philosopher of science Robert Johnson provides a similar criticism to Harris's argument. Johnson argues that Harris's approach lacks justification for morals being factual and objective:

"Harris still appears to be trapped in the problem of admitting that he is just assuming that the moral fact relating to 'wellbeing' exists. Will we find this moral fact while studying the ground under rocks? No. Will we be able to imply its existence when examining the issue like with the laws of quantum mechanics? No. In fact the only thing backing up our intuitions that these moral facts simply exist independently is just that: our intuitions... The problem itself can be explained fairly simply: just because Harris correctly identifies *how* morality is currently defined, it does not mean that morality *should* therefore be taken as factual. Indeed, Harris himself admits there are plenty of things we currently allow for which are immoral...."[308]

You cannot test the personal

Science prides itself on testing ideas. Without testing there is no science. However, at some point testing must give way to trust. For instance, how do we know what people have intended? How do we know what a person is feeling? The scientist may argue that they can tell someone is lying by using a lie detector; they may also assert that an entire array of physiological and behavioural indicators correlates to certain feelings (this is not true and will be discussed below). They have a point, but it is not as simple as that. Consider friendships as an example. Your friend asks you about your day and how you are feeling, and you respond by saying it has been a great day and that you are feeling quite happy. Imagine, you meet him the following day and he asks you the same question, but will only believe you if you hook yourself up to a lie detector to capture essential physiological data. Would that harm your friendship? If he continued to make the same request every time you responded to his question, would the relationship you have built with him be affected? Of course it would. The realm of personal friendship is preserved if we are trustworthy in our responses and if we trust what people say.

Another example is emotions. How do we know if someone is feeling depressed? Do we have a depression detector that we could use? Although physiological data provides some input, a significant portion of the vital information is in the personal interaction between the psychiatrist and the patient. This usually takes the form of questions, answers and even a completed questionnaire. These all require that we trust some of the patient's answers. Therefore, it seems to me that observations alone are not enough for certain domains of human life, such as friendship and mental health. Science, therefore, must rely on trusting rather than depending solely on testing.

As discussed in Chapter 7, science can only deal with third-person data, whereas personal attributes, such as feelings and experiences, are first-person data. Frank Jackson's Mary argument I expounded upon in Chapter 7 shows that knowing all the physical third-person facts do not lead to all the facts. In other words, they can tell us nothing about the personal first-person data. Science cannot tell us anything about what it is like for an organism to experience an internal subjective conscious state (*see Chapter 7*). The only way of getting close to an answer is by trusting someone's description of their personal subjective conscious experience (although you will still never be able to truly know what it is like for them to have that experience; see Chapter 7). The point is simple: science cannot test the personal.

Cannot answer 'why?'

My aunty knocks on your door and presents you with a lovely home-baked chocolate cake. You accept the gift and place the cake on your kitchen table. Once my aunty has gone, you open the box to have a slice. Before you indulge, you ask yourself a question: *Why has she baked me this cake?* As a scientist you cannot do much apart from explore the only piece of data you have at hand: the cake. After doing many tests, you find out that the cake was probably baked at 350 degrees Fahrenheit, and the ingredients included cocoa powder, sugar, eggs and milk. However, knowing all of this information does not help you to answer the question. The only way you can find out is if you ask her.

This example shows us that science can tell us the 'what' and the 'how', but it fails to give us the 'why'. What is meant by 'why' here is that there is a purpose behind things. Science can answer why mountains exist from the point of view that they were formed via geological processes, but it cannot provide the purpose behind the formation of the mountains. Many would simply deny the concept of purpose altogether.

Asking why implies a purpose, and many atheists maintain that purpose is an illusion, based on outdated religious thinking. This is a very unhelpful way of looking at our existence in the universe. In such a world, everything can be explained via physical processes that we have no control over. We are just one of the dominoes in a falling row of dominoes. We have to fall, because the domino behind us fell. Not only is it counterintuitive, but it highlights some striking contradictions in the way we reason in normal day-to-day activities. Imagine while reading this book you reach the final chapter and you see the following sentence: "There is no purpose behind this book". Would you even consider taking such a statement seriously?

Cannot answer some metaphysical questions

Science can address some metaphysical questions. However, these are the questions that can be empirically addressed. For example, science has been able to address the beginning of the universe via its field known as cosmology. Nevertheless, some valid questions cannot be answered scientifically. These include: *Why do conclusions in deductive reasoning necessarily follow from the previous premises? Is there an afterlife? Do souls exist? What is it like for a conscious organism to experience a subjective conscious experience? Why is there something rather than nothing?* The reason that science cannot address these questions is because they refer to things that go beyond the physical, observable world.

Necessary truths

Scientism cannot prove necessary truths such as mathematics and logic. As discussed in Chapter 3, the conclusion of a valid deductive argument necessarily follows from its premises. Consider the following argument:

1. Conclusions based on limited observations are not absolute.
2. Scientific conclusions are based on limited observations.
3. Therefore, scientific conclusions are not absolute.

The validity of this argument (not to be confused with its soundness) is not based on empirical evidence. Its validity refers to the logical flow of the argument and has nothing to do with the truth of the premises. There is a logical connection between the conclusion and the premises. This connection is not based on anything empirical; it is happening in one's mind. Can science justify the logical connection between the premises and the conclusion? No, it cannot. As discussed in Chapter 3, there is an insight in our minds that moves us from the premises to the conclusion. We see something that is not based on empirical evidence. There seem to be internal logical structures or aspects of our minds that facilitate this type of reasoning. No form of observation can justify or prove the logical flow of a deductive argument.

Mathematical truths such as 3 + 3 = 6 are also necessary truths and are not purely empirical generalisations.[309] For instance, if I were to ask what is one Fufulah plus one Fufulah, the answer would obviously be two. Even though you do not know what a Fufulah is, and you have never sensed one, you know that one of them plus another one is going to be two.

Other sources of knowledge

Science cannot justify other sources of knowledge, such as testimony. This is a branch of epistemology "concerned with how we acquire knowledge and justified belief from the say-so of other people".[310] Therefore, one of the key questions it tries to answer is: How do we gain "knowledge on the basis of what other people tell us?"[311] Professor Benjamin McMyler provides a summary of testimonial knowledge:

"Here are a few things that I know. I know that the copperhead is the most common venomous snake in the greater Houston area. I know that Napoleon lost the Battle of Waterloo. I know that, as I write, the average price for gasoline in the U.S is $4.10 per gallon... All of these things I know on the basis of what epistemologists call testimony, on the basis of being told of them by another person or group of persons."[312]

McMyler's summary seems quite intuitive and highlights why we claim some knowledge solely based on testimonial transmission. The world being a sphere is a striking example. The belief that the world is a sphere is—for most of us—not based on mathematics or science. It is purely centred on testimony. Your initial reactions may entail the following statements: "I have seen pictures", "I have read it in science books", "All my teachers told me", "I can go on the highest mountain peak and observe the curvature of the Earth", and so on. However, upon intellectual scrutiny, all of our answers fall under testimonial knowledge. Seeing pictures or images is testimonial because you have to accept the say-so of the authority or person who said it is an image of the world. Learning this fact from science textbooks is also due to testimonial transmission, as you have to accept what the authors say as true. This also applies when referring to your teachers. Talk of attempting to empirically justify your current conviction by standing on the highest peak is still based on testimony, as many of us have never done such a thing. Your assumption that standing on the highest peak will provide you with evidence for the roundness of the Earth is still based ultimately on the say-so of others. Even if you have done it before, it does not in any way prove the roundness of the Earth. Standing on a peak will only indicate that the Earth has some form of curvature— and not a complete sphere (after all, it can be semi-circular or shaped like a flower). In summary, for the majority of us, the fact that the world is round is not based on anything else apart from testimony.

Knowledge is impossible without testimony. Professor of Epistemology C. A. J. Coady summarises the points made so far, and lists some of the things that are solely accepted on the basis of testimonial transmission: "...many of us have never seen a baby born, nor have most of us examined the circulation of the blood nor the actual geography of the world nor any fair sample of the laws of the land, nor have we made the observations that lie behind our knowledge that the lights in the sky are heavenly bodies immensely distant...."[313]

The significance of testimonial knowledge needs no further discussion (for a lengthier discussion on testimony please refer to Chapter 13).

In summary, scientism, which is the view that the scientific method is the only way to form conclusions about reality, is false. Scientism is self-defeating; it also cannot account for moral truths, logical and mathematical truths, and indispensable sources of knowledge such as testimony. Science is a limited method of study that cannot answer all the questions.

Assumption #2: It works, therefore it's true

It does not logically follow that just because something works, it is true. Despite this, popular ignorance of the philosophy of science has allowed popularisers such as Richard Dawkins to publicly maintain that scientific conclusions are true because they work. During a public lecture, Dawkins was asked about the level of certainty that we can attribute to science; his answer was—as mentioned previously—crude. Dawkins was obviously mistaken; it does not follow that just because something works, it is in fact true. The phlogiston theory is an apt example to prove this point.

Early chemists postulated a theory that in all combustible objects was an element called phlogiston. According to this theory, when a combustible object burned, it would release phlogiston. The more combustible a material was, the more phlogiston it contained. This theory was adopted as a fact by the scientific community. The theory worked so well that in 1772 Dan Rutherford used it to discover nitrogen, which he called 'phlogisticated air' at the time. However, phlogiston was later found to be a false theory; phlogiston did not exist. This is one of many examples to show that a theory can work and produce new scientific truths, and yet later be found to be false. The lesson is obvious: just because something works, does not mean it is true. Some untrained objectors would argue that the example above is specific and cannot apply to modern science. They maintain that the theory of phlogiston was not a complete theory and had assumptions. However, today's scientific theories do not suffer from these problems. This is completely false. Take Darwinian evolution as an example of a well-established theory. According to mainstream secular academics it is based on assumptions, considered relatively speculative, and there are disputes about its core ideas.[314]

Scientific U-turns do not care about who is sitting in the passenger seat. Even things which seemed obvious, undeniable and observable can be overturned. A relatively recent example of this is the study of Neanderthal skulls in Europe. Darwinian biologists argued that Neanderthals must have been the ancestors to our species. In textbooks, documentaries and museums this 'scientific fact' was taught; in 1997 biologists announced the Neanderthal simply could not be our forerunner, based on modern DNA testing.

Every aspect of science, and even the subtheories that make up the bigger theories in every field, will eventually revise their conclusions. The history of science has shown us this trend, so to speak of 'scientific facts' as immutable is not accurate. It is also impractical. All scientific theories are 'work in progress' and 'approximate models'. If someone claims there is such a thing as scientific truths, then how would he or she explain the fact that 'quantum mechanics' and 'general relativity', which are both seen as true by physicists, contradict each other at a fundamental level? They both cannot be true in an absolute sense. Knowing this, physicists assume both to be true working models and use this approach to make further progress. The idea that 'scientific facts' are final is therefore misleading, impractical and dangerous for scientific progress. Historians and philosophers of science have been vocal in their opposition to use of such language. Philosophers of science Gillian Barker and Philip Kitcher drive the point home: "Science is revisable. Hence, to talk of scientific 'proof' is dangerous, because the term fosters the idea of conclusions that are graven in stone."[315]

Assumption #3: Science leads to certainty

Some atheists have a gross misunderstanding of the philosophy of science. They assume that once science declares something is a fact, then it is absolutely true and will never change. This, however, exposes a lack of knowledge of the basic unresolved issues in science. One of these issues, which is relevant to our discussion, is induction. Although there are many ways scientists confirm a theory or form conclusions about the empirical data they have tested, inductive arguments remain the bedrock of most of them. Yet inductive arguments can never lead to certainty.

Inductive arguments

Inductive arguments concern our knowledge of the unobserved. They play a central role in human knowledge, specifically scientific knowledge. Inductive arguments use instances of what we have observed to make conclusions for what we have not observed. They can be applied to include the present and the past. For example:

- Past—Premise: The bodybuilders I have spoken to have increased muscle mass as a result of eating a lot of animal protein. Conclusion: All bodybuilders in the past increased muscle mass by eating a lot of animal protein.
- Present—Premise: My friend has always experienced friendly dogs. Conclusion: All dogs are friendly.
- Future—Premise: All of the US presidential campaigns have had a Democrat candidate. Conclusion: The next presidential campaign will have a Democrat candidate.

The above conclusions obviously do not reach the level of true certainty because they are not deductive arguments. The explanations below show why the conclusions in the above inductive arguments do not necessarily follow:

- Vegetarian bodybuilders in the past gained muscle mass from eating only vegetable protein.
- It could be the case that some dogs are unfriendly.
- In the future, there could be a political paradigm shift in US politics, the Democrats could dissolve and a new party could emerge.

The uncertain nature of inductive arguments has caused many philosophers to question the validity of induction as a means to knowledge: this is an area of philosophy known as epistemic justification. This questioning led to what is now known as the problem of induction. It must be noted that inductive arguments are not the same as inductive reasoning, as this type of reasoning refers to the use of the senses and not how conclusions are made. For example, you observe frogs in your garden, and you mirror what you have observed by stating that there are frogs in your garden. You do not make a conclusion for unknown phenomena (in this case all frogs, or the next frog you have not yet observed).

The problem of induction

The challenge to induction can be traced back to the Greek, sceptical, philosophical school known as Pyrrhonism.[316] However, it was David Hume who comprehensively explained the failure of inductive arguments to provide knowledge of reality. Hume argued that the nature of our reasoning was based upon cause and effect, and that the foundation of cause and effect was experience. He maintained that since our understanding of cause and effect was based on experience, it would not lead to certainty. Hume argued that to use a limited set of experiences to conclude for an unobserved experience would not give rise to certainty.[317]

The previous examples show that inductive arguments make a conclusion by moving from the particular to the general. In other words, one moves from a limited set of experiences to conclude for experiences that have not been experienced. Inductive arguments are not deductively valid, in that the conclusion does not necessarily follow from its premises.

Hume does not restrict his argument to the uncertainty of induction; he claims that they are not justified in any way. Inductive arguments are based on an assumption that "the future will resemble the past",[318] which implies that nature is uniform. However, the only way to justify this assumption would be to use an inductive argument. Hume argues that this reasoning is circular because the assumption is based on the thing that we are seeking to justify. To justify an inductive argument with this assumption would be tantamount to justifying induction arguments with inductive arguments. After all, it could be that nature is not uniform.[319]

In summary, Hume's argument is that we cannot justify inductive arguments. The assumption that nature is uniform is based on an inductive argument, and therefore to use this assumption as a means to validate inductive arguments "is like underwriting your promise to pay back a loan by promising you will keep your promises".[320]

Inductive arguments as a problem for science

Given that inductive arguments cannot give rise to certainty, it then becomes a problem for scientific conclusions. These conclusions heavily rely on inductive arguments to form conclusions about the data that scientists have observed. However, since all observations are limited or based on a particular set of observed data, then deriving a conclusion based on limited data will not be certain.

The history of science provides many examples that highlight its dynamic nature. Prevailing theories in every field of science are very different from past eras. Samir Okasha, a lecturer of philosophy at the University of York, argues that if we were to pick any scientific disciples we could be "sure that the prevalent theories in that discipline will be very different from those 50 years ago, and extremely different from 100 years ago."[321]

At the beginning of the 20th century, physics looked neat and tidy with its Newtonian model of the universe. No one had challenged it for around 200 years as it was 'scientifically proven' to work. However, quantum mechanics and general relativity shattered the Newtonian view of the world. Newtonian mechanics assumed time and space to be fixed entities, but Albert Einstein showed these were relative and dynamic. Eventually, after a period of upheaval, the 'Einstein Model' of the universe replaced the 'Newtonian Model'. A cursory glance at the history of science confirms the problem of induction: a new observation can always contradict previous conclusions.

Science and religious scripture

Since scientific conclusions are inductive in nature, and inductive arguments do not lead to certainty, it follows that what we call scientific facts should not be considered absolute. There are no Moses tablets in science. There are, however, some things that we should not be sceptical about, such as: the roundness of the Earth, the existence of gravity and the elliptical nature of orbits.

Many atheists mock religious scripture for its inability to represent the facts. There are many online and off-line discussions on science and religious orthodoxy. Even mainstream television programmes host debates on religious perspectives on the natural world. However, in light of the discussion above, we have created a false dichotomy of religion versus science. It is not as simple as accepting one over the other.

Science is the application of reason to the natural world. It seeks to understand how the world works. The Qur'an also refers to natural phenomena, and inevitably there have been direct conflicts about scientific conclusions. When a conflict arises, there is no reason to panic or to deny the Qur'anic verse that is not in line with science; nor can anyone use this situation to claim that the Qur'an is wrong. To do so would be to assume that scientific conclusions are true in an absolute sense and will not change; this is patently false. History has shown that science revises its conclusions. Believing this does not make one anti-science. Imagine how much progress we would make if scientists were not allowed to challenge past conclusions: there would be none. Science is not a collection of eternal facts and was never meant to be.

Since there are good arguments to justify the Qur'an's claim of being God's word (*see Chapter 13*), then if the Qur'an conflicts with limited human knowledge it should not create massive confusion. Remember, God has the picture, we have just a pixel. Until the 1950s, all physicists, including Einstein, believed that the universe was eternal; all the data supported this, and this belief conflicted with the Qur'an. Yet the Qur'an explicitly states that the universe had a beginning. New observations using powerful advanced telescopes made physicists drop the 'steady state' model (eternal universe) and replace that with the Big Bang Model (universe with a beginning, possibly about 13.7 billion years ago). So, science came into line with the Qur'an. The same thing happened with the Qur'anic view of the sun. The Qur'an states that the sun has an orbit; astronomers disagreed, saying it was stationary. This was the most direct contradiction between observations of scientists and the Qur'an. However, after the discoveries of the Hubble telescope, astronomers revised their conclusions and found the Sun was orbiting around the centre of the Milky Way galaxy.

Yet this does not mean that the Qur'an is a book of science. It's a book of signs. The Qur'an does not give any details concerning natural phenomena. Most of the things it refers to can be understood and verified with the naked eye. The main objective of verses that point towards the natural world is to expose a metaphysical power and wisdom. Their role does not include elucidating scientific details. These can change over time; however, the fact that natural phenomena have a power and wisdom behind them is a timeless reality. From this perspective, conflict between the Qur'an and scientific conclusions will probably continue, as they are two completely different types of knowledge.

This discussion should not, however, encourage Muslims and religious people to deny scientific conclusions. To do so would be absurd. Rather, both well-confirmed scientific theories and the revelational truths should be accepted, even if they contradict each other. Scientific conclusions can be accepted practically as working models that can change and are not absolute, and the revelational truths can be accepted as part of one's beliefs. If there is no hope of reconciling a scientific conclusion and a statement of the Qur'an, then you do not have to reject revelation and accept the science of the day. Conversely, the science should not be rejected either. As previously mentioned, it is within your epistemic right to accept both scientific and revelational truths. The balanced and nuanced approach concerning science and revelation is to accept the science and allow the evidence to speak for itself. However, this should be in the context of not making massive epistemic leaps of faith and concluding that the evidence we have acquired and the conclusions we have made are the *gospel truth*. Science can change. In addition, this approach includes accepting the revelation. In summary, we can accept scientific conclusions practically and as working models, but if anything contradicts revelation (after attempting to reconcile the two), you do not have to accept the scientific conclusion into your belief system. This is why Muslims should not need to deny Darwinian evolution; they can accept it practically as the current best-working model, but understand that some aspects of it cannot be reconciled with orthodoxy. Remember, just because something is the current best-working model, it is not the absolute truth.

Islamic inductive arguments?

Critical and learned observers of this discussion will notice that although this is a mainstream understanding of science (amongst academics and philosophers), it also brings to light potential criticisms of Islamic epistemology. They can argue that in the Islamic tradition, inductive arguments are used to preserve the Qur'an and Prophetic traditions (known as *hadith*; *ahadith*, pl.). Therefore, Muslims cannot claim certainty in these vital source texts for Islam. This is a misplaced contention. To explain why, refer back to the earlier distinction between inductive reasoning and inductive arguments. Inductive reasoning provides certainty for basic types of knowledge. For instance, if I observe X in Y, it follows that Y allows X; I observe that crows fly, so it necessarily follows that some crows fly. As you can see, this form of induction just 'mirrors' the observation. It states the plain facts without making a conclusion for something that is yet to be observed. This type of induction was used in the preservation of the Qur'an and the Prophetic traditions. For example, a companion of the Prophet Muhammad ﷺ heard the Qur'an, and he simply repeated what he had heard. He never made a conclusion for a verse that he never heard. For example, a companion wouldn't hear "Iyyaka na'abudu wa iyyaka nasta'een" (it is You we worship and it is You we ask for help) and then conclude "Qul huwa Allahu ahad" (Say, He is God, the uniquely One). Hence this objection is false, as it misunderstands the type of induction involved in the preservation of the Qur'an and the Prophetic traditions.

Assumption #4: Philosophical and methodological naturalism

Naturalism heavily influences scientific thinking, theories and observations. There are two types of naturalism: philosophical and methodological. Philosophical naturalism is the view that the universe is like a closed system; there is nothing outside the universe that interferes with it, and there is nothing supernatural. A key aspect of philosophical naturalism is that all phenomena can be explained via physical processes. Methodological naturalism maintains that for anything to be described as scientific, it cannot refer to God's creative power or activity.

Philosophical naturalism is simply a faith. The atheist Professor Michael Ruse admits this fact: "If you want a concession, I've always said that naturalism is an act of faith...."[322] Why is it a faith? Well, naturalism is incoherent, as it blindly believes that everything can be explained via physical processes, despite a number of recalcitrant facts; in other words, facts that resist a theory.[323] For example, we both meet today at a restaurant at six o'clock, and the following day the police come to my house to arrest me on suspicion of murdering someone at the same time we were having dinner. The recalcitrant fact would be that I was with you eating at the time of the murder. My proven whereabouts resist the police's suspicions that I committed the murder. You may be wondering, what are these recalcitrant facts that render philosophical naturalism as incoherent? Well, many of the previous chapters are a good starting point. Philosophical naturalism cannot adequately explain the hard problem of consciousness (*see Chapter 7*), the finitude and dependency of the universe (*see Chapters 5 and 6*), the fine-tuning of the laws and the order in the universe (*see Chapter 8*), the existence of objective morals (*see Chapter 9*) and much more. In light of this, why would anyone blindly adopt such a philosophy, which prevents one from allowing reality to speak for itself? Many atheists have such naturalistic presuppositions. Therefore, it is not surprising that they dismiss the conclusions of theistic arguments. Usually they reject good arguments because they are blinded with the false assumption that everything has to be explained by physical processes and that they can never entertain supernatural explanations.

Methodological naturalism is also an incoherent position. It restricts the intellectual breadth of scientific conclusions. Do not misunderstand me here; I agree that science has to stick to physical explanations. The Islamic tradition argues that God uses physical causes to manifest His will and power. Therefore, methodological naturalism does not cause a problem for a Muslim. However, God provides an additional explanatory framework to put physical causes and processes into their correct context. For example, instead of speculating that the first living cell was brought to Earth via aliens and a meteorite (as Richard Dawkins once claimed),[324] it would be far more reasonable to assert God's creative power and ability, as it does not lead to an absurd infinite regress and argument that life can come from non-life (or even that rationality can come from non-rational physical processes and causes; *see Chapter 3*).

So has science disproved God?

In light of the above, the answer is no. Science is a beautiful method of study that has benefited humanity tremendously. However, its conclusions are not engraved in stone. As a method, it cannot directly reject God's existence, answer all questions, and it is not the only way to form conclusions about reality. Many of the assumptions that some atheists hold about science are incoherent and based on a gross misunderstanding of the philosophy of science.

Chapter 13
God's Testimony
The Divine Authorship of the Qur'an

Thus far, our concern has been with the evidence for God's existence and responses to key arguments against the Divine. Previous chapters have argued that God is the necessarily existing creator, designer, and moral lawgiver of the universe. However, that only tells us so much about the Divine Reality. The next question is: *If this Being indeed created us, then how do we know who He is?* Following that line of thought, we will be looking at the Qur'an as a candidate for Divine revelation. Although the previous chapters have referenced many Qur'anic verses, the following chapter will go into detail about the rational basis for God's word.

Most of what we know is based on the say-so of others. This holds true for facts we would never deny. For many of us, these truths include the existence of Amazonian native tribes, photosynthesis, ultraviolet radiation, and bacteria. Let me elaborate further by using your mother as an example. How would you prove to me—a perfect stranger—that your mother did in fact give birth to you? As bizarre as this question sounds, it will help clarify a very important yet underrated source of knowledge. You might say "my mother told me so", "I have a birth certificate", "my father told me, he was there", or "I have checked my mother's hospital records". These responses are valid; however, they are based on the statements of other people. Sceptical minds may not be satisfied. You may try to salvage an empirical basis for your conviction by using the 'DNA card' or by referring to video footage. The conviction that your mother is who she says she is isn't based on a DNA home test kit. The reality is that most of us have not taken a DNA test. It is also not based on video footage, as you still have to rely on the say-so of others to claim that the baby is actually you. So why are we so sure? This admittedly quirky example reemphasises an important source of knowledge that was introduced in Chapter 12: *testimony*.

Many of our beliefs are based on a form of reasoning which begins with a collection of data, facts or assertions, and then seeks the best explanation for them. Let's welcome your mother back briefly, again. She is heavily pregnant with you inside her womb and the due date was last week. Suddenly, her waters break and she starts having contractions, so your father and the relevant medical staff safely assume that she's started labour. Another example: some years on, your mother notices an open packet of biscuits and crumbs around your mouth and on your clothes. She *infers* that you opened the packet and helped yourself to some biscuits. In both examples, the conclusions are not *necessarily* true or indisputable, but they are the best explanations considering all of the facts available. This thinking process is known as *inference to the best explanation*.

So why have I introduced the above scenarios? Because using the concepts and principles from these examples, this chapter will put forward the case that the Qur'an is an inimitable expression of the Arabic language, and that God best explains its inimitability. What is meant by inimitability is that no one has been able to produce or emulate the Qur'an's linguistic and literary features. These can include—but are not limited to—its unique literary form and genre, in the context of sustained eloquence. Though this assertion seems quite disconnected to what I have elaborated so far, consider the following outline:

The Qur'an was revealed in Arabia to the Prophet Muhammad ﷺ in the 7th century. This period was known as an era of literary and linguistic perfection. The 7th century Arabs were socialised into being a people who were the best at expressing themselves in their native tongue. They would celebrate when a poet rose amongst them, and all they knew was poetry. They would start with poetry and end with poetry. The cultivation of poetic skills and linguistic mastery was everything for them. It was their oxygen and life-blood; they could not live or function without the perfection of their linguistic abilities. However, when the Qur'an was recited to them they lost their breath; they were dumbfounded, incapacitated, and stunned by the silence of their greatest experts. They could not produce anything like the Qur'anic discourse. It got worse. The Qur'an challenged these linguists *par excellence* to imitate its unique literary and linguistic features, but they failed. Some experts accepted the Qur'an was from God, but most resorted to boycott, war, murder, torture and a campaign of misinformation. In fact, throughout the centuries experts have acquired the tools to challenge the Qur'an, and they too have testified that the Qur'an is inimitable, and appreciate why the best linguists have failed.

How can a non-Arab or non-expert of the Arabic language appreciate the inimitability of the Qur'an? Enter now the role of testimony. The above assertions are based on an established written and oral testimonial transmission of knowledge from past and present scholars of the Arabic language. If this is true, and the people best placed to challenge the Qur'an failed to imitate the Divine discourse, then who was the author? This is where testimony stops and the use of inference begins. In order to understand the inference to the best explanation, the possible rationalisations of the Qur'an's inimitable nature must be analysed. These include that it was authored by an Arab, a non-Arab, Muhammad ﷺ or God. Considering all of the facts that will be discussed in this essay, it is implausible that the Qur'an's inimitability can be explained by attributing it to an Arab, a non-Arab or Muhammad ﷺ. For that reason, God is the inference to the best explanation.

The main assumptions in the above introduction are that testimony is a valid source of knowledge, and inference is a suitable and rational method of thinking to form conclusions about reality. This chapter will introduce the epistemology of testimony, and elaborate on the rational use of testimonial transmission. It will highlight the effective use of inferring to the best explanation, and apply both concepts to the Qur'an's inimitability. This chapter will conclude that God is the best explanation for the fact that no one has been able to imitate the Divine book. All this will be achieved without the reader requiring any knowledge or expertise of the Arabic language.

The epistemology of testimony

As briefly discussed in Chapter 12, testimony is an indispensable and fundamental source of knowledge. There are some very important questions epistemologists are trying to answer in the field of the epistemology of testimony. These include: *When and how does testimony yield evidence? Is testimonial knowledge based on other sources of knowledge? Is testimony fundamental?* Although it is not the scope of this chapter to solve or elaborate on all the issues in this area of epistemology, it will summarise some of the discussions to further substantiate the fact that testimony is a valid source of knowledge.

Is testimony fundamental?

The examples on testimonial transmission in Chapter 12 expose our epistemic dependence on the say-so of others. This reminds me of a public discussion I had with outspoken atheist Lawrence Krauss. I highlighted the fact that observations were not the only source of knowledge and therefore wanted to expose his empirical presupposition. I raised the issue of testimony and asked him if he believed in evolution. He replied that he did, and so I asked him if he had done all the experiments himself. He replied in the negative.[325] This uncovered a serious issue in his—and by extension, many of our—assumptions about why we believe what we believe. Most of our beliefs are based on the say-so of others and are not empirical simply because they are couched in scientific language.

Until relatively recently, testimony was neglected as an area of in-depth study. This academic silence came to an end with various studies and publications, most notably Professor C. A. J. Coady's *Testimony: A Philosophical Discussion*. Coady argues for the validity of testimony, and attacks David Hume's reductionist account of testimonial transmission. The *reductionist* thesis asserts that testimony is justified via other sources of knowledge such as perception, memory and induction. In other words, testimony on its own has no warrant and must be justified *a posteriori*, meaning knowledge based on experience. Coady's account for testimony is fundamental; he asserts that testimonial knowledge is justified without appealing to other sources of knowledge, like observation. This account of testimony is known as the *anti-reductionist* thesis. Coady contends the reductionist thesis by attacking Hume's approach. Hume is seen as the main proponent of the reductionist thesis due to his essay, *On Miracles*, which is the tenth chapter of his *Enquiry Concerning Human Understanding*. Hume's reductionist approach does not entail denying testimonial knowledge. He actually highlights its importance: "We may observe, that there is no species of reasoning more common, more useful, and even necessary to human life, than that which is derived from the testimony of men...."[326] Hume argues that our trust in testimony is based on a conformity between testimonial knowledge and experience. This is where Coady seeks to dismantle the basis of Hume's approach. His criticism is not limited to the following argument, but elaborating on it here demonstrates the strength of his overall contentions.

Coady argues that Hume's appeal to collective observation exposes a vicious circle. Hume claims that testimony can only be justified if the knowledge that someone is testifying to is in agreement with observed facts. However, what Hume implies by observed facts is not personal observation, but rather collective experience, and Coady argues that we cannot always rely on personal observed generalisations. This is where the vicious circle is exposed; we can only know what others have observed based upon their testimony. Relying on one's own direct observations would not suffice, as that knowledge would be too limited and unqualified to justify anything—or at least very little. Therefore, the reductionist thesis is flawed. Its claim that testimony must be justified via other sources of knowledge, such as observation, actually assumes that which it tries to deny: the fundamental nature of testimony. The key reason which affirms this point is that in order to know what our collective observations are, you must rely on other people's testimony, as we have not observed them ourselves.

Relying on experts

The modern scientific progress we all are proud of could never have happened without trusting an authority's claim to experimental data. Take evolution as an example. If Richard Dawkins's belief in evolution required that he must perform all of the experiments himself and personally observe all of the empirical data, he could never be so bold in claiming its truth. Even if he could repeat some of the observations and experiments himself, he would still have to rely on the say-so of other scientists. This area of study is so vast that to verify everything ourselves would be impossible, and to maintain such a claim would make scientific progress unattainable.

The previous example raises an important question: *What if the testimonial transmission of knowledge is based on the say-so of an expert?* The fact is that we are not all experts and thus must, at times, accept the testimony of others. University lecturer in philosophy Dr. Elizabeth Fricker elaborates:

"But that there are some occasions on which it is rational deferentially to accept another's testimony, and irrational to refuse to do so, is entailed by her background knowledge of her own cognitive and physical nature and limitations, together with her appreciation of how other people are both like and in other respects unlike herself, hence on some occasions better epistemically placed regarding some matter than she is herself. I may rationally regret that I cannot fly, or go for a week without sleep without any loss of performance, or find out for myself everything which I would like to know. But given my cognitive and physical limitations as parametric, there is no room for rational regret about my extended but canny trust in the word of others, and enormous epistemic and consequent other riches to be gained from it."[327]

Trust

This is where the concept of trust enters the discussion of testimonial transmission. To accept the word of others based on their authority on a particular subject requires us to not only trust them, but to be trustworthy in our assessments of their trustworthiness.

Discussions about the nature and validity of testimony have moved on from the reductionist and anti-reductionist paradigms. Professor of Philosophy Keith Lehrer argues that the justification for testimony is neither of the two approaches. Lehrer's argument rests on trust. He argues that testimony leads to the acquisition of knowledge under "some circumstances but not all circumstances."[328] He maintains that testimony is "itself a source of evidence when the informant is trustworthy in the testimony. The testimony in itself does not constitute evidence otherwise."[329] The person who testifies does not need to be "infallible to be trustworthy",[330] but "the person testifying to the truth of what she says must be trustworthy in what she accepts and what she conveys."[331] Lehrer admits that trustworthiness is not sufficient for the conversion of the say-so of others into knowledge, that the person's trustworthiness must be assessed (something he refers to as "truth-connected") and that we must be trustworthy and reliable in our assessment.[332] The assessment of a testimonial transmission can include background information on a topic, the testimonies of others on a particular field of knowledge, as well as personal and collective experiences.

Lehrer claims that in order for us to be trustworthy about the way we evaluate the trustworthiness of others, we need to refer to previous experiences in our assessments and whether we were accurate or mistaken. However, when we learn that the testimony of a person is not trustworthy, it is usually due to relying on the testimony of others about that person.[333] This may expose a vicious circle, because to assess the testimony of others, other testimonies are relied upon. Lehrer asserts this is more of a "virtuous loop".[334] How is this the case? The professor provides two answers:

"First, any complete theory of justification or trustworthiness will have to explain why we are justified or trustworthy in accepting the theory itself. So the theory must apply to itself to explain why we are justified or trustworthy in accepting it. Secondly, and equally important, our trustworthiness at any given time must result from what we have accepted in the past, including what we have accepted from the testimony of others. The result is that there is a kind of mutual support between the particular things we have accepted and our general trustworthiness in what we accept, including, of course, the particular things we have accepted. It is the mutual support among the things that we accept that results in the trustworthiness of what we accept."[335]

The right of deferral

Lehrer's discussion on trustworthiness raises the question of how we can establish trust to rely on the authority or the say-so of others. Professor Benjamin McMyler develops an interesting argument that aids in answering this question. McMyler argues that the epistemological problem of testimony can be "recast as a problem of explaining the epistemic right of deferral."[336] McMyler argues that if an audience is entitled to defer challenges back to the speaker, it provides a new way in framing the problem of testimony. This requires that both parties acknowledge a responsibility. The speaker must accept responsibility for espousing testimonial knowledge, and the audience must accept that they can defer challenges back to the speaker.[337]

Trustworthiness can be built by exercising this right to defer challenges back to the speaker (or writer). If coherent answers to these challenges are given, this can potentially increase trust. The following example explains this point. A professor of linguistics claims that the Qur'an is inimitable, and elaborates on its eloquence, unique literary form and genre. The audience takes responsibility and challenges the professor. The challenge is in the form of questions, including: *Can you give us more examples from the Qur'an? What have other authorities said about the Qur'an's genre? How can you explain the views of academics who disagree with you? Given the historical background information on the Qur'an, in what way does it support your assertion?* The professor provides coherent answers to the questions, and gradually builds trust.

A note on eyewitness testimony

The discussion so far refers to the testimonial transmission of knowledge, and not the recollection of what was witnessed during an event or a crime. The existing material concerning eyewitness testimony is vast, and this chapter does not intend to discuss the conclusions and implications of such studies and research. However, given that there is an academic concern over eyewitness testimony with regards to its reliability, it should not be conflated with the testimonial transmission of knowledge. These are distinct areas. Eyewitness testimony may suffer due to our imperfect short-term memories and the psychological influences and constraints on recalling the sequence of a particular event. The testimony of knowledge, ideas or concepts does not suffer from such issues because the acquisition of knowledge is usually a result of repetition, a relatively longer duration, internalisation and study.

This point leads to a slight but useful diversion—David Hume's treatise on miracles. Hume argued that the only evidence we have for miracles is eyewitness testimony. He concluded that we should only believe in miracles if the probability of the eyewitnesses to be mistaken, is greater than the probability for the miracle to occur.[338]

Notwithstanding the concerns over single eyewitness reports, eyewitness testimony can be taken seriously in the context of multiple witnessing (which is related to the concept of *tawaatur* in Islamic studies). If there exists a large (or large enough) number of independent witnesses who transmitted the testimony via varying chains of transmission, and many of these witnesses never met each other, then to reject that report would be bordering on the absurd. Even Hume himself recognized the power of this type of eyewitness report and maintained that miracles may be possible to prove if the testimonial transmission is large enough:

"I beg the limitations here made may be remarked, when I say, that a miracle can never be proved, so as to be the foundation of a system of religion. For I own, that otherwise, there may possibly be miracles, or violations of the usual course of nature, of such a kind as to admit of proof from human testimony; though, perhaps, it will be impossible to find any such in all the records of history. Thus, suppose, all authors, in all languages, agree, that, from the first of January 1600, there was a total darkness over the whole Earth for eight days: suppose that the tradition of this extraordinary event is still strong and lively among the people: that all travellers, who return from foreign countries, bring us accounts of the same tradition, without the least variation or contradiction: it is evident, that our present philosophers, instead of doubting the fact, ought to receive it as certain...."[339]

The focus of this chapter is on the testimonial transmission of knowledge and not events or eyewitness reports—the conceptual distinctions between the two are obvious. However, it has been mentioned here to remind the reader of the distinction between the two types of testimony.

To conclude this section, testimony is a necessary source of knowledge. Without testimonial transmission we could not have had the scientific progress characteristic of our era, many of our established claims to knowledge would be reduced to a sceptic's musings, and we would not be justified in easily dismissing the flat-earther's assertions. For testimony to turn into knowledge, we must be trustworthy in our assessments of the trustworthiness of others and take responsibility for deferring challenges back to the one testifying. We must also ensure that there is some truth connected to their claims, which can include other testimonies or background information.

Inference to the best explanation

Inference to the best explanation is an invaluable way of thinking. It involves trying to coherently explain a particular set of data and/or background knowledge. For example, when we are asked by our doctor how we are feeling, we present her with the following symptoms: nasal stuffiness, sore or itchy throat, sneezing, hoarseness, coughing, watery eyes, fever, headache, body aches, and fatigue. Based on this information, the doctor attempts to best explain why we are unwell. Coupled with her background knowledge accumulated via her medical education, she concludes that the above symptoms are best explained by the common cold. Professor of History and Philosophy Peter Lipton similarly explains the practical and indispensable role of inference:

"The doctor infers that his patient has measles, since this is the best explanation of the evidence before him. The astronomer infers the existence of motion of Neptune, since that is the best explanation of the observed perturbations of Uranus... According to the Inference to the Best Explanation, our inferential practices are governed by explanatory considerations. Given our data and our background beliefs, we infer what would, if true, provide the best of the competing explanations we can generate of those data...."[340]

As with most things, we can have competing explanations for the data at our disposal. What filters these explanations is not only their plausibility, but the availability of other pieces of data that could help us discriminate between them. Lipton explains: "We begin by considering plausible candidate explanations, and then try to find data that discriminate between them... An inference may be defeated when someone suggests a better alternative explanation, even though the evidence does not change."[341]

The accessibility to additional data is not the only way to assess which of the competing explanations is the most convincing. The best explanation is one that is the simplest. Simplicity, however, is just the beginning, as there must be a careful balance between simplicity and comprehensiveness.

Comprehensiveness entails that an explanation must have explanatory power and scope. The explanation must account for all of the data, including disparate or unique observations.

Another criterion to assess the comprehensiveness of an explanation includes explaining data or observations that were previously unknown, unexpected or inexplicable. An important principle in assessing the best explanation is that it is most likely to be true, compared to competing explanations, given our background knowledge. The academic philosopher at Princeton University Gilbert H. Harman asserts that when alternative explanations exist, one "must be able to reject all such alternative hypotheses before one is warranted in making the inference. Thus one infers, from the premise that a given hypothesis would provide a 'better' explanation for the evidence than would any other hypothesis, to the conclusion that the given hypothesis is true."[342]

In light of the above, inference to the best explanation is an indispensable form of reasoning. It can also lead to certainty. If the data at our disposal is limited and the explanations are finite, then the best explanation would be, to some extent, certain—as there would not be a possibility of another better explanation, or a chance of new data that could change what we consider the best explanation. The Qur'an coming from the Divine is based on this type of certainty. There are no other rational explanations for the Qur'an's authorship and the data that the explanations are based on are finite. For example, there will never be a new letter of the classical Arabic language and a brand new history of Arabic is untenable.

Formulating an argument

The discussion so far has highlighted the importance of testimony and inference to the best explanation in arriving at knowledge. However, merely quoting testimonies will not suffice, because there are competing expert testimonies about the Qur'an's inimitability. Therefore, we will need to present well-established background information to show why the testimonies in support of the Qur'an's inimitability should be favoured.

This background information includes the fact that the Qur'an presents a linguistic and literary challenge, and that the 7th century Arabs achieved mastery in expressing themselves in the Arabic language, yet failed to imitate the Qur'an. Once this is established, adopting the testimony in favour of the inimitability of the Qur'an would be the rational choice, as it provides the basis to accept them. The testimonies that disagree with the Qur'an's uniqueness are reduced to absurdity, as they deny what has been established (to be explained later). Once the testimonial transmission is adopted, the competing explanations for the Qur'an's inimitability must be assessed in order to make an inference to the best explanation; the Qur'an was produced either by an Arab, a non-Arab, Muhammad ﷺ or God. A summary of the argument is as follows:

1. The Qur'an presents a literary and linguistic challenge to humanity.
2. The 7th century Arabs were best placed to challenge the Qur'an.
3. The 7th century Arabs failed to do so.
4. Scholars have testified to the Qur'an's inimitability.
5. Counter-scholarly testimonies are not plausible, as they have to reject the established background information.
6. Therefore (from 1-5), the Qur'an is inimitable.
7. The possible explanations for the Qur'an's inimitability are authorship by an Arab, a non-Arab, Muhammad ﷺ or God.
8. It could not have been produced by an Arab, a non-Arab or Muhammad ﷺ.
9. Therefore, the best explanation is that it is from God.

The remaining part of this chapter will elaborate on the premises above.

1. The Qur'an presents a literary and linguistic challenge to humanity.

"Read in the name of your Lord".[343] These were the first words of the Qur'an revealed to the Prophet Muhammad ﷺ over 1,400 years ago. Muhammad ﷺ, who was known to have been meditating in a cave outside Mecca, had received revelation of a book that would have a tremendous impact on the world we live in today. Not known to have composed any piece of poetry and not having any special rhetorical gifts, Muhammad ﷺ had just received the beginning of a book that would deal with matters of belief, legislation, rituals, spirituality, and economics in an entirely new genre and literary form.[344]

The unique literary and linguistic features of the Qur'an have been used by Muslims to articulate a number of arguments to substantiate their belief that the book is from the Divine. The failure of anyone to imitate the Qur'an developed into the Muslim theological doctrine of the Qur'an's inimitability or *al-i'jaaz al-Qur'an*. The word *i'jaaz* is a verbal noun that means 'miraculousness' and comes from the verb *a'jaza*, which means 'to render incapable', or 'to make helpless'. The linguistic meaning of the term brings to light the theological doctrine that Arab linguistics *par excellence* were rendered incapable of producing anything like it. Jalal al-Din al-Suyuti, prolific 15th century writer and scholar, summarises this doctrine:

"...when the Prophet brought [the challenge] to them, they were the most eloquent rhetoricians so he challenged them to produce the [entire] likes [of the Qur'an] and many years passed and they were unable to do so as God says, *Let them then produce a recitation similar to it, if indeed they are truthful.* Then, [the Prophet] challenged them to produce 10 chapters like it where God says, *Say, bring then ten chapters like it and call upon whomever you can besides God, if you are truthful.* Then, he challenged them to produce a single [chapter] where God says, *Or do they say he [i.e. the Prophet] has forged it? Say, bring a chapter like it and call upon whomever you can besides God, if you are truthful...* When the [Arabs] were unable to produce a single chapter like [the Qur'an] despite there being the most eloquent rhetoricians amongst them, [the Prophet] openly announced the failure and inability [to meet the challenge] and declared the inimitability of the Qur'an. Then God said, *Say, if all of humankind and the jinn gathered together to produce the like of the Qur'an, they could not produce it—even if they helped one another....*"[345]

According to classical exegesis, the various verses in the Qur'an that issue a challenge to produce a chapter like it daringly call for the linguistic experts of any era to imitate the Qur'an's linguistic and literary features.[346] The tools needed to meet this challenge are the finite grammatical rules, literary and linguistic devices, and the twenty-eight letters that comprise the Arabic language; these are independent and objective measures available to all. The fact that it has not been matched since it was first revealed does not surprise most scholars familiar with the Arabic language and the Qur'an.

2. The 7th century Arabs were best placed to challenge the Qur'an.

The Qur'an posed a challenge to the greatest Arabic linguists, the 7th century Arabs. The fact that they reached the peak of eloquence is affirmed by western and eastern scholarship. The scholar Taqi Usmani asserts that for the 7th century Arab "eloquence and rhetoric were their life blood."[347] According to the 9th century biographer of the poets, Al-Jumahi, "Verse was to the Arabs the register of all they knew, and the utmost compass of their wisdom; with it they began their affairs, and with it they ended them."[348] The 14th century scholar Ibn Khaldun highlights the importance of poetry in Arab life: "It should be known that Arabs thought highly of poetry as a form of speech. Therefore, they made it the archives of their history, the evidence for what they considered right and wrong, and the principal basis of reference for most of their sciences and wisdom."[349]

Linguistic ability and expertise was a highly influential feature of the 7th century Arab's social environment. The literary critic and historian Ibn Rasheeq illustrates this: "Whenever a poet emerged in an Arab tribe, other tribes would come to congratulate, feasts would be prepared, the women would join together on lutes as they do at weddings, and old and young men would all rejoice at the good news. The Arabs used to congratulate each other only on the birth of a child and when a poet rose among them."[350] The 9th century scholar Ibn Qutayba defined poetry as the Arabs saw it: "The mine of knowledge of the Arabs, the book of their wisdom... the truthful witness on the day of dispute, the final proof at the time of argument."[351]

Navid Kermani, a writer and expert in Islamic studies, explains the extent to which the Arabs had to study to master the Arabic language, which indicates that the 7th century Arab lived in a world that revered poetry: "Old Arabic poetry is a highly complex phenomenon. The vocabulary, grammatical idiosyncrasies and strict norms were passed down from generation to generation, and only the most gifted students fully mastered the language. A person had to study for years, sometimes even decades under a master poet before laying claim to the title of poet. Muhammad ﷺ grew up in a world which almost religiously revered poetic expression."[352]

The 7th century Arab lived in a socio-cultural environment that had all the right conditions to facilitate the unparalleled expertise in the use of the Arabic language.

3. The 7th century Arabs failed to do so.

Their linguistic abilities notwithstanding, they collectively failed to produce an Arabic text that matched the Qur'an's linguistic and literary features. The linguistics expert Professor Hussein Abdul-Raof asserts, "The Arabs, at the time, had reached their linguistic peak in terms of linguistic competence and sciences, rhetoric, oratory, and poetry. No one, however, has ever been able to provide a single chapter similar to that of the Qur'an."[353]

Professor of Qur'anic Studies Angelika Neuwrith argued that the Qur'an has never been successfully challenged by anyone, past or present: "...no one has succeeded, this is right... I really think that the Qur'an has even brought Western researchers embarrassment, who weren't able to clarify how suddenly in an environment where there were not any appreciable written text, appeared the Qur'an with its richness of ideas and its magnificent wordings."[354]

Labid ibn Rabi'ah, one of the famous poets of the Seven Odes, embraced Islam due to the inimitability of the Qur'an. Once he embraced Islam, he stopped composing poetry. People were surprised, for "he was their most distinguished poet".[355] They asked him why he stopped composing poetry; he replied, "What! Even after the revelation of the Qur'an?"[356]

E. H. Palmer, Professor of Arabic and of the Qur'an, argues that the assertions made by academics like the one above should not surprise us. He writes, "That the best of Arab writers has never succeeded in producing anything equal in merit to the Qur'an itself is not surprising."[357]

Scholar and Professor of Islamic Studies M. A. Draz affirms how the 7th century experts were absorbed in the discourse that left them incapacitated: "In the golden age of Arab eloquence, when language reached the apogee of purity and force, and titles of honour were bestowed with solemnity on poets and orators in annual festivals, the Qur'anic word swept away all enthusiasm for poetry or prose, and caused the Seven Golden Poems hung over the doors of the Ka'ba to be taken down. All ears lent themselves to this marvel of Arabic expression."[358]

The number of testimonial transmissions from the 7th century that affirm the Arabs' inability to produce anything like the Qur'an excludes any doubt in this context. It would be unreasonable to dismiss the fact that the Arabs were incapacitated. Similar to what was mentioned in the section on eyewitness testimony, the narratives that conclude the Arabs' failure to imitate the Qur'an have reached the status of *tawaatur* (mass concurrent reporting). There exist a large number of experts who have conveyed this knowledge via varying chains of transmission, and many of them never met each other.

A powerful argument that supports the assertion that the 7th century Arabs failed to imitate the Qur'an relates to the socio-political circumstances of the time. Central to the Qur'anic message was the condemnation of the immoral, unjust and evil practices of the 7th century Meccan tribes. These included the objectification of women, unjust trade, polytheism, slavery, hoarding of wealth, infanticide and the shunning of orphans. The Meccan leadership was being challenged by the Qur'anic message, and this had the potential to undermine their leadership and economic success. In order for Islam to stop spreading, all that was needed was for the Prophet's ﷺ adversaries to meet the linguistic and literary challenge of the Qur'an. However, the fact that Islam succeeded in its early, fragile days in Mecca testifies to the fact that its primary audience was not able to meet the Qur'anic challenge. No movement can succeed if a claim fundamental to its core is explicitly proven false. The fact that the Meccan leadership had to resort to extreme campaigns, such as warfare and torture, to attempt to extinguish Islam demonstrates that the easy method of refuting Islam—meeting the Qur'anic challenge—failed.

4. Scholars have testified to the Qur'an's inimitability.

Multitudes of scholars from western, eastern, religious and non-religious backgrounds have testified to the Qur'an's inimitability. Below is a non-exhaustive list of the scholarship that forms the testimony that the Qur'an cannot be emulated:

- Professor of Oriental Studies Martin Zammit: "Notwithstanding the literary excellence of some of the long pre-Islamic poems... the Qur'an is definitely on a level of its own as the most eminent written manifestation of the Arabic language."[359]
- The scholar Shah Waliyyullah: "Its highest degree of eloquence, which is beyond the capacity of a human being. However, since we come after the first Arabs we are unable to reach its essence. But the measure which we know is that the employment of lucid words and sweet constructions gracefully and without affectation that we find in the Tremendous Qur'an is to be found nowhere else in any of the poetry of the earlier or later peoples."[360]
- Orientalist and litterateur A. J. Arberry: "In making the present attempt to improve on the performance of predecessors, and to produce something which might be accepted as echoing however faintly the sublime rhetoric of the Arabic Koran, I have been at pain to study the intricate and richly varied rhythms which—apart from the message itself—constitutes the Koran's undeniable claim to rank amongst the greatest literary masterpieces of mankind."[361]
- Scholar Taqi Usmani: "None of them was able to compose even a few sentences to match the Qurānic verses. Just think that they were a people who according to 'Allāmah Jurjāni, could never resist ridiculing the idea in their poetry if they heard that there was someone at the other end of the globe who prided himself on his eloquence and rhetorical speech. It is unthinkable that they could keep quiet even after such repeated challenges and dare not come forward... They had left no stone unturned for persecuting the Prophet ﷺ. They tortured him, called him insane, sorcerer, poet and sooth-sayer, but failed utterly in composing even a few sentences like the Qurānic verses."[362]
- Imam Fakhr al-Din: "It is inimitable because of its eloquence, its unique style, and because it is free of error."[363]

- Al-Zamlakani: "Its word structures for instance, are in perfect harmony with their corresponding scales, and the meaning of its phraseology is unsurpassed, such that every linguistic category is unsurpassed in the case of every single word and phrase."[364]
- Professor Bruce Lawrence: "As tangible signs, Qur'anic verses are expressive of an inexhaustible truth, they signify meaning layered with meaning, light upon light, miracle after miracle."[365]
- Professor and Arabist Hamilton Gibb: "Like all Arabs they were connoisseurs of language and rhetoric. Well, then if the Koran were his own composition other men could rival it. Let them produce ten verses like it. If they could not (and it is obvious that they could not), then let them accept the Koran as an outstanding evidential miracle."[366]

The above confirmations of the inimitability of the Qur'an are a small sample from the innumerable testimonies available to us.

Other instances of 'inimitability': Al-Mutannabi and Shakespeare

Abu at-Tayyib Ahmad ibn al-Husayn al-Mutanabbi al-Kindi was considered an inimitable poetic genius by many Arabs. Some have argued that although other poets have used the same panegyric genre and poetic metre as the great poet, they have not been able to match his level of eloquence and stylistic variance. Therefore, they conclude that Al-Mutannabi is inimitable because we have the blueprint of his work and the linguistic tools at our disposal, but cannot emulate anything like his poetic expression. If this is true, then it undermines the Qur'an's inimitability. However, this acclamation of Al-Mutanabbi is unfounded. There have been imitations of Al-Mutanabbi's work by the Jewish poets Moses ibn Ezra and Solomon ibn Gabriol. Interestingly, the Andalusian poet Ibn Hani' al-Andalusi was known as the Al-Mutannabi of the West.[367]

One significant point is that medieval Arabic poetry did not create new literary genres. This was due to the fact that it depended on previous poetic work. The academic Denis E. McAuley writes that medieval poetry largely hinged "more on literary precedent than on direct experience."[368]

In classical Arabic poetry, it was not unusual for a poet to attempt to match a predecessor's poem by writing a new one in the same poetic metre, rhyme, and theme. This was considered normal practice.[369] It is not surprising that Professor of Religion Emil Homerin explored the literary expression of Ibn al-Farid, and described his work as "very original improvisations on al-Mutanabbi".[370]

To highlight further the fact that Al-Mutanabbi can be emulated, he disclosed that he borrowed work from another poet, Abu Nuwas.[371] Many medieval Arab literary critics such as Al-Sahib ibn 'Abbad and Abu Ali Muhammad ibn al-Hasan al-Hatimi wrote criticisms of Al-Mutanabbi. Ibn 'Abbad wrote *al-kashf 'an masawi' shi'r al-Mutanabbi* and Al-Hatimi wrote a biographical account of his encounter with Al-Mutanabbi in his *al-Risala al-Mudiha fi dhikr sariqat Abi al-Tayyib al-Mutanabbi*.[372] The conclusions of these literary criticisms imply that although his work is the product of genius, they can be emulated. Al-Hatimi presents a stronger polemic against Al-Mutanabbi and argues the case that his poetry does not have a unique style and contains errors. Professor Seeger A. Bonebakker, who studied Al-Hatimi's literary criticism of Al-Mutanabbi, concludes that his "judgement is often well-founded and one almost ends up feeling that Mutanabbi was, after all, a mediocre poet who was not only lacking in originality, but also had insufficient competence in grammar, lexicography, and rhetoric, and sometimes gave evidence of incredibly bad taste."[373]

Consider the general consensus that Shakespeare is thought to be unparalleled with regards to the use of the English language. However, his work is not considered inimitable. His sonnets are written predominantly in a frequently used meter called the iambic pentameter, a rhyme scheme in which each sonnet line consists of ten syllables. The syllables are divided into five pairs called iambs or iambic feet.[374] Since the blueprint of his work is available, it is not surprising that the English dramatist Christopher Marlowe has a similar style, and that Shakespeare has been compared to Francis Beaumont, John Fletcher and other playwrights of his time.[375]

Testifying to the Qur'an's inimitability does not imply accepting its Divinity

A valid contention concerning academic testimonies of the Qur'an's inimitability is that these scholars agree that the Qur'an cannot be imitated, yet they have not concluded that it is a divine text. The problem with this contention is that it conflates testifying to the Qur'an's inimitability with inference to the best explanation. The argument I am presenting in this chapter does not conclude the divinity of the Qur'an from the statements of scholars. Rather, it articulates that the best explanation to elucidate the inimitability of the Qur'an is that it came from God. Whether these scholars accept the inference, or the divinity of the Qur'an, is irrelevant. The statements of the scholars are used as evidence for the Qur'an's inimitability, not that it is best explained by God. The argument infers from the text's inimitability, not from conclusions the scholars may have drawn from the fact that it cannot be imitated. It must be pointed out that these scholars may not have been presented with an argument that presents an inference to the best explanation, or they may have not reflected on the philosophical implications of the Qur'an's inimitability. These academics may even deny the God explanation because they adopt philosophical naturalism. The belief in naturalism will deter them from concluding anything about the supernatural.

Also, many academics, especially living in today's postmodernist culture, have a restricted approach to many of the sciences. Therefore, many of these scholars are interested in the Qur'an not to be convinced of its divinity or to accept Islam, but to appreciate its literature for the sake of literary studies. This is a very common trend in modern academia. So when these scholars probe into the inimitability of the Qur'an, it is very likely that they are focusing exclusively on its literary merit, not on its claim to divinity. They want to find out whether the Qur'an is inimitable or sophisticated, and if so, to what extent. They are entirely uninterested in the question of what inimitability implies about its Divine origin.

5. Counter scholarly testimonies are not plausible, as they have to reject the established background information

In light of the above, the testimonial transmission concerning the inimitability of the Qur'an would be the most rational to adopt. This does not mean there is a complete consensus on the issue, or that all scholarship asserts that the Qur'an is unchallenged. There are some (albeit in the minority) scholarly opinions that contend against the Qur'an's inimitability. If valid testimony does not require unanimity, why would someone accept one testimonial transmission over another?

The testimony concerning the Qur'an's inimitability is more reasonable because it rests on strong background knowledge. This knowledge has been discussed in premises 1, 2 and 3, which highlight the fact that the Qur'an presents a literary and linguistic challenge to humanity. The 7th century Arabs were best placed to challenge the Qur'an, yet these linguistic masters failed to meet this challenge.

Adopting the counter testimonies leads to absurdity. This is because an explanation is required to answer why those who were best placed to challenge the Qur'an failed to do so. Possible explanations would include rejecting the validity of this established history, or claiming a greater understanding and appreciation of classical Arabic than the 7th century linguist masters. These explanations render the counter testimonies without a rational basis. Rejecting the established history would require a remaking of the history of Arabic literature. Assuming superior linguistic abilities than the 7th century specialists is debased by the fact that these experts had a relatively homogenous linguistic environment. These environments are areas where the purity of the language is maintained, and there is a limited amount of linguistic borrowing and degeneration. Contemporary Arab linguistic environments suffer from excessive linguistic borrowing and degeneration. Therefore, to claim superiority over a people coming from a culture that had the fertile ground for linguistic perfection is untenable.

Despite the weakness of these contentions, when an analysis of the work of the scholars who testify against the Qur'an's inimitability is performed, the results conclude the linguistic meagreness of this type of scholarship. An example of its inadequacy can be found in the work of the highly acclaimed German orientalist and scholar Thedor Nöldeke. He was an academic critic of the linguistic and literary features of the Qur'an, and therefore rejected the doctrine of the Qur'an's inimitability. However, his criticism brings to light the unsubstantiated nature of such claims. For instance, Nöldeke remarks, "The grammatical persons change from time to time in the Qur'an in an unusual and not beautiful way *(nicht schoner Weise)*."[376]

The Qur'anic linguistic feature that Nöldeke refers to is actually the effective rhetorical device known as *iltifaat* or grammatical shifts. This literary device enhances the text's literary expression and it is an accepted, well-researched part of Arabic rhetoric.[377] One can find references to it in the books of Arabic rhetoric by Al-Athir, Suyuti and Zarkashi.[378]

These grammatical shifts include: change in person, change in number, change in addressee, change in tense, change in case marker, using a noun in place of a pronoun and many other changes.[379] The main functions of these shifts include the changing of emphasis, to alert the reader to a particular matter, and to enhance the style of the text.[380] Its effects include creating variation and difference in a text to generate rhythm and flow, and to maintain the listener's attention in a dramatic way.[381]

The 108th Qur'anic chapter provides a good example of the use of grammatical shifts:

"Verily, We have granted you The Abundance. Therefore turn in prayer to your Lord and sacrifice. For he who hates you, he will be cut off."[382]

In this chapter, there is a change from the first-person plural "We" to the second person "...your Lord". This change is not an abrupt shift; it is calculated and highlights the intimate relationship between God and the Prophet Muhammad ﷺ. The use of "We" is used to emphasize the Majesty, Power and Ability of God. This choice of personal pronoun calls attention to the fact that God has the Power and Ability to grant Muhammad ﷺ "...The Abundance", whereas "your Lord" has been used to emphasise intimacy, closeness and love; the phrase has a range of meanings that imply master, provider, and the One that cares. This is an apt use of language, as the surrounding concepts are about prayer, sacrifice and worship: "Therefore turn in *prayer* to your Lord and *sacrifice*". Furthermore, the purpose of this chapter is also to console Prophet Muhammad ﷺ, as using such intimate language enhances the psycholinguistic effect.

Theodor Nöldeke's criticism of the Qur'an was not only a personal value judgement, but exposed his crude understanding of classical Arabic. It also confirmed his inability to reach the level of expertise that was attained by 7th century Arabs. These grammatical shifts contribute to the dynamic style of the Qur'an and are obvious stylistic features and an accepted rhetorical practice. The Qur'an uses this feature in such a way that conforms to the theme of the text while enhancing the impact of the message it conveys. It is not surprising that in his book, *Discovering the Qur'an: A Contemporary Approach to a Veiled Text*, Professor Neal Robinson concludes that the grammatical shifts used in the Qur'an, "...are a very effective rhetorical device."[383]

To conclude, counter testimonies that argue against the Qur'an's inimitability do not hold water because they create far more problems than they solve. The scholarship that provides a basis for these counter-testimonies is meagre and based on a crude understanding of the Arabic language. Rejecting the inimitability of the Qur'an requires an answer to the following question: *Why did the best-placed Arabs fail to challenge the Qur'an?* The possible answers to this question are rationally absurd. For these reasons, adopting the counter-testimonies is flawed.

6. Therefore (from 1-5) the Qur'an is inimitable.

It follows from points 1 to 5 that the Qur'an's inimitability is justified.

7. The possible explanations for the Qur'an's inimitability are authorship by an Arab, a non-Arab, Muhammad ﷺ or God

To articulate the Divine origins of the Qur'an without referring to specifics about the Arabic language, the use of testimony and inference are required. What has been discussed so far is that there is a valid testimonial transmission that the Qur'an is inimitable, and that the possible explanation for its inimitability can be explained by attributing its authorship to an Arab, a non-Arab, Muhammad ﷺ or God. However, it can be argued that there are other possible competing explanations, but we do not know what they are. This assertion commits a type of fallacy that some have called "the fallacy of the phantom option". If there are genuine competing explanations, then they must be presented on the intellectual table for discussion. Otherwise, this kind of reasoning is no different from claiming that the leaves do not fall from trees because of gravity, but because of another explanation that we do not know about.

8. It could not have been produced by an Arab, a non-Arab or Muhammad ﷺ.

To understand who could have possibly produced the Qur'an, the rest of this chapter will break down the three main theories.

An Arab?

There are a few key reasons why the Qur'an could not have come from an Arab. Firstly, they achieved unparalleled linguistic and literary mastery, yet they failed to challenge the Qur'an and the leading experts of the time testified to the inimitable features of the Qur'an. One of the best linguists of the time, Walid ibn al-Mughira, exclaimed:

> "And what can I say? For I swear by God, there is none amongst you who knows poetry as well as I do, nor can any compete with me in composition or rhetoric—not even in the poetry of jinns! And yet, I swear by God, Muhammad's speech [meaning the Qur'an] does not bear any similarity to anything I know, and I swear by God, the speech that he says is very sweet, and is adorned with beauty and charm."[384]

Secondly, the Arab polytheists in the 7th century initially accused the Prophet ﷺ of being a poet. This was an easier thing to do than going to war and fighting the Muslims. However, anyone who aspired to master the Arabic language and Arabic poetry required years of study under poets. None of them came out to expose Muhammad ﷺ as being one of his students. The very fact that Muhammad ﷺ was successful in his message demonstrates that he succeeded in showing the poets and linguists of the time that the Qur'an is indeed a supernatural genre. If the Qur'an was not inimitable, any poet or linguist could have produced something better or similar to the Qur'anic discourse. The expert in Islamic studies Navid Kermani makes this point clear: "Obviously, the Prophet succeeded in this conflict with the poets, otherwise Islam would not have spread like wildfire."[385]

An even more fundamental point is that the Qur'an was revealed throughout the Prophet's ﷺ life. If an Arab other than the Prophet ﷺ had produced it, he would have had to constantly shadow the Prophet ﷺ wherever he went, and spew out revelations whenever the occasion called for it. Is one seriously to believe such a fraud would go unexposed for the entire 23-year period of revelation?

What about today's Arabs? To assert that a contemporary Arabic-speaking person might emulate the Qur'an is unfounded. A few reasons substantiate this point. Firstly, the Arabs in the 7th century were better placed to challenge the Qur'an, and since they failed to do so, it would be unreasonable to assert that a linguistically impoverished modern Arab might surpass the abilities of their predecessors. Secondly, modern Arabic has suffered from greater linguistic borrowing and degeneration than the classical Arabic tradition. So how can an Arab who is a product of a relatively linguistically degenerated culture be equal to an Arab who was immersed in an environment of linguistic purity? Thirdly, even if a contemporary Arab learns classical Arabic, his linguistic abilities could not match someone who was immersed in a culture that mastered the language.

A non-Arab?

The Qur'an could not have come from a non-Arab, as the language in the Qur'an is Arabic, and the knowledge of the Arabic language is a prerequisite to successfully challenge the Qur'an. This has been addressed in the Qur'an itself: "And indeed We know that they [polytheists and pagans] say: 'It is only a human being who teaches him (Muhammad).' The tongue of the man they refer to is foreign, while this is a speech *Arabeeyun mubeen* [clear Arabic]."[386]

The classical exegete Ibn Kathir explains this verse to mean: "How could it be that this Qur'an with its eloquent style and perfect meanings, which is more perfect than any Book revealed to any previously sent Prophet, might have been learnt from a foreigner who hardly speaks the language? No one with the slightest amount of common sense would say such a thing."[387]

What if a non-Arab learned the language? This would make that person an Arabic speaker, and I would refer to the first possible explanation above.

However, there are differences between native and non-native speakers of languages, as various academic studies in applied linguistics and similar fields have concluded. For instance, in the English language, there are differences between native and non-native speakers in reliably discriminating between literal and idiomatic speech.[388] Differences exist between English-speakers with one non-native parent and those with native parents. The speakers with one non-native parent exhibit worse linguistic performance on certain tasks than those with native parents.[389] Even in cases of non-native speakers having indistinguishable linguistic competence with native speakers, there are still subtle linguistic differences. Research conducted by Kenneth Hyltenstam and Niclas Abrahamsson in *Who can become native-like in a second language? All, some, or none?* concluded that competent non-native speakers exhibit features that are imperceptible except under detailed and systematic linguistic analysis.[390] Therefore, to conclude that the Qur'an, with its inimitable features and as a linguistic masterpiece, is a product of a non-Arab, or non-native speakers, is untenable.

Prophet Muhammad ﷺ?

It is pertinent to note that the Arab linguists at the time of revelation stopped accusing the Prophet ﷺ of being the author of the Qur'an after their initial false assertion that he became a poet. Professor Mohar Ali writes:

> "It must be pointed out that the Qur'an is not considered a book of poetry by any knowledgeable person. Nor did the Prophet ﷺ ever indulge in versifying. It was indeed an allegation of the unbelieving Quraysh at the initial stage of their opposition to the revelation that Muhammad [ﷺ] had turned a poet; but soon enough they found their allegation beside the mark and changed their lines of criticism in view of the undeniable fact of the Prophet's ﷺ being unlettered and completely unaccustomed to the art of poetry-making, saying that he had been tutored by others, that he had got the 'old-worst stories' written for him by others and read out to him in the morning and evening."[391]

Significantly, the Prophet ﷺ was not considered a master of the language and did not engage in the craft of poetry or rhymed prose. Therefore, to claim that he somehow managed to conjure up a literary and linguistic masterpiece is beyond the pale of rational thought. Kermani writes, "He had not studied the difficult craft of poetry, when he started reciting verses publicly... Yet Muhammad's recitations differed from poetry and from the rhyming prose of the soothsayers, the other conventional form of inspired, metrical speech at the time."[392]

The scholar Taqi Usmani similarly argues, "Such a proclamation was no ordinary thing. It came from a person who had never learned anything from the renowned poets and scholars of the time, had never recited even a single piece of poetry in their poetic congregations, and had never attended the company of soothsayers. And far from composing any poetry himself, he did not even remember the verses of other poets."[393]

Further, the established Prophetic traditions of the Prophet Muhammad ﷺ are in a distinct style from that of the Qur'an. Dr. Draz argues the difference between the Qur'anic style and the Prophet's ﷺ:

"When we consider the Qur'ānic style we find it the same throughout, while the Prophet's own style is totally different. It does not run alongside the Qur'ān except like high flying birds which cannot be reached by man but which may 'run' alongside him. When we look at human styles we find them all of a type that remains on the surface of the Earth. Some of them crawl while others run fast. But when you compare the fastest running among them to the Qur'ān you feel that they are no more than moving cars compared to planets speeding through their orbits."[394]

Nonetheless, Dr. Draz's argument on the differences between styles may not have much rational force in light of poets and spoken-word artists. Poets and spoken-word artists maintain key stylistic differences between their normal speech and their work over a long period of time. Thus, to use this as an argument to disprove that the Prophet Muhammad ﷺ authored the Qur'an is weak. However, it has been mentioned here because if the styles were the same or even similar, then that would rule out any possibility of the Qur'an being inimitable Divine speech.

The Prophet Muhammad ﷺ experienced many trials and tribulations during the course of his Prophetic mission. For example, his children died, his beloved wife Khadija passed away, he was boycotted, his close companions were tortured and killed, he was stoned by children, he engaged in military campaigns; throughout all this, the Qur'an's literary nature remains that of the Divine voice and character.[395] Nothing in the Qur'an expresses the turmoil and emotions of the Prophet Muhammad ﷺ. It is almost a psychological and physiological impossibility to go through what the Prophet ﷺ went through, and have none of the resultant emotions manifest themselves in the literary character of the Qur'an.

From a literary perspective, the Qur'an is known as a work of unsurpassed excellence. However, its verses were many times revealed for specific circumstances and events that occurred during the period of revelation. Each verse was revealed without revision, yet they collated to create a literary masterpiece. In this light, the explanation that the Qur'an is a result of the Muhammad's ﷺ literary abilities is obviously unfounded. All literary masterpieces written by geniuses have undergone revision and deletion to achieve literary perfection, yet the Qur'an was revealed instantaneously and remained unchanged.[396] In the process of making good literature, editing and amending are absolutely necessary. No one can produce sophisticated literature 'on the go'. However, that is exactly what we see in the case of the Qur'an. Disparate Qur'anic verses were revealed in different contexts and occasions, and once these verses had been recited by the Prophet ﷺ to an audience, he could not take them back to improve their literary quality. This constitutes strong circumstantial evidence that the Qur'an, given its inimitability, could not have been produced by the Prophet ﷺ. When we consider this and other evidences cited above, the cumulative impression we get is that it is extremely unlikely, if not downright impossible, for the Qur'an to have been produced by the Prophet Muhammad ﷺ.

An example to highlight this point is the work of the highly acclaimed poet Abu at-Tayyib Ahmad ibn al-Husayn al-Mutanabbi al-Kindi. Al-Mutanabbi was considered the greatest of all Arab poets and an unparalleled genius. Therefore, some have concluded that since his work was unparalleled, and that he was a human being, it follows the Qur'an was written by a human author too. This reasoning does not logically follow because Al-Mutannabi would correct his work and produce various versions until he was satisfied.[397] This was obviously not the case with Muhammad ﷺ, as he did not edit, amend, or change the Qur'an once it was revealed. This can only mean that the Qur'an is not the work of a literary genius, who, in general, would need to revise their work.

To conclude, attributing the authorship of the Qur'an to genius, specifically Muhammad's ﷺ genius, is unfounded. Even a literary genius edits, amends and improves their work. This was not the case with the Qur'an. All human expressions can be imitated if we have the blueprint and the tools at our disposal. This has been shown for literary geniuses such as Shakespeare and Al-Mutanabbi. Therefore, if the Qur'an had been a result of Muhammad's ﷺ genius, it should have been imitated.

A central argument that dismisses the assertion that the Qur'an was a consequence of the Prophet Muhammad's ﷺ literary abilities concerns the existence of blueprints for human expressions, and the tools required to replicate them. All types of human expression—whether the result of a genius or not—can be imitated if the blueprint of that expression exists, given that the tools are available for us to use. This has been shown to be true for various human expressions, such as art, literature and even complex technology. For example, artwork can be imitated even though some art is thought to be extraordinary or amazingly unique.[398] But in the case of the Qur'an, we have its blueprint (the Qur'an itself) and the tools (the finite words and grammatical rules of the classical Arabic language) at our disposal. Yet no one has been able to imitate its eloquence, unique literary form and genre.

9. Therefore, the best explanation is that the Qur'an is from God.

Since the Qur'an could not have been produced by an Arab, a non-Arab or the Prophet Muhammad ﷺ, then it follows that the best explanation is that it came from God. This provides the best explanation for the Qur'an's inimitability because the other explanations are untenable in light of the available knowledge. A possible disagreement with this conclusion is that God is assumed to exist in order for this inference to work; therefore, it begs the question of the existence of the Divine. Although it will make the argument easier to appreciate, and can work without any previous conviction in the existence of the Divine, this argument is best articulated to fellow theists. That is not a real problem, however, because a sustained case for God's existence has been made throughout this book.

Conversely, the point can be made that a previous conviction in God's existence is not necessary, and that the inimitability of the Qur'an is a signpost to the existence of the Divine. If a human being (an Arab, a non-Arab or the Prophet Muhammad 🕊) could not have produced the Qur'an—and all possible explanations have been exhausted—then who else could be the author? It must be something that has greater linguistic capacity than any known text producer. The intuitive conclusion is that the concept that describes a being with greater linguistic capacity than any human is the concept of God. God is indeed greater. Therefore, the inimitability of the Qur'an provides a rational basis for God's existence, or at least a signpost to the transcendent.

Similar reasoning is adopted by scientists. Take the recent discovery of the Higgs-Boson. The Higgs-Boson particle is the building-block of the Higgs field. This field was switched on during the early universe to give particles mass. Before the discovery of this particle, it was still accepted as the best explanation for the fact that during the early universe, particles changed state from having no mass to having mass (with the exception of photons). So, the Higgs-Boson particle was the best explanation for the available data even before it was empirically verified. Applying this reasoning back to the inimitability of the Qur'an, the fact that the book has unique literary and linguistic features is best explained by God. All other competing explanations fail, and God is the best explanation for the information and knowledge available to us.

Alternative inferences

Alternative inferences could include the fact that the inimitability of the Qur'an is best explained by a higher being or that it could have come from the devil. These alternative inferences are unlikely; hence they have not been incorporated into the central argument presented in this essay. Nevertheless, addressing them here will demonstrate why they have not been included in the main discussion.

Postulating that the Qur'an comes from a higher being seems to be a semantic replacement for God. What is meant by "a higher being"? Is not the best explanation of a higher being God Himself? If "a higher being" implies a greater linguistic power, capacity and ability than a human, then who can best fit these criteria than God Himself? This book has articulated independent evidence for God's existence, and it is very likely that God would want to communicate with us. This follows from the fact that not only is God the creator and designer of the entire cosmos we inhabit, but He has also made it fit for our existence. In addition, He has created us with souls or consciousness, and instilled in us a sense of morality. Clearly, God is extremely invested in our existence and flourishing. As such, it is entirely likely that He would want to communicate to us in the form of revelation. So, when we have evidence that the Qur'an—a book that claims to be from God—does have properties that are entirely in line with Divine activity, it makes perfect sense to attribute its authorship to God. To say that the Qur'an could have been produced by some unknown "higher beings" of unknown motives would be tantamount to invoking the existence of any unknown entity to explain anything.

Theistic responses to this discussion usually entertain the possibility of the devil being the author of the Qur'an. This explanation is untenable. The Qur'an could not have come from the devil, or some type of spirit, because the basis of their existence is the Qur'an and revelation itself, not empirical evidence. Therefore, if someone claims that the source of the Qur'an is the devil, they would have to prove his existence and ultimately have to prove revelation. In the case of using the Qur'an as the revelation to establish the devil's existence, then that would already establish it as a Divine text, because to believe in the devil's existence would presuppose the Qur'an to be Divine, and therefore this contention is self-defeating. If, however, the revelation that is referred to is the Bible, it must be shown to be a valid basis to justify the belief in the devil. In light of contemporary studies into the textual integrity and historicity of the Bible, this is not feasible.[399] Further, a content analysis of the Qur'an would strongly indicate that the book is not the teachings of the devil, as the Qur'an rebukes him and promotes morals and ethics not in line with an evil worldview. Despite this, the devil objection does not conform to our intellectual practices. We can realistically explain anything by citing the activity of the devil; from this perspective it is an intellectual cop-out.

Conclusion

This chapter has presented an argument for the Divine nature of the Qur'anic discourse using testimony and inference to the best explanation. The crucial and fundamental role of testimony has been highlighted, and inference to the best explanation has been shown to be a rational and valid method of thinking to form conclusions about reality. The Qur'an's inimitability can be established using testimony. Arabic linguists and literary experts confirm the inimitability of the Qur'an, and their testimonial knowledge on the topic is warranted based on established background knowledge. This knowledge includes the fact that the Qur'an poses an intellectual linguistic and literary challenge to the world, that the Arabs in the 7th century were best placed to challenge the Qur'an, and the fact that they failed to produce anything like the Qur'an's unique content and literary form. Given that it is reasonable to accept the testimony in favour of the Qur'an's inimitability—based on established background information—inference is then used to best explain the book's unique linguistic and literary features. The possible explanations comprise an Arab, a non-Arab, Muhammad ﷺ and God. Since attributing this unique discourse to an Arab, a non-Arab or Muhammad ﷺ is untenable in light of the information available to us, the best explanation is that it came from God.

To reject the conclusions made in this chapter is epistemically equivalent to rejecting the spherical nature of the Earth and the conclusions of qualified medical staff. The spherical nature of the Earth, for most of us, is ultimately based on testimonial transmission, and the conclusions of trained medical experts are based on inferences to the best explanation. A retort to this assertion may include the fact that trust in the spherical nature of the Earth and the medical diagnosis of experts is justified based on other knowledge we have acquired, and it does not lead to extraordinary claims such as postulating the supernatural. This contention is common. However, it presupposes a naturalistic ontology. This means that a hidden assumption behind such concerns is the rejection of anything supernatural and that all phenomena can be explained via physical processes. Such a daring and presumptuous worldview is unjustified and incoherent in light of modern studies on the philosophy of the mind, the development and acquisition of language, and objective moral truths and cosmology, as the preceding chapters in this book demonstrate. Significantly, we are not postulating the existence of the supernatural here; we have already established His existence on the basis of evidences in the earlier chapters. We are merely claiming that the Being whose existence we have already established serves as the best explanation for certain facts.

To end, if someone with an open mind and heart—without the intellectual constraints of non-negotiable assumptions about the world—has access to the argument presented in this chapter, especially in light of the stage-setting in the previous ones, they should make the most rational conclusion that the Qur'an is from the Divine. Nevertheless, whatever is said or written about the Qur'an will always fall short in describing and exploring its words and their meanings: "Say, 'If the sea were ink for [writing] the words of my Lord, the sea would be exhausted before the words of my Lord were exhausted, even if We brought the like of it as a supplement.'"[400]

Chapter 14
The Prophetic Truth
The Messenger of God

The Qur'an teaches that we must believe in all the prophets and messengers, and that they were all chosen to help guide humanity to the ultimate truth of God's oneness and our servitude to Him. The Qur'an mentions many of the prophets and messengers whom we have been accustomed to at school or at home. The Divine book mentions many of them by name, including Abraham, Moses, Jesus, David, John, Zacharias, Elias, Jacob and Joseph, may God's peace be upon them all. However, there is a distinction between a prophet and a messenger. A prophet is a person who has been inspired by God to guide his people to the truth. A messenger is very similar, but the difference is that a messenger has been given Divine revelation. The role of these messengers and prophets is to be a manifestation of what has been revealed to them, and to exemplify God-consciousness, piety and compassion. Since messengers have been given God's revealed word, their role also includes teaching the correct interpretation and understanding of what God has revealed. Additionally, messengers and prophets act as practical and spiritual examples as they embody the meaning, message and values conveyed by the Divine text. From this perspective, the Divine revelation tells us what to do and the Prophet's ﷺ life shows us how to do it.

The Qur'an mentions the Prophet Muhammad's ﷺ name five times,[401] and confirms that the book was revealed unto him via the angel Gabriel. The Qur'an affirms that Muhammad ﷺ is God's final messenger.[402] From this perspective, intellectually affirming this status of the Prophet Muhammad ﷺ is quite simple. Once the Qur'an has been established as a Divine book, it necessarily follows that whatever it says will be the truth. Since it mentions Muhammad ﷺ as God's messenger, and what comes from truth is true, then the fact that Muhammad ﷺ was a recipient of Divine revelation is also true. Despite this undeniable conclusion, the fact that the

Prophet Muhammad ﷺ was the final messenger of God can also be deduced from his experiences, teachings, character and the impact he has on the world.

The Prophet Muhammad's ﷺ life experiences comprise one of the strongest arguments in support of his claim—and by extension the Qur'an's claim—that he was God's final messenger. Once an analysis of his life is performed, to conclude that he was lying or deluded would be tantamount to concluding that no one has ever spoken the truth. It would be the epistemic equivalent of denying that the person you call your mother gave birth to you. The teachings of the Prophet Muhammad ﷺ cover a wide range of topics including spirituality, society, economy and psychology. Studying his statements, and taking a holistic approach to his teachings, will force any rational mind to conclude that there was something very unique and special about this man. Significantly, scrutinising his character in the context of a myriad of difficult situations and circumstances will facilitate the conclusion that he had unparalleled levels of tolerance, forbearance and humility—key signs of a prophetic character. Muhammad's ﷺ life and teachings, however, not only influenced the Arab world, but had a tremendous impact on the whole of humanity. Simply put, Muhammad ﷺ was responsible for unprecedented tolerance, progress and justice.

Denying Muhammad ﷺ, denying your mother

As mentioned in Chapter 13, the only real source of knowledge that we have to confirm that the lady we call our mother gave birth to us is testimonial knowledge. Even if we claim to have a birth certificate, hospital records, or a DNA test certificate, these still are all examples of testimonial knowledge. You have to believe in the say-so of others. In this case, the one who filled in the birth certificate, the one responsible for the hospital records, and the person who completed the DNA test certificate. Fundamentally, it is just based on a testimonial transmission; there is not a shred of physical evidence that can empirically verify the claim that your mother gave birth to you. Even if you do the DNA test yourself (which is highly unlikely), your conviction now that she gave birth to you is not based on the fact that you can potentially acquire the results. The irony is that the only reason you believe a DNA test can be used to verify that your mother gave birth to you is based on the testimonial transmission of some authority

242 | The Divine Reality

telling you so, because you haven't done it yourself yet. So, from an epistemic perspective, the basis for your belief that your mother gave birth to you is based on a few instances of testimonial transmission. Since we have far more authentic testimonial evidence to conclude that the Prophet Muhammad ﷺ was the final prophet of God, then to deny Muhammad ﷺ would be equivalent to denying your own mother.

The argument

The Prophet Muhammad ﷺ claimed prophethood over 1,400 years ago with the following simple, yet profound message: *There is none worthy of worship but God, and the Prophet Muhammad is the final messenger of God.*

The Prophet Muhammad ﷺ became a prophet at the age of 40, after spending some time meditating and reflecting in a cave outside Mecca. The dawn of prophethood began with the revelation of the first verses of the Qur'an. Its message was simple: our ultimate purpose in life is to worship God. Worship is a comprehensive term in the Islamic spiritual tradition; it means to love, know, obey, and dedicate all acts of worship to God alone (*see Chapter 15*).

To test the truth of his message and claim to prophethood, we must rationally investigate the historical narratives and testimonies concerning the life of the Prophet ﷺ. Once we do this, we will be in a position to come to a balanced conclusion in this regard.

The Qur'an provides a rational approach to testing the claim of the Prophet ﷺ. It argues that the Prophet ﷺ is not a liar, mad, astray, or deluded, and denies that he speaks from his own desire. The Qur'an affirms that he is indeed the messenger of God; therefore, he is speaking the truth:

"Your companion is not mad."[403]

"Your companion has not strayed; he is not deluded; he does not speak from his own desire."[404]

"Muhammad is the messenger of God."[405]

We can summarise the argument in the following way:

- The Prophet Muhammad ﷺ was either a liar, or deluded, or speaking the truth.
- The Prophet ﷺ could not have been a liar or deluded.
- Therefore, the Prophet ﷺ was speaking the truth.

Was he a liar?

Early historical sources on the Prophet Muhammad's ﷺ life illustrate the integrity of his character. He was not a liar and to assert as much is indefensible. The reasons for this abound—for instance, he was known even by the enemies of his message as the "Trustworthy"[406].

The Prophet Muhammad's ﷺ message undermined the economic and power structures of society. Seventh century Meccan society was based on trade and commerce. The leaders of Meccan society would attract these traders with the 360 idols they had in the Ka'bah—the cube-shaped structure built by Abraham as a house of worship. The Prophet's ﷺ message was simple, yet it powerfully challenged 7th century Arabian polytheism. The leaders of that society initially mocked him, thinking the Prophet ﷺ would not have an impact. However, as his message was gradually taking root with high-profile conversions, the leadership started to abuse the Prophet ﷺ, both physically and emotionally.

He was persecuted for his beliefs, boycotted and exiled from his beloved city—Mecca. He was starved of food and stoned by children to the point where blood drenched his legs. His wife passed away and his beloved companions were tortured and persecuted.[407] Further proof of the Prophet's ﷺ reliability and credibility is substantiated by the fact that a liar usually lies for some worldly gain. Muhammad ﷺ suffered tremendously for his message[408] and rejected outright the riches and power he was offered to stop promulgating his message. He was uncompromising in his call to God's oneness.

Montgomery Watt, late Emeritus Professor in Arabic and Islamic Studies, explores this in *Muhammad at Mecca* and argues that calling the Prophet ﷺ an impostor is irrational: "His readiness to undergo persecution for his beliefs, the high moral character of the men who believed in him and looked up to him as a leader, and the greatness of his ultimate achievement—all argue his fundamental integrity. To suppose Muhammad an impostor raises more problems than it solves."[409]

Was he deluded?

To claim that the Prophet Muhammad ﷺ was deluded is to argue that he was misled to believe that he was the messenger of God. If someone is deluded, they have a strong conviction in a belief despite any evidence to the contrary. Another way of looking at the issue of delusion is that when someone is deluded, they speak falsehood whilst believing it to be true. The Prophet Muhammad ﷺ had many experiences during his career that, if he were deluded, he would have used as evidence to support his delusion. One example is the passing away of his son, Ibrahim. The boy died at an early age and the day he died there was a solar eclipse. Many Arabs thought that God made the eclipse happen because His prophet's son passed away. If the Prophet ﷺ were deluded, he would have used such an opportunity to reinforce his claim. However, he did not and rejected the people's assertions. The Prophet ﷺ replied to them in the following way: "The sun and the moon do not eclipse because of the death of someone from the people but they are two signs amongst the signs of God. When you see them, stand up and pray."[410]

The Prophet ﷺ foretold many things that would happen to his community after his death. These events occurred exactly as Muhammad ﷺ stated, and this is not consistent with a deluded individual. For example:

The Mongol invasion

Six hundred years or so after the death of the Prophet Muhammad ﷺ, the Mongols invaded the Muslim lands and massacred millions of people. A significant milestone in the invasion was the ransacking of Baghdad. At that time, it was known as a city of learning and culture. The Mongols arrived in Baghdad in 1258 and spent a whole week spilling blood. They were hell-bent on demolishing the city. Thousands of books were destroyed and up to one million people were killed. This was a major event in Islamic history.

The Mongols were non-Arabs who had flat noses, small eyes, and their boots were made of hair; the Mongols had fur covers over their boots called *degtii*. This was foretold by the Prophet Muhammad ﷺ hundreds of years before the Mongol invasion: "The Hour will not be established till you fight with the Khudh and the Kirman from among the non-Arabs. They will be of red faces, flat noses and small eyes; their faces will look like flat shields, and their shoes will be of hair."[411]

Competing in constructing tall buildings

"Now, tell me of the Last Hour," said the man.

The Prophet ﷺ replied, "The one asked knows no more of it than the one asking."

"Then tell me about its signs," said the man.

The Prophet ﷺ replied, "That you see barefoot, unclothed bedouins competing in the construction of tall buildings."[412]

Notice the detail in the prophecy: a specific people (the Arab bedouins of the region) were identified. Prophet Muhammad ﷺ could have easily played it safe by using more general language such as, "That you see competition in the construction of tall buildings...." This would have been flexible enough to be applied to anyone in the world. Today we find in the Arabian Peninsula that the Arabs who used to be impoverished herders of camels and sheep are competing in building the tallest tower blocks. Today the Burj Khalifa in Dubai is the world's tallest man-made structure at 828 metres.[413] A short time after it was completed, a rival family in Saudi Arabia announced that they would build a taller one (1,000 metres), the Kingdom Tower—currently estimated to be completed in 2019. Thus, they are literally competing with each other over who can build the tallest building.[414]

Now, what is remarkable is that until only 50 or 60 years ago, the people of the region hardly had any houses at all. In fact, most of them were still Bedouins, living in tents. The discovery of oil in the 20th century led to the transformation of the region. If not for oil, chances are the region would still be the barren desert that it was at the time of the revelation of the Qur'an. If this were mere guesswork on his part, the discovery of oil would represent a massive stroke of luck. Moreover, if Prophet Muhammad ﷺ were merely guessing, wouldn't it have made more sense to relate this prophecy to the superpowers of his time—Rome and Persia—who (unlike the Arabs) already had a tendency to construct extravagant buildings and palaces?[415]

Tunnels in Mecca and tall buildings surpassing its mountains

The Prophet Muhammad ﷺ prophesised tunnels in Mecca and that the buildings of the city would surpass the tops of the mountains: "When you see tunnels built in Mecca and you see its buildings taller than its mountains, know that the matter is close at hand."[416]

Today in 2016, anyone who visits the city—and you can find pictures online—can see these tunnels and the buildings that surpass some of the mountains of Mecca. Here are some pictures below:

Dishes will be constantly communicating

The Prophet Muhammad ﷺ foretold the use of satellite dishes and the impact they would have on family relations: "The dishes will communicate continuously and people will sever their family ties."[417]

This can refer to the satellite technology that is now widespread in households. The use of such technology has kept people 'in doors' watching television, and has created a society that is increasingly individualistic and less family-centric. In other words, people do not visit family as much as they used to. This observation is not anecdotal and has been supported by research.[418]

The Prophet Muhammad's ﷺ teachings, character and unprecedented global impact are also strong evidence to show that he was not deluded and therefore must have been speaking the truth. These will be elaborated on later in this chapter.

Was he both lying and deluded?

It is not possible for an individual to be both deluded and a liar. Lying is done with intent, whereas a delusion is when a person believes in something that is

248 | *The Divine Reality*

actually not true. The two are diametrically opposed phenomena. The assertion that the Prophet Muhammad ﷺ was both lying and deluded is logically impossible, as the Prophet ﷺ could not have been intentionally untruthful about his claims and at the same time believe them to be true.

He was speaking the truth

Considering what has been discussed so far, the most reasonable conclusion is that the Prophet Muhammad ﷺ was speaking the truth. This conclusion is echoed by the historian Dr. William Draper: "Four years after the death of Justinian, A.D. 569, was born in Mecca, in Arabia, the man who, of all men, has exercised the greatest influence upon the human race... To be the religious head of many empires, to guide the daily life of one-third of the human race, may perhaps justify the title of a messenger of God."[419]

Objections

Before we discuss the profound teachings, sublime character and the unprecedented impact of the Prophet Muhammad ﷺ, there are some objections that need to be addressed.

Legend

An objection to the argument that has been presented includes that there can be another option to explain the Prophet Muhammad's ﷺ claim to prophethood. This additional option is that the Prophet's ﷺ claim is based on a legend. In other words, it is has no ground in established history. This objection maintains that the narratives and testimonies that underpin the life of the Prophet Muhammad ﷺ cannot be trusted or independently verified. In essence, the proponent of this contention does not trust Islamic history.

The 'legend' objection is incoherent and exposes a lack of knowledge concerning how scholars ensured the historical integrity of the sources of the life of the Prophet ﷺ. The Islamic approach to preserving history is based on two main elements: the *isnaad*, known as 'the chain of narration', and the *matn*, meaning 'the text or report'. There are robust criteria used to establish a sound chain of narration and a report. This is not the place to go into detail about this Islamic science (referred to as *'ilm ul-hadith* in the Islamic intellectual tradition; the knowledge of narrations); however, a brief summary of what it entails will be enough to demonstrate its robustness.

- In order for the chain of narration to be authentic, many rational criteria for each narrator would have to be fulfilled. Some of these include:

  o The name, nickname, title, parentage and occupation of the narrator should be known.
  o The original narrator should have stated that he heard the narration directly from the Prophet ﷺ.
  o If a narrator referred his narration to another narrator, the two should have lived in the same period and have had the possibility of meeting each other.
  o At the time of hearing and transmitting the narration, the narrator should have been physically and mentally capable of understanding and remembering it.
  o The narrator should have been known as a pious and virtuous person.
  o The narrator should not have been accused of having lied, given false evidence or committed a crime.
  o The narrator should not have spoken against other reliable people.

- In order for the text of the report to be accepted the number of rational criteria must be fulfilled. Some of these include:

  o The text should have been stated in plain and simple language as this was the undisputed manner of speech of the Prophet Muhammad ﷺ.
  o A text which referred to actions that should have been commonly known and practised by others but were not known and practised, was rejected.
  o A text contrary to the basic teachings of the Qur'an was rejected.

    o A text inconsistent with well-known historical facts was rejected.[420]

Unsound logic

Another objection to the argument is that its logical form is unsound. For example, it could be that the Prophet Muhamad ﷺ was not lying from the perspective of being immoral. He was falsely attributing to himself prophethood for a greater good. As a social reformer he believed that he had to make such a radical claim to transform the immoral and decadent society he was living in. This would not make him deluded, as he knew that he was not speaking the truth, and it would not make him a liar from the perspective of being immoral. He would be a moral reformer, and like most reformers he had to choose the lesser of the two evils for a greater good.

    This interesting objection is misplaced for a few reasons. Firstly, it is irrational to assert that a claim to prophethood would be required to make the necessary moral changes. In actual fact, the Prophet's ﷺ claim to receiving Divine revelation was the very thing that initially prevented him from gaining any ground in changing society. He was mocked, ridiculed and abused. A reformer would not make up such a claim, especially if that claim created more obstacles to reaching his objectives. Secondly, the Prophet ﷺ went through immense hardship, yet he did not compromise or sacrifice his message. He was offered conditional political power, which meant he could change the moral fabric of society, yet he rejected power because his acceptance would mean that he would have to abandon his noble call that there is no deity worthy of worship except God (*see Chapter 15*). If he had been a moral reformer he would have amended his strategy. However, he did not.

The teachings, character and impact of the Prophet ﷺ

The teachings of Muhammad ﷺ are not those of someone who is deluded or a liar. Amongst many of his teachings, he taught humanity about compassion, mercy, humility, peace, love and how to benefit and serve others. The Prophet's ﷺ character was one of perfection. He reached the summit of virtues; he was compassionate, humble, tolerant, just, and showed great humanity, forbearance and piety. His guidance also had an unprecedented impact on the world. The Prophet's ﷺ profound leadership and sublime teachings of tolerance, justice, progress, freedom of belief and many other areas of life strongly indicate that he was not deluded; rather, he was a man of truth.

<u>His teachings and character</u>

The Prophet Muhammad's ﷺ teachings and character are clear signs that he was a mercy to mankind and a noble human being given a Divinely inspired message to take people out of darkness, into the light of truth. Below are selections of his teachings and examples of his sublime character. I believe they speak for themselves. The more we study, reflect and ponder on the Prophetic wisdom, the more we will fall in love with and appreciate who Muhammad ﷺ really was:

His teachings

Mercy and compassion

"The Merciful One shows mercy to those who are themselves merciful [to others]. So show mercy to whatever is on Earth, then He who is in heaven will show mercy to you."[421]
"God is compassionate and loves compassion."[422]
"He is not of us who has no compassion for our little ones and does not honour our old ones."[423]
"May God have mercy on a man who is kind when he buys, when he sells, and when he makes a demand."[424]

Contentment and spirituality

"Richness is not having many possessions. Rather, true richness is the richness of the soul."[425]
"Indeed, God does not look towards your bodies nor towards your appearances. But, He looks towards your hearts and your deeds."[426]
"Do not talk too much without remembrance of God. Indeed, excessive talking without remembrance of God hardens the heart. And

indeed the furthest of people from God are the harsh-hearted."[427]

"Be mindful of God, you will find Him before you. Get to know God in prosperity and He will know you in adversity. Know that what has passed you by was not going to befall you; and that what has befallen you was not going to pass you by. And know that victory comes with patience, relief with affliction, and ease with hardship."[428]

"Islam has been built on five [pillars]: testifying that there is no deity worthy of worship except God and that Muhammad is the Messenger of God, establishing the prayer, paying the obligatory charity, making the pilgrimage to the House, and fasting in Ramadan."[429]

"God, the Exalted, has said: 'O son of Adam, I forgive you as long as you pray to Me and hope for My forgiveness, whatever sins you have committed. O son of Adam, I do not care if your sins reach the height of the heaven; then you ask for my forgiveness, I would forgive you. O son of Adam, if you come to Me with an Earth load of sins, and meet Me associating nothing with Me, I would match it with an Earth load of forgiveness.'"[430]

"God says: 'I am as My servant thinks I am [or: as he expects Me to be]. I am with him when he makes mention of Me. If he makes mention of Me to himself, I make mention of him to Myself. And if he makes mention of Me in an assembly, I make mention of him in an assembly better than it. And if he draws near to Me a hand's span, I draw near to him an arm's length. And if he draws near to Me an arm's length, I draw near to him a fathom's length. And if he comes to Me walking, I go to him at speed.'"[431]

Love

"By the one who has my soul in His hand, you will not enter the Garden until you believe, and you will not believe until you love one another. Shall I point out to you something, which will make you love one another if you do it? Make the greeting of peace be widespread among you."[432]

"The servant of God does not reach the reality of faith until he loves for the people what he loves for himself of goodness."[433]

"Love for the people what you love for yourself and you will be a believer. Behave well with your neighbours and you will be a Muslim."[434]

"There have come to you the diseases of the nations before you: envy and hatred, and hatred is the razor. It shaves the religion and it does not shave hair. By the one in whose hand is the soul of Muhammad, you will not believe until you love one another. Shall I tell you something which, if you did it, you would love each other? Spread peace between yourselves."[435]

"None of you has faith until he loves for the people what he loves for himself."[436]

"When a man loves his brother he should tell him that he loves him."[437]

"Love for humanity what you love for yourself."[438]

"The best deed after belief in God is benevolent love towards people."[439]

Community and peace

The Prophet Muhammad ﷺ was asked: "What sort of deeds or traits of Islam are good?" The Messenger of God replied: "To feed others, and to greet those whom you know and those whom you do not know."[440]

"He who makes peace between the people by inventing good information or saying good things is not a liar."[441]

"He who does not thank people, does not thank God."[442]

"By God, he does not [truly] believe! By God, he does not [truly] believe! By God, he does not [truly] believe" Someone asked: "Who, O Messenger of God?" He said: "He whose neighbour is not safe from his mischief."[443]

"All mankind is from Adam and Eve, an Arab has no superiority over a non-Arab nor a non-Arab has any superiority over an Arab; also a white has no superiority over a black nor a black has any superiority over a white, except by piety and good action."[444]

"The believer is not he who eats his fill while his neighbour is hungry."[445]

Charity and humanitarianism

"God said: 'Spend [i.e. on charity], O son of Adam, and I shall spend on you.'"[446]

"Charity does not diminish wealth."[447]

"Visit the sick, feed the hungry and free the captives."[448]

"Make things easy, and do not make them difficult, and give good tidings and do not make people run away."[449]

"Give the labourer his wages before his sweat dries."[450]

"Every act of goodness is charity."[451]

Character and manners

"The believers who show the most perfect faith are those who have the best character, and the best of you are those who are best to their wives."[452]

"[God] has revealed to me that you should adopt humility so that no one oppresses another."[453]

"Neither nurse grudge nor sever [the ties of kinship], nor nurse enmity, and become as fellow brothers and servants of God."[454]

"He who truly believes in God and the last Day should speak good or keep silent."[455]

"The best among you is he who has the best manners."[456]

"Beware of suspicion, for suspicion is the worst of false tales."[457]

"The strong man is not the one who is strong in wrestling, but the one who controls himself in anger."[458]

Environment and animals

"If the Hour [the day of Resurrection] is about to be established and one of you is holding a palm shoot, let him take advantage of even one second before the Hour is established to plant it."[459]

"If a Muslim plants a tree or sows seeds, and then a bird, or a person or an animal eats from it, it is regarded as a charitable gift (*sadaqah*) for him."[460]

"Removing harmful things from the road is an act of charity."[461]

The companions asked the Prophet Muhammad 🌸, "O God's Messenger! Is there a reward for us in serving the animals?" He replied: "There is a reward for serving any living being."[462]

"Whoever kills a sparrow or anything bigger than that without a just cause, God will hold him accountable on the Day of Judgment."[463]

"A prostitute saw a dog lolling around a well on a hot day and hanging his tongue from thirst. She drew some water for it in her shoe, so God forgave her."[464]

Abdullah ibn Amr ibn al-ʿAas reported that the Prophet ﷺ passed one day by Saʿd ibn Abi Waqqas while he was performing *wudoo'* (ritual ablution). The Prophet ﷺ asked Saʿd, "Why this wastage?" Saʿd replied "Is there wastage in ritual ablution also?" The Prophet ﷺ said, "Yes, even if you are at a flowing river."[465]

His character

The following testimonies and narrations describe some of the qualities of the character of the Prophet Muhammad ﷺ:

Forbearance, forgiveness and compassion

When the Prophet ﷺ had his tooth broken and his face cut during one of the battles when he was defending the Muslims and non-Muslims under his protection, his companions asked him to curse the aggressors. However, he replied: "I was not sent to curse, but I was sent as a summoner and as a mercy. O God, guide my people for they do not know."[466]

Anas ibn Malik said, "I served the Messenger of God ﷺ for ten years and he never said 'Uff!' to me. He did not say about anything I had done, 'Why did you do it?' nor about anything I had not done, 'Why did you not do it?'"[467]

Anas said, "I was with the Prophet ﷺ when he was wearing a thick cloak. A bedouin pulled him so violently by his cloak that the edge of the cloak made a mark on the side of his neck. Then he said, 'Muhammad! Let me load up these two camels of mine with the property of God you have in your possession! You will not let me load up from your property or your father's property.' The Prophet ﷺ was silent and then he said, 'Shall I take retaliation from you, bedouin, for what you have done to me?' He replied, 'No.' The Prophet ﷺ asked, 'Why not?' The bedouin replied, 'Because you do not repay back a bad action with a bad action.' The Prophet ﷺ laughed and ordered that one camel be loaded up with barley and the other camel with dates.'"[468]

Once a man demanding repayment for a debt seized hold of the Prophet Muhammad ﷺ and behaved very badly. The Prophet's ﷺ

companion was present and chased him off and spoke harshly to him. However, the Prophet ﷺ said, "He and I needed something else from you. Command me to repay well and command him to ask for his debt well." The Prophet ﷺ repaid the loan and added more to it because his companion had alarmed him. The man, known as Zayd ibn Sa'na, later became a Muslim. Zayd explains: "There were only two remaining signs of Prophethood which I had not yet recognised in Muhammad or noticed: forbearance overcoming quick-temperedness and extreme ignorance only increasing him in forbearance. I tested him for these and I found him as described."[469]

Anas ibn Malik recalls the compassion of the Prophet Muhammad ﷺ towards children: "I never saw anyone who was more compassionate towards children than God's Messenger ﷺ." [470]

The Prophet's ﷺ companions were killed and tortured; he himself was boycotted, starved and abused. There were many injustices and wrongs committed against the Prophet ﷺ and his followers. However, when he peacefully took Mecca, known as the conquest of Mecca, he delivered a universal forgiveness and pardon. He described the day as a day of "piety, faithfulness and loyalty."[471]

Appearance and approachability

The Prophet Muhammad's ﷺ companions narrate about his appearance:

Abdullah ibn al-Harith said, "I did not see anyone who smiled more than the Messenger of God."[472]

Al-Baraa' ibn 'Aazib narrated, "The Messenger of God ﷺ was the most handsome of all people, and had the best appearance."[473]

Jaabir ibn Samurah narrated, "I saw the Messenger of God ﷺ on a brightly moonlit night wearing a red garment. Then I started looking at him and at the moon. And for me, he was more beautiful than the moon."[474]

Ali ibn Abi Talib narrated, "Those who saw him suddenly stood in awe of him and those who shared his acquaintanceship loved him. Those who described him said they had never seen anyone like him before or since."[475]

Umm Ma'bad al-Khuza'iyah described to her husband what the

Prophet ﷺ looked like: "He was innocently bright and had broad countenance. His manners were fine. Neither his belly bulged out nor was his head deprived of hair. He had black attractive eyes finely arched by continuous eyebrows. His hair glossy and black, inclined to curl, he wore long. He was extremely commanding. His head was large, well-formed and set on a slender neck. His expression was pensive and contemplative, serene and sublime. The stranger was fascinated from the distance, but no sooner he became intimate with him than this fascination was changed into attachment and respect. His expression was very sweet and distinct. His speech was well set and free from the use of superfluous words, as if it were a rosary of beads. His stature was neither too high nor too small to look repulsive... He was always surrounded by his Companions. Whenever he uttered something, the listeners would hear him with rapt attention and whenever he issued any command, they vied with each other in carrying it out. He was a master and commander. His utterances were marked by truth and sincerity, free from all kinds of falsehoods and lies."[476]

Humility and modesty

The Prophet Muhamad ﷺ said, "Do not exaggerate in praising me as the Christians praised the son of Mary, for I am only a servant. So, call me the servant of God and His Apostle."[477]

The Prophet's ﷺ wife, Aishah (may God be pleased with her) was asked, "What did God's messenger do at home?" She said, "He was like any other human being, cleaning and mending his garment, milking the goat, mending his shoes, serving himself, and be of service to his family, till he hears the call to prayer, then he goes out [to pray in the mosque]."[478]

The Prophet ﷺ showed humility when he said, "I am but a man like yourselves. I am prone to forget just as you are."[479]

When the Prophet ﷺ saw a man trembling with fear when he saw him, he said to him, "Relax, I am not a king; I am the son of a woman from *Quraysh* [an Arab people] who would eat dried/jerked meat."[480]

The Prophet ﷺ would invoke his Lord saying, "O God, make me live humbly and make me die humbly, and gather me among the humble on the day of resurrection."[481]

Abu Sa'eed al-Khudri said, "I saw the messenger of God ﷺ prostrating in mud and water so that I saw the marks of mud on his forehead."[482]

Anas said, "The Prophet ﷺ would be invited to eat barley bread and rancid fat and he would accept it."[483]

Aisha (may God be pleased with her) said, "At our home [that is, the home of the Prophet's household], fire would not be kindled (sometimes) for a whole month; we subsisted merely on water and dates."[484]

Muhammad's ﷺ impact on the world

The Prophet Muhammad ﷺ was truly a mercy to mankind. This assertion is not only justified by his message and his teachings, but it also includes his unprecedented impact on our world. There are two key reasons why his teachings on a social level were so transformative: the justice and compassion of Islam.

Compassion and justice are its central values, expressed through a sincere belief in the existence and worship of one God. By singling Him out for worship and being conscious of one's accountability, a Muslim is encouraged to act compassionately, fairly and justly. The Qur'an clearly states in this regard:

"O you who believe, be steadfast in your devotion to God and bear witness impartially: do not let the hatred of others lead you away from justice, but adhere to justice, for that is closer to being God-conscious. Be mindful of God: God is well acquainted with all that you do."[485]

"O you who believe, uphold justice and bear witness to God, even if it is against yourselves, your parents, or your close relatives. Whether the person is rich or poor, God can best take care of both. Refrain from following your own desire, so that you can act justly— if you distort or neglect justice, God is fully aware of what you do."[486]

"What will explain to you what the steep path is? It is to free a slave, to feed at a time of hunger an orphaned relative or a poor person in distress, and to be one of those who believe and urge one another to steadfastness and compassion."[487]

Tolerance and coexistence

When these values were practised and internalised, the Muslims created a society that was unmatched in history. At a time when Europe was entrenched in sectarian violence, racism, tribalism and hatred, the teachings of the Prophet Muhammad 🕮 were a light for the world. Consider the treatment of minorities such as the Jews and the Christians. The Prophet Muhammad 🕮 in the treaty of Medina said: "It is incumbent on all the Muslims to help and extend sympathetic treatment to the Jews who have entered into an agreement with us. Neither an oppression of any type should be perpetrated on them nor their enemy be helped against them."[488]

The popular historian Karen Armstrong points out how the values of the Prophet Muhammad 🕮 established an unprecedented coexistence: "The Muslims had established a system that enabled Jews, Christians, and Muslims to live in Jerusalem together for the first time."[489]

The Jewish academic historian Amnon Cohen illustrates the practical application of Islamic values, and how the Jews of Ottoman Jerusalem were free and contributed to society:

"No one interfered with their internal organisation or their external cultural and economic activities... The Jews of Ottoman Jerusalem enjoyed religious and administrative autonomy within an Islamic state, and as a constructive, dynamic element of the local economy and society they could—and actually did—contribute to its functioning."[490]

'Umar ibn al-Khattab, the companion and student of the Prophet Muhammad 🕮, granted the Christians of Palestine religious freedom, security and peace. His treaty with the Palestinian Christians stated:

"This is the protection which the servant of God, the Leader of the faithful, grants to the people of Palestine. Thus, protection is for their lives, property, church, cross, for the healthy and sick and for all their co-religionists. In this way their churches shall not be turned into dwelling houses, nor will they be pulled down, nor any injury will be done to them or to their enclosures, nor to their cross, and nor will anything be deducted from their wealth. No restrictions shall be made regarding their religious ceremonies."[491]

In 869 CE, patriarch Theodosius of Jerusalem confirmed the Muslims' adherence to the values of their beloved Prophet ﷺ: "The Saracens [i.e. the Muslims] show us great goodwill. They allow us to build our churches and to observe our own customs without hindrance."[492]

These historical narratives are not historical accidents. They are grounded in the Prophet's ﷺ timeless values of tolerance and mercy.

Safety and protection

Europe in the 7ᵗʰ century was in utter darkness when it came to ensuring the safety and protection of minorities and foreign people living in or visiting a particular land. However, the Prophet Muhammad's ﷺ teachings ensured that minorities were protected and lived in peace:

"He who harms a person under covenant, or charges him more than he can pay, I will argue against him on the Day of Judgement."[493]

"He who hurts a non-Muslim under protection hurts me."[494]

The 13ᵗʰ century jurist Al-Qarafi explains the above Prophetic teachings:

"The covenant of protection imposes upon us certain obligations toward the non-Muslims under Muslim protection. They are our neighbours, under our shelter and protection upon the guarantee of God, His Messenger, and the religion of Islam. Whoever violates these obligations against any one of them by so much as an abusive word, by slandering his reputation, or by doing him some injury or assisting in it, has breached the guarantee of God, His Messenger ﷺ, and the religion of Islam."[495]

In light of the above, it is no wonder the Qur'an describes the Prophet ﷺ as "a mercy for the worlds"[496] and that God's mercy "encompasses all things"[497].

When the Prophet's ﷺ teachings were realised in history, minorities were protected, experienced peace and praised the Muslim authorities. For example, Bernard the Wise, a pilgrim monk, visited Egypt and Palestine in the reign of Al-Mu'tazz (866-9 CE), and he had the following to say:

> "...the Christians and the Pagans [i.e. Muslims] have this kind of peace between them there that if I was going on a journey, and on the way the camel or donkey which bore my poor luggage were to die, and I was to abandon all my goods without any guardian, and go to the city for another pack animal, when I came back I would find all my property uninjured: such is the peace there."[498]

The unprecedented impact and effect of Islamic values made people prefer the mercy and tolerance of Islam. Reinhart Dozy, an authority on early Islamic Spain, explains:

> "...the unbounded tolerance of the Arabs must also be taken into account. In religious matters they put pressure on no man... Christians preferred their rule to that of the Franks."[499]

Professor Thomas Arnold, commenting on an Islamic source, states that Christians were happy and at peace with Islam to the point where they "called down blessings on the heads of the Muslims."[500]

Freedom of belief

During a time when freedom of belief was a relatively alien concept, the Prophet Muhammad ﷺ created a society that never forced anyone to convert to Islam. Forced conversion is utterly forbidden in Islam. This is due to the following Qur'anic verse: "There is no compulsion in religion: true guidance has become distinct from error...."[501]

Michael Bonner, an authority on the history of early Islam, explains the historical manifestation of the verse above: "To begin with, there was no forced conversion, no choice between 'Islam and the Sword'. Islamic law, following a clear Qur'anic principle (2:256), prohibited any such things: *dhimmis* [non-Muslims under Muslim protection] must be allowed to practice their religion."[502]

Economic liberation

The teachings of the Prophet Muhammad ﷺ caused the economic liberation of people under his leadership. Taxes were low and anyone who could not afford to pay their taxes would not have to pay anything.[503]

It was incumbent on the authorities to ensure that everyone, including non-Muslim citizens, had enough to feed their families and maintain a decent standard of living. For example, 'Umar ibn 'Abd al-'Aziz, one of the Muslim leaders, wrote to his agent in Iraq: "Search for the people of the covenant in your area who may have grown old, and are unable to earn, and provide them with regular stipends from the treasury to take care of their needs."[504]

A practical manifestation of the Prophet's ﷺ teachings can be found in the following letter written by a rabbi in 1453. He was urging his co-religionists to travel to Muslim lands after Europe's persecution of the Jews, and that they were economically emancipated: "Here in the land of the Turks we have nothing to complain of. We possess great fortunes; much gold and silver are in our hands. We are not oppressed with heavy taxes and our commerce is free and unhindered. Rich are the fruits of the Earth. Everything is cheap and every one of us lives in peace and freedom...."[505]

Inter-racial co-operation

Far from being a source of racial conflict, the Prophet ﷺ offered a viable model of inter-racial co-operation. The Qur'an eloquently states: "People, we created you all from a single man and a single woman, and made you into races and tribes so that you should recognize one another. In God's eyes, the most honoured of you are the ones most mindful of Him: God is all knowing, all aware."[506]

The Prophet Muhammad ﷺ made it clear that racism has no place in Islam: "All mankind is from Adam and Eve, an Arab has no superiority over a non-Arab nor a non-Arab has any superiority over an Arab; also a white has no superiority over a black nor has a black any superiority over a white, except by piety and good action."[507]

As Hamilton A. R. Gibb, a historian on Orientalism, stated:

"But Islam has a still further service to render to the cause of humanity. It stands after all nearer to the real East than Europe does, and it possesses a magnificent tradition of interracial understanding and co-operation. No other society has such a record of success uniting in an equality of status, of opportunity, and of endeavour so many and so various races of mankind... Islam has still the power to reconcile apparently irreconcilable elements of race and tradition. If ever the opposition of the great societies of East and West is to be replaced by co-operation, the mediation of Islam is an indispensable condition. In its hands lies very largely the solution of the problem with which Europe is faced in its relation with East. If they unite, the hope of a peaceful issue is immeasurably enhanced—but if Europe, by rejecting the co-operation of Islam, throws it into the arms of its rivals, the issue can only be disastrous for both."[508]

The respected historian A. J. Toynbee also confirms: "The extinction of race consciousness as between Muslims is one of the outstanding achievements of Islam and in the contemporary world there is, as it happens, a crying need for the propagation of this Islamic virtue...."[509]

Scientific progress

The Prophet Muhammad ﷺ was the bearer of the message of the Qur'an, both in word and deed. His message and teachings created the much-needed tranquillity, tolerance and peace that facilitated one of the most successful civilisations in history. While Europe was plunged in the darkness of ignorance, the Islamic civilisation inspired by the Prophet ﷺ produced a society that was a beacon of light for the entire world. Historian of science Victor Robinson succinctly summarises the contrast between medieval Europe and Islamic Spain:

"Europe was darkened at sunset, Cordova shone with public lamps; Europe was dirty, Cordova built a thousand baths; Europe was covered with vermin, Cordova changed its undergarments daily; Europe lay in mud, Cordova's streets were paved; Europe's palaces had smoke-holes in the ceiling, Cordova's arabesques were exquisite; Europe's nobility could not sign its name, Cordova's children went to school; Europe's monks could not read the baptismal service, Cordova's teachers created a library of Alexandrian dimensions."[510]

Islamic civilisation produced advances in mathematics, medicine, astronomy and chemistry. Consider the mathematician Al-Khawarizmi, who played a significant role in the development of algebra. He also developed the idea of algorithms, which has earned him the title of the grandfather of computer science, because without algorithms there would be no computers. Abu al-Qasim Az-Zahrawi has been described as the greatest medieval surgeon because of his inventions in surgical procedures and instruments.

Muslims and Arab scientists who understood and internalised Islamic values were also pioneers in dealing with mental and psychological disorders. For example, in the 8th century, the physician Razi built the first psychiatric ward in Baghdad. The 11th century physician Ibn Sina (known in the West as Avicenna—the founder of modern medicine) understood that most mental illness is physiologically based.[511]

Interestingly, Abu Zayd al-Balkhi, a 9th century physician, wrote a book on what is now known as cognitive behavioural therapy. His book, *Sustenance of the Soul,* was probably the first written account to distinguish between endogenous and reactive depression.[512]

These pioneers and Muslim intellectuals were directly influenced by the values of Islam. These include the words of the Prophet Muhammad ﷺ that encourage seeking the cure for illnesses: "There is no disease that God has sent down except that He also has sent down its treatment."[513]

The Qur'an encourages reading, acquiring knowledge, reflection, and the empirical sciences. It is a book that mentions knowledge over 100 times and makes us reflect upon ourselves, and the world around us:

"The example of this worldly life is but like rain which We have sent down from the sky that the plants of the Earth absorb—those from which men and livestock eat—until, when the Earth has taken on its adornment and is beautified and its people suppose that they have capability over it, there comes to it Our command by night or by day, and We make it as a harvest, as if it had not flourished yesterday. Thus do We explain in detail the signs for a people who give thought."514

"Read! In the name of your Lord who created: He created man from a clinging form. Read! Your Lord is the Most Bountiful One who taught by [means of] the pen, who taught man what he did not know."515

"Say, 'How can those who know be equal to those who do not know?' Only those who have understanding will take heed."516

"Then do they not look at the camels—how they are created? And at the sky—how it is raised? And at the mountains—how they are erected? And at the Earth—how it is spread out?"517

"There truly are signs in the creation of the heavens and Earth, and in the alternation of night and day, for those with understanding, who remember God standing, sitting and lying down, who reflect on the creation of the heavens and Earth...."518

The teachings of the Prophet Muhammad ﷺ not only created an environment conducive to scientific progress, but also helped shaped the intellectual growth of a very important man in the history of science. His name was Ibn al-Haytham, and he is considered one of the world's first scientists.519 According to many historians of science, such as David C. Lindberg, Ibn al-Haytham is considered to be amongst the first to have formalised the scientific method with emphasis on systematic experimentation.520

Ibn al-Haytham wrote *The Book of Optics*, which had a huge impact on Europe. Without his formalisation of the scientific method, it could be argued that we would not be enjoying the scientific advancements that we enjoy today.

Ibn al-Haytham was also a student of theology and the Qur'an. He clearly cites the Qur'an as his inspiration to study science and the natural world: "I decided to discover what it is that brings us closer to God, what pleases Him most, and what makes us submissive to His ineluctable Will."521

Many academics recognise Europe's indebtedness to Islam.[522] Professor George Saliba argues, "There is hardly a book on Islamic civilization, or on the general history of science, that does not at least pretend to recognize the importance of the Islamic scientific tradition and the role this tradition played in the development of human civilisation in general."[523]

Professor Thomas Arnold was of the view that Islamic Spain facilitated the European Renaissance: "...Muslim Spain had written one of the brightest pages in the history of Medieval Europe... bringing into birth a new poetry and a new culture, and it was from her that Christian scholars received what of Greek philosophy and science they had to stimulate their mental activity up to the time of the Renaissance."[524]

Perhaps one of the most poignant summaries of the greatness of the civilisation that the Prophet Muhammad ﷺ created is in a speech by the former CEO of Hewlett Packard, Carly Fiorina:

"There was once a civilization that was the greatest in the world. It was able to create a continental super-state that stretched from ocean to ocean, and from northern climes to tropics and deserts. Within its dominion lived hundreds of millions of people, of different creeds and ethnic origins. One of its languages became the universal language of much of the world, the bridge between the peoples of a hundred lands. Its armies were made up of people of many nationalities, and its military protection allowed a degree of peace and prosperity that had never been known.

"And this civilization was driven more than anything, by invention. Its architects designed buildings that defied gravity. Its mathematicians created the algebra and algorithms that would enable the building of computers, and the creation of encryption. Its doctors examined the human body, and found new cures for disease. Its astronomers looked into the heavens, named the stars, and paved the way for space travel and exploration. Its writers created thousands of stories. Stories of courage, romance and magic.

"When other nations were afraid of ideas, this civilization thrived on them, and kept them alive. When censors threatened to wipe out knowledge from past civilizations, this civilization kept the knowledge alive, and passed it on to others. While modern Western civilization shares many of these traits, the civilization I'm talking about was the Islamic world from the year 800 to 1600, which included the Ottoman Empire and the courts of Baghdad, Damascus and Cairo, and enlightened rulers like Suleiman the Magnificent.

"Although we are often unaware of our indebtedness to this other civilization, its gifts are very much a part of our heritage. The technology industry would not exist without the contributions of Arab mathematicians. Leaders like Suleiman contributed to our notions of tolerance and civic leadership. And perhaps we can learn a lesson from his example: It was leadership based on meritocracy, not inheritance. It was leadership that harnessed the full capabilities of a very diverse population that included Christianity, Islamic, and Jewish traditions. This kind of enlightened leadership—leadership that nurtured culture, sustainability, diversity and courage—led to 800 years of invention and prosperity."[525]

The key reason the Prophet Muhammad ﷺ was able to directly influence such tolerant and compassionate societies was because affirming the Oneness of God, pleasing and worshipping Him, was the spiritual and moral basis of his life and the lives of those who loved and followed him. This provided timeless, objective moral grounding to achieve what the 18th century economist Adam Smith claimed was the first nation: "...under which the world enjoyed that degree of tranquillity which the cultivation of the sciences requires...."[526]

The Prophet Muhammad's ﷺ trustworthiness, high moral character and the impact he has had on the world establishes a strong case for his being the final messenger of God. Studying his life and understanding his teachings in a holistic and nuanced way will lead to only one conclusion: he was a mercy to the world and the one chosen by God to lead the world into Divine guidance and light.

Chapter 15
The Free Slave
Why God is Worthy of Our Worship

"The one who is imprisoned is the one whose heart is imprisoned from God and the captive is the one whose desires have enslaved him."[527]

Imagine a friend of yours gave you £100 pounds each day because, without any fault of your own, you required financial assistance. This kindness did not last for a few days; it continued for years. The money kept on appearing in your bank account. However, you started to forget who the benefactor was, and in this state of immense ingratitude, you then began to thank the money and not the one who gave it to you. This describes polytheism and atheism in a nutshell. From a spiritual perspective, it is the height of ingratitude and irrationality. The emotionally intelligent and rational person would always thank the one who gave him something that he did not earn or own. This is a non-negotiable moral principle.

Why, however, does this describe polytheism and atheism?

There is something in your life that you receive freely, yet you do not earn it and do not own it. There is no good reason to believe that you deserve it either. This thing is this moment, and the next moment, and all of the moments of your existence. You do not earn these moments, so what can you possibly do to earn another instant in your life? This is exactly why in popular culture we call it a gift: the gift of life. That's why we all consider it to be so precious. You do not own these moments because you do not have the capacity to bring anything into existence; you cannot even create a fly. You do not deserve another moment of your existence because it is not yours; you do not have the ability to produce life, even for a second. Therefore, nothing that you do can be deserving of something that you can never acquire by yourself. In light of these basic truths, you must always be in a state of gratitude, because you always receive something that you neither earn, nor own, nor deserve.

Since polytheism and atheism either have no one to thank or thank the wrong being (usually a created dependent and finite entity), it follows that their worldviews are not only irrational but the height of ingratitude. As discussed in Chapter 6, God is independent and everything depends upon Him. Therefore, everything that we say, do, use and acquire is fundamentally dependent on God alone. It inevitably follows—if one is sane and moral—that we must be thankful to God, and acknowledge that all gratitude belongs to Him alone. Thankfulness and gratitude are a key aspect of worship. However, the concept of worship in the Islamic tradition is not restricted to gratitude, it is quite comprehensive. Worship entails that we must love, know, and obey God, as well as dedicate all acts of worship to Him alone. Acts of worship in Islam include prayer, repentance, supplication, and purifying our hearts from their spiritual diseases and praise. These aspects of worship are not only rational; they are also repeatedly mentioned in the Qur'an.

I started this chapter by discussing gratitude because gratitude is a key to worship. If you are not grateful, you completely deny the fact that you are dependent on God alone, and you deny that He is the One who provides you with everything, no matter how small. So apart from being grateful to the One who gives us life, why is God worthy of and entitled to our worship?

Knowing God

Before I answer this question, it is important to elaborate on what is meant by knowing God. Knowledge of God is essential to understanding why God is worthy of our worship, because we cannot worship something we are ignorant of. This is why, in the Islamic tradition, traversing a path of knowing God is a form of worship:

"So know, that there is no deity except God."[528]

To know God means that we affirm that He is the sole creator and maintainer of everything that exists (known as *Oneness of God's Lordship*). It also entails that we affirm His names and attributes in the context of recognising that they are unique and that nothing can compare to God (known as *Oneness of God's Names and Attributes*). Knowledge of God also involves that we must know that He is unique in His Divinity; He alone is entitled to all acts of worship (known as *Oneness of God's Divinity*). It must be noted that in Islamic theology it is critical to affirm that nothing whatsoever shares in God's creative power and ability, names and attributes, and Divinity. All forms of anthropomorphism are completely rejected. God is transcendent and maximally perfect. He has no imperfections. The concept of oneness in the Islamic spiritual tradition is referred to as *tawheed*, which linguistically means to affirm oneness or to make something one or unique.

Oneness of Lordship

The oneness of God's Lordship is to affirm and recognise that God is the sole creator, master and owner of everything that exists. God is the One who sustains, takes care of, and nourishes everything. According to the Islamic doctrine of *tawheed*, anyone who denies this has associated partners with God, which is polytheism (known as *shirk* in Islamic theology). Anyone who believes that these descriptions of God can be shared by any created thing has deified that thing. Therefore, they have associated partners with God.

Oneness of God's names and attributes

The 'oneness of God's names and attributes' means to describe God only by the names and attributes that He has described Himself by, in the Qur'an and the Prophetic teachings (some names such *Al-Khaaliq*, The-Creator, and *Al-Qadeer*, The-Powerful, can be affirmed by a sound rational mind). These names and attributes, such as The-Loving and The-Subtle, are affirmed but they are not comparable to creation. God's names and attributes are perfect without any deficiency or flaw. God's names are described by God Himself as the most beautiful:

> "The most beautiful names belong to God: so call on Him by them."[529]

As has been mentioned throughout this book, God is maximally perfect. The one who compares these names and attributes to creation has committed humanisation, and therefore has associated partners with God. The one who compares any created thing to God has committed deification, which is also a form of associating partners with God.

Oneness of God's Divinity

The oneness of God's Divinity is that we must affirm that all acts of worship must be directed to Him alone. Someone who directs acts of worship to anything other than God, and the one who seeks reward from anything other than God in any act of worship, has associated partners with Him.

The gravest sin

Associating partners with God is the gravest sin. The consequence of this sin is that the one who dies in such a state and has not repented dies in a state of disbelief. This will never be forgiven by God:

"Indeed, God does not forgive association with Him, but He forgives what is less than that for whom He wills. And he who associates others with God has certainly committed a tremendous sin."[530]

However, if one associates partners with God and repents to Him and returns to the path of oneness, he or she will be forgiven, and their transgressions will be transformed into good deeds:

"And those who invoke not any other deity along with God... Except those who repent and believe, and do righteous deeds; for those, God will change their sins into good deeds, and God is Oft Forgiving, Most Merciful."[531]

The one who has associated partners with God and has never repented, and dies in that state (and has no excuse), has essentially oppressed themselves by closing the door to God's mercy. Their hearts have 'eternally' rejected God's guidance and mercy; therefore, they have alienated themselves from the Divine. Those who reject God will plead to go back to earth to do righteousness, but their hearts have 'eternally' rejected:

"[For such is the state of the disbelievers], until, when death comes to one of them, he says, 'My Lord, send me back that I might do righteousness in that which I left behind.' No! It is only a word he is saying."[532]

This self-imposed spiritual reality is a form of denial. The person has denied all the just and fair opportunities that God has given them to embrace His mercy and love:

"And God has not wronged them, but they wrong themselves."[533]

"This because of that which your hands had sent forward. And indeed, God is not unjust to His slaves."[534]

It must be noted that according to Islamic theology, if someone was not given the right message of Islam they will have an excuse and will be tested on the Day of Judgment.[535] God is The-Just and no one will be treated unjustly. This is why, when a non-Muslim has passed away, it is considered un-Islamic to pass judgement on their final abode. No one knows what is in someone else's heart and whether someone was given the right message in the right way. However, from a creedal and societal point of view, non-Muslims who died will be buried as non-Muslims. This does not mean that this is their final judgement. In reality, God is maximally and perfectly just and merciful, so no one will be treated unmercifully and no one will be treated unjustly.

People who have heard the message of Islam in a sound and correct way will have to account for their denial. However, whoever dies without having heard the message of Islam, or heard it in a distorted form, will be given an opportunity to accept the truth. Echoing the principles from the various verses of the Qur'an and the Prophetic traditions, Al-Ghazali summarises this nuanced approach. He argues that people who never heard the message of Islam will have an excuse: "In fact, I would say that, God willing, most of the Byzantine Christians and the Turks of this age will be included in God's mercy. I'm referring here to those who live in the farthest regions of Byzantium and Anatolia who have not come into contact with the message... They are excused."[536]

Al-Ghazali also argues that the people who heard negative things of the Prophet Muhammad and his message will also be excused: "These people knew the name 'Muhammad', but nothing of his character or his qualities. Instead, all they heard since childhood is that a liar and imposter called 'Muhammad' claimed to be a prophet... This party, in my opinion, is like the first party. For even though they've heard his name, they heard the opposite of what his true qualities were. And this does not provide enough incentive for them to investigate [his true status]."[537]

The true teachings of Islam are a barrier to extremism. In my view, all forms of extremism are based on an 'ideological hardness' that hardens people's hearts. What I mean by this is that people adopt non-negotiable, binary and negative assumptions about the world and other people. This makes one group of people 'otherize' another. Otherization is not simply labelling people as belonging to other groups. This is natural and part of modern society. Otherization usually happens when one group describes another group in a negative way and maintains that each member is the same. This hardens people's hearts and prevents them from positively engaging with other people who seem to be different. Islam does not otherize people. It does not assert that everyone who is not a Muslim is ultimately doomed or evil. The Qur'an makes it quite clear that people constituting other groups "are not all alike"[538] and describes some of them as "upright"[539]. The Qur'an also applies this concept to believers too; some are righteous and some are not. Nevertheless, Islam teaches that every human being must be treated with mercy, compassion and fairness (*see Chapter 14*).

The essence of worship

In the Islamic tradition, a key act of worship is supplication (known as *dua* in Islamic theology). The Prophet Muhammad ﷺ taught that supplication is "the essence of worship"[540]. Supplications are to God alone, because only He can help us when we ask for help for something that we need or want. Supplicating to anything other than God is an act of polytheism, because the person is asking for something from an entity that does not have the ability to provide or fulfil that request. For example, if someone were to ask a stone idol to grant them twin girls, it would be an act of polytheism because they are supplicating to an entity that has no power to fulfil that request. This does not mean, however, that asking someone who has the ability to assist you for help is polytheism. It would only be polytheism if one were to believe that God was not the ultimate creator of their ability to help you. Supplicating to God is part of making our worship pure, and the way we supplicate to Him should be with humility. God says: "Invoke your Lord with humility"[541] and "So invoke God making your worship pure for Him"[542].

According to the Islamic spiritual tradition, acts of worship are accepted if they fulfil two conditions. The first is that the act of worship should be done purely for the sake of God. The second is that the action itself is prescribed by the Islamic source texts: the Qur'an and the Prophetic traditions. So a natural question that follows from this is: *What are these acts of worship?* The acts of worship are many. As previously mentioned, any good action that is done to please God is an act of worship. However, there are some basic acts of worship which are essential to Islamic spiritual practice. These have been summarised by the Prophet Muhammad 🕮 as the five pillars of Islam. They include: affirming and recognising in one's heart that there is no deity worthy of worship except God and that Muhammad 🕮 is God's final messenger; praying five times a day; giving the obligatory charity if one can afford to; fasting in Ramadan (the 9th month of the Islamic calendar) and performing the pilgrimage if one is able to do so. These acts of worship have profound meanings and inner dimensions. These are the basic pillars of Islam. However, in developing one's spiritual practice one can engage in a plethora of additional spiritual activities. These include: reciting the Qur'an; remembrance of God; removing the spiritual diseases in one's heart; voluntary charity; conveying the message of Islam to others; feeding the poor; taking care of animals; studying the life of the Prophet Muhammad 🕮; memorising the Qur'an; the night prayer; reflecting on natural phenomena and much more.

So why do all our acts of worship have to be dedicated to God alone?
I will elaborate on the following points to answer this question:

- God's right to worship is a necessary fact of His existence.
- God has created and sustains everything.
- God provides us with innumerable favours.
- If we love ourselves, we must love God.
- God is The-Loving, and His love is the purest form of love.
- Worship is part of who we are.
- Obeying God is part of worshipping Him.

God's right to worship is a necessary fact of His existence
The best place to start is to understand who God is. God, by definition, is the One who is entitled to our worship; it is a necessary fact of His own existence. The Qur'an repeatedly highlights this fact about God,

> "Indeed, I am God. There is no deity except Me, so worship Me and establish prayer for My remembrance."[543]

Since God is the only Being whose right is our worship, then all of our acts of worship should be directed to Him alone.

In the Islamic tradition, God is considered a maximally perfect Being. He possesses all the perfect names and attributes to the highest degree possible. For example, in Islamic theology, God is described as the The-Loving, and this means that His love is the most perfect and greatest love possible. It is because of these names and attributes that God must be worshipped. We always praise people for their kindness, knowledge and wisdom. However, God's kindness, knowledge and wisdom are to the highest degree possible with no deficiency or flaw. Therefore, He is worthy of the most extensive form of praise, and praising God is a form of worship. God is also the only One entitled to our supplications and prayers. He knows best what is good for us, and He wants what is good for us. Such a Being with these attributes must be prayed to, and be asked assistance of. God is worthy of our worship because there is something about God that makes Him so. He is the Being with the most perfect names and attributes.

An important point regarding worshipping God is that it is His right, even if we are not recipients of any type of comfort. If we were to live a life full of suffering, God must still be worshipped. Worshipping God is not dependent on some kind of reciprocal relationship; He gives us life, and we worship Him in return. Do not misunderstand what I am saying here: God showers us with many blessings (as I will discuss below); however, He is worshipped because of who He is and not necessarily how He decides—via His boundless wisdom—to distribute His bounty.

God has created and also sustains everything

God has created everything; He continually sustains the entire cosmos and provides for us out of His bounty. The Qur'an continually repeats this concept in various ways, which evokes a sense of gratitude and awe in the heart of the listener or reader:

> "It is He who created for you all of that which is on the Earth."[544]

> "Do they indeed ascribe to Him as partners things that can create nothing but are themselves created?"[545]

> "O mankind, remember the favour of God upon you. Is there any creator other than God who provides for you from the heaven and Earth? There is no deity except Him, so how are you deluded?"[546]

Therefore, everything we use in our daily lives, and all of the essential things that we require to survive, are due to God. It follows then that His is all gratitude. Since God created everything that exists, He is the owner and master of everything, including us. Hence, we must be in a sense of awe and gratitude to Him. Since God is our Master, we must be His servants. To deny this is not only rejecting reality, but it is the height of ingratitude, arrogance and thanklessness, as discussed earlier in this chapter.

Since God created us, our very existence is solely dependent on Him. We are not self-sufficient, even if some of us are deluded in thinking that we are. Whether we live a life of luxury and ease or poverty and hardship, we are ultimately dependent on God. Nothing in this universe is possible without Him and whatever happens is due to His will. Our success in business and the great things that we may achieve are ultimately because of

God. He created the causes in the universe that we use to achieve success, and if He does not will our success it will never happen. Understanding our ultimate dependency on God should evoke an immense sense of gratitude and humility in our hearts. Humbling ourselves before God and thanking Him is a form of worship. One of the biggest barriers to Divine guidance and mercy is the delusion of self-sufficiency, which is ultimately based on ego and arrogance. The Qur'an makes this point clear:

"But man exceeds all bounds when he thinks he is self-sufficient."[547]

"There is the one who is miserly, and is self-satisfied, who denies goodness—We shall smooth his way towards hardship and his wealth will not help him as he falls. Our part is to provide guidance."[548]

God provides us with innumerable favours

"And if you should [try to] count the favours of God, you could not enumerate them. Indeed mankind is [generally] most unjust and ungrateful."[549]

We should be eternally grateful to God because we could never thank Him for His blessings. The heart is an appropriate example to illustrate this point. The human heart beats around 100,000 times a day, which is approximately 35,000,000 times a year. If we were to live up to the age of 75, the number of heartbeats would reach 2,625,000,000. How many of us have even counted that number of heartbeats? No one ever has. To be able to count that many times, you would have had to start counting each heartbeat from the day you were born. This would interfere with your ability to live a normal life, as you would always be counting every time your heart started a new beat. However, every heartbeat is precious to us. Anyone of us would sacrifice a mountain of gold to ensure that our hearts function properly to keep us alive. Yet we forget and deny the One who created our hearts and enables them to function. This illustration forces us to conclude that we must be grateful to God, and gratitude is a form of worship. The above discussion just refers to heartbeats, so imagine the gratitude we must express for all the other blessings God has given us. From this perspective anything other than a heartbeat is a bonus. God has given us favours we cannot enumerate, and if we could count them we would have to thank Him for these, too.

If we love ourselves, we must love God

Loving God is a fundamental aspect of worship. There are many types of love and one of these includes self-love. This occurs due to the desire to prolong our existence, feel pleasure and avoid pain, as well as the need to satisfy our human needs and motivations. We all have this natural love for ourselves because we want to be happy and content. The psychologist Erich Fromm argued that loving oneself is not a form of arrogance or egocentricity. Rather, self-love is about caring, taking responsibility and having respect for ourselves. This type of love is necessary in order to love others. If we cannot love ourselves, how then can we love other people? There is nothing closer to us than our own selves; if we cannot care for and respect ourselves, how then can we care for and respect others? Loving ourselves is a form of 'self-empathy'. We connect with our own feelings, thoughts and aspirations. If we cannot connect with our own selves, how then can we empathise and connect with others? Eric Fromm echoes this idea by saying that love "implies that respect for one's own integrity and uniqueness, love for an understanding of one's own self, cannot be separated from respect and love and understanding for another individual."[550]

If a person's love for himself is necessary, this should lead him to love the One who made him. Why? Because God created the physical causes and means for human beings to achieve happiness and pleasure, and avoid pain. God has freely given us every precious moment of our existence, yet we do not earn or own these moments. The great theologian Al-Ghazali aptly explains that if we love ourselves we must love God:

"Therefore, if man's love for himself be necessary, then his love for Him through whom, first his coming-to-be, and second, his continuance in his essential being with all his inward and outward traits, his substance and his accidents, occur must also be necessary. Whoever is so besotted by his fleshy appetites as to lack this love neglects his Lord and Creator. He possesses no authentic knowledge of Him; his gaze is limited to his cravings and to things of sense."[551]

God is The-Loving, and His love is the purest form of love

God is The-Loving. He has the purest form of love. This should make anyone want to love Him, and loving Him is a key part of worship. Imagine if I were to tell you that there was this person who was the most loving person ever, and that no other love could match his love; wouldn't that instil a strong desire to get to know this person, and eventually love him too? God's love is the purest and most intense form of love; therefore, any sane person would want to love him too.

Given that the English word for love encompasses a range of meanings, the best way to elaborate on the Islamic conception of God's love is to look into the actual Qur'anic terms used to describe Divine love: His mercy (*rahmah*) and His special love (*muwadda*). By understanding these terms and how they relate to the Divine nature, our hearts will learn to love God.

Mercy

It is said that another word for love is mercy. One of God's names is The-Merciful; the Arabic word used is *Ar-Rahmaan*. This English translation does not fully represent the depth and intensity that the meaning of this word carries. The name *Ar-Rahmaan* has three major connotations: the first is that God's mercy is an intense mercy; the second is that His mercy is an immediate mercy; and the third is a mercy so powerful that nothing can stop it. God's mercy encompasses all things and He prefers guidance for people. In God's book, the Qur'an, He says,

"...but My mercy encompasses all things...."[552]

"It is the Lord of Mercy who taught the Qur'an."[553]

In the above verse, God says He is The-Merciful, which can be understood as the "Lord of Mercy", and that He taught the Qur'an. This is a linguistic indication to highlight that the Qur'an was revealed as a manifestation of God's mercy. In other words, the Qur'an is like one big love-letter to humanity. As with true love, the one who loves wants good for the beloved, and warns them of pitfalls and obstacles, and shows them the way to happiness. The Qur'an is no different: it calls out to humanity, and it also warns and expresses glad tidings.

Special Love

According to the Qur'an, God is The-Loving. The Arabic name is *Al-Wadood*. This refers to a special love that is apparent. It comes from the word *wud*, which means expressing love through the act of giving: "And He is the Forgiving, The Loving."[554]

God's love transcends all of the different types of love. His love is greater than all worldly forms of love. For example, a mother's love, although selfless, is based on her internal need to love her child. It completes her, and through her sacrifices she feels whole and fulfilled. God is an independent Being who is self-sufficient and perfect; He does not require anything. God's love is not based on a need or want; it is therefore the purest form of love, because He gains absolutely nothing from loving us.

In this light, how can we not love the One who is more loving than anything we can imagine? The Prophet Muhammad ﷺ said, "God is more affectionate to His servants than a mother to her children."[555]

If God is the most loving, and His love is greater than the greatest worldly love we have experienced, this should instil in us a deeper love for God. Significantly, this should make us want to love Him by being one of His servants. Al-Ghazali aptly said, "For those endowed with insight there is in reality no object of love but God, nor does anyone but He deserve love."[556]

From a spiritual perspective, God's love is the greatest blessing anyone can ever achieve, as it is a source of internal tranquillity, serenity, and eternal bliss in the hereafter. Not loving God is not only a form of ingratitude, but the greatest form of hate. Not loving the One who is the source of love is a rejection of that which enables love to occur and fill our hearts.

God does not force His special love on us. Although, by His mercy, He lovingly gives us every moment of our lives, to fully embrace God's love and be recipients of His special love, one must enter into a relationship with Him. It is as if God's love is waiting for us to embrace it. However, we have closed the door and put up the shutters. We have kept the door shut by denying, ignoring and rejecting God. If God were to force His special love on us, love would lose all meaning. We have the choice: to follow the right path and thereby gain God's special love, or reject His guidance and face the spiritual consequences.

The most loving Being loves you, but in order for you to fully embrace that love, and for it to be meaningful, you have to choose to love Him and follow the path that leads to His love. This path is the Prophetic path of the Prophet Muhammad ﷺ (*see Chapter 14*):

"Say, [O Muhammad]: 'If you love God, then follow me, [so] God will love you and forgive your sins. And God is Forgiving and Merciful'."[557]

Worship is part of who we are

God is worthy of our worship because worship is part of who we are. Just like our need to eat, drink and breathe, worship is an innate tendency (*see Chapter 4*). From this perspective, we are natural-born worshippers, because that is who we are and it is our Divinely given purpose. Worshipping God is a logical necessity, just as when we say a car is red. It is red because we have defined that colour as red; it is red by definition. Likewise, we are worshippers by definition, because God defined and made us that way: "I did not create the *Jinn* [spirit world], nor mankind, except to worship Me."[558]

Even people who do not believe in God, including those who reject the fact that He is entitled to worship, manifest signs of adoration, reverence and devotion. If you do not worship God, you'll still end up worshipping something. From an Islamic perspective, the object that you love and revere the most, including whatever you attribute ultimate power to and believe you are ultimately dependent on, is essentially your object of worship. For many people, this can include an ideology, a leader, a family member, and even your own self. In other words, many people idolise these things. Polytheism or idolatry is not just about praying to or bowing down in front of an object.

God is rooted in our innermost nature, and when God commands us to worship Him it is actually a mercy and act of love. It is as if every human being has a hole in his or her heart. This hole is not physical, it is spiritual, and it needs to be filled to achieve spiritual tranquillity. We attempt to fill this hole with a new job, a holiday, a new house, a new car, a hobby, travel or taking up a popular self-help course. However, every time we fill our hearts with these things, a new hole appears. We are never truly satisfied, and after a while we seek something else to fill the spiritual void. Yet, once we fill our hearts with the love of God, the hole remains permanently closed. Thus, we feel at peace and experience a tranquillity that can never be put into words, and a serenity that is undisturbed by calamity.

Obeying God is part of worshipping Him

"[A]nd obey God and the Prophet[559] so that you may be given mercy."[560]

When I travel by plane, I usually hear the pilot announce—via the inflight audio system—to fasten our seat belts due to oncoming turbulence. My typical response involves sitting down, fastening my belt and hoping for the best. The reason I obey the pilot's command is that I understand he is the authority concerning the plane, how it works and the effects of turbulence. My obedience is a result of using my rational faculties. Only an arrogant person would disobey a valid authority. Would any of us take seriously a seven-year-old telling us that our maths professor does not know how to teach calculus?

In a similar light, disobeying God is foolish and unfounded. Obeying to God, even if we do not know the full wisdom behind some of His commands, is the most rational thing to do. God's commands are based on His boundless knowledge and wisdom. He is the ultimate authority. To deny this authority is like a two-year-old child scribbling on a piece of paper and claiming that he is more eloquent than Shakespeare. (Actually, it is worse.)

This does not mean that we suspend our minds when obeying God. We are told by God Himself to use our reason. However, once we have established what God has said, then that should result in obedience.

Obeying God entails that one should fear Him. A believer should fear God if he wants to be in a state of servitude and obedience. This fear, however, is not the type of fear that is associated with being scared of an enemy or an evil force. God wants good for us. Rather, this fear is associated with skin-shivering awe, loss, love and unhappiness. We fear God from the perspective of fearing losing His love and good pleasure.[561] To explain this point, consider the following illustration:

Imagine you are walking through a mall. You notice a young child being told off by her mother. The child starts to cry and holds on to her mother's leg. The child begs for her mother's forgiveness and asks for a hug. The mother smiles and tells her child that she was telling her off to protect her and ensure she stays safe. The child's fear is a fear of losing her mother's love and pleasure. The child does not want to lose her mother's love and make her unhappy. This is the type of fear we must have for God.

We should want to obey God because we fear the spiritual consequences of disobedience. These include losing God's special love; including breaking the connection we have built with Him through our acts of worship. Disobedience is our way of running away from God's mercy, and an absence of His mercy leads to a terrible abode of self-inflicted suffering; hell. Al-Ghazali summarises this type of fear by describing it as a fear of losing something that is loved: "Whoever loves something must fear to lose it. Hence love cannot be without fear, for the object of love is something that can be lost."[562]

The Qur'an mentions the fear of God, and this fear must be understood in the way I have just explained above. However, the Divine book also mentions God-consciousness, known as *taqwaa* in Islamic theology. A good translation of the Qur'an would distinguish the two terms. Their meanings are different, and they overlap. While fear of God entails fearing loss and the spiritual consequences of disobedience, God-consciousness refers to being mindful and aware of the Divine presence; He knows what we are doing and, as lovers of God, we should want to seek His good pleasure and love.

Does God need our worship?

This common question arises due to a misunderstanding of God in the Islamic tradition. The Qur'an and the Prophetic traditions clearly explain that God is transcendent and free of any need; in other words, He is absolutely independent (*see Chapter 6*).

Therefore, God does not need us to worship Him at all. He gains nothing from our worship, and our lack of it takes nothing away from God. We worship God because—through God's wisdom and mercy—He created us that way. God made worship good and beneficial for us, from both worldly and spiritual perspectives.

Why did He create us to worship Him?

What follows from this answer is usually the question: *Why did God create us to worship Him?* God is a maximally good Being, and therefore His actions are not only good, they are expressions of His nature. In addition, God loves good. The fact that God has created rational creatures who would freely choose to worship Him and do good—some to the point of becoming exalted in virtue like the prophets, and then being given eternal life in the presence of God—to pass an eternity of intimate love and companionship, is the greatest story ever told. Since God loves all good, it is clear why He would make this story a reality. In summary, God created us to worship Him because He wants good for us; in other words, He wants us to go to paradise. He has made it clear that those who attain paradise have been created to experience His mercy:[563] "If your Lord had pleased, He would have made all people a single community, but they continue to have their differences—except those on whom your Lord has mercy—for He created them to be this way." [564]

God creating us to worship Him was inevitable. His perfect names and attributes were going to manifest themselves. An artist inevitably produces art work because he has the attribute of being artistic. By greater reason, God would inevitably create us to worship Him because He is the One worthy of worship. This inevitability is not based on need but rather a necessary manifestation of God's names and attributes.

Another way of answering this question is to understand that our knowledge is fragmentary and finite, so we will never be able to fathom the totality of God's wisdom. As previously mentioned, if we comprehended all of God's wisdom, it would mean we would become Gods or that God would be like us. Both are impossibilities. Hence, the very fact that there may be no answer to this question indicates the transcendence of God's knowledge. In summary, He created us to worship Him due to His eternal wisdom; we just cannot comprehend why.

A practical way of looking at this question is explained in the following illustration. Imagine you were on the edge of a cliff and someone pushed you into the ocean below. This water is infested with sharks. However, the one who pushed you gave you a waterproof map and an oxygen tank to enable you to navigate to a beautiful tropical island, where you will stay forever in bliss. If you were intelligent, you would use the map and reach the safety of the island. However, being stuck on the question, *why did you throw me in here?* will probably cause you to be eaten by the sharks. For the Muslim, the Qur'an and Prophetic traditions are the map and the oxygen tank. They are our tools to navigate the path of life safely. We have to know, love and obey God, and dedicate all acts of worship to Him alone. Fundamentally, we have the choice of harming ourselves by ignoring this message, or embracing the love and mercy of God by accepting it.

The free slave

From an existential perspective, worshipping God is true liberation. If worship entails knowing, loving and obeying God, then in reality many of us also have other gods in our lives. Many of us know, love and obey our own egos and desires. We think we are always right, we never want to be wrong, and we always want to impose ourselves on others. From this perspective, we are enslaved to ourselves. The Qur'an points out such a debased spiritual state and describes the one who considers his desires, passions and whims as his god, to be worse than an animal: "Think of the man who has taken his own passion as a god: are you to be his guardian? Do you think that most of them hear or understand? They are just like cattle— no, they are further from the path."[565]

From self-worship, sometimes we move to worship various forms of social pressures, ideas, norms and cultures. They become our point of reference, we start to love them, want to know more about them, and are led to 'obey' them. Examples abound; take, for instance, materialism. We have become preoccupied with money and material belongings. Obviously, to want money and possessions is not necessarily a bad thing, but we have allowed our pursuit to define who we are. Our time and efforts are devoted to the accumulation of wealth, making the false notion of material success the primary focus in our lives. From this perspective, material things start to control us, and lead us to serve the culture of avid materialism rather than serving God. I appreciate that this does not apply to everyone, but this form of excessive materialism is very common.

Research by Jean M. Twenge and Tim Kasser concluded that materialism amongst youth has increased over generations—this study was based on data from 1976 to 2007—and it has remained very high. Social instability such as divorce, unemployment, racism, antisocial behaviour, decreased life-satisfaction and other social problems have some association with higher levels of materialism.[566] This is supported by research conducted by S. J. Opree and others, where they conclude that a high level of materialism during childhood years may decrease life-satisfaction in adulthood.[567] Obviously, research of this kind is not entirely conclusive, and much more research needs to be done, but it supports a collective intuition that such priorities are clearly not right. Our sense of who we are is based on our jobs, earnings, wealth and possessions. Our identities are slowly becoming contingent on material factors and not on—what many would consider—higher values such as our ethics, moral standards, humanitarianism, and connecting with God and other human beings.

Essentially, if we are not worshipping God, we are still worshipping something else. This can be our own egos and desires, or ephemeral things like material possessions. In the Islamic tradition, worshipping God defines who we are, as it is part of our nature. If we forget God, and start to worship things that are not worthy of worship, we will slowly forget our own selves: "And be not like those who forgot God, so He made them forget themselves."[568]

Our understanding of who we are is dependent on our relationship with God, which is shaped by our servitude and worship. In this sense, when we worship God we are freed from submission to other 'gods', whether ourselves or things that we own or desire.

As previously mentioned, the Qur'an presents us with a profound analogy: "God puts forward this illustration: can a man who has for his masters several partners at odds with each other be considered equal to a man devoted wholly to one master? All praise belongs to God, though most of them do not know."[569]

God is essentially telling us that if we do not worship God, we end up worshipping something else. These things enslave us and they become our masters. The Qur'anic analogy is teaching us that without God, we have many 'masters' and they all want something from us. They are all 'at odds with each other', and we end up in a state of misery, confusion and unhappiness. However, God, who knows everything, including our own selves, and who has more mercy than anyone else, is telling us that He is our master, and that only by worshipping Him alone will we truly free ourselves from the shackles of the things we have taken as replacements for Him.

To conclude this chapter, lovingly worshipping God and peacefully submitting to Him frees you from the degraded worship of the ephemeral world and the lustful submission to the carnal and egotistical realities of the human condition. The following lines of poetry by the Poet of the East, Muhammad Iqbal, eloquently summarises this point:

"This one prostration which you deem too exacting liberates you from a thousand prostrations."[570]

Chapter 16
Conclusion
Transforming Our Hearts

My father is a free man. What I mean by freedom is not that he lives in a country that gives him his liberties and human rights. Rather, he is emotionally free. When he decides to express himself, he does so without a care in the world. He expresses himself as if there are no external hindrances. I remember when I was in secondary school, I used to play for the school band. Since my father encouraged me to take up classical guitar lessons, attending the school band was a natural consequence of my extracurricular activity. During a school concert, my father would attend and enjoy the amazing talents and abilities of the students. One performance artist had phenomenal abilities. While she was on stage, she reached the climactic point of her performance, emotionally and passionately expressing herself. It was a breath-taking display of talent. My father stood up and gave her an ovation. He did this all alone, but he did not care. He remained standing and continued praising her flair and aptitude.

We have all experienced such a reaction to human ability. When we see amazing spectacles of skill by one of our sporting heroes, or when we observe great feats of courage, or when we listen to a motivational speech— we are compelled to praise what we have experienced. We stand. We clap. We give an ovation. We are moved, inspired, encouraged, elated and overwhelmed by what we have experienced. We never forget these moments in our lives. Just think and reflect on similar experiences. Sink back into the feelings you had. Something affected your soul; you had to give due praise.

However, we live in this amazing universe. We hope, love, seek justice and believe in the ultimate value of human life. We reason, infer, deduce, and discover. We live in a vast universe with billions of stars, galaxies and planets. The universe contains sentient beings that can have a unique stream of consciousness. We have an immaterial mind that interacts with the physical world. The universe has laws and a precise arrangement that, if different, would have prevented the emergence of conscious life. We feel— deep down inside—the wrongness of evil, and the rightness of good.

In our universe, there are animals that can withstand their own body weight many times over, and seeds that can germinate from the heat of fire. We live on a planet with over 6,000 languages and over eight million species. We live in a universe where the human mind can discover weapons that can wipe out the Earth, and produce ideas that can prevent those weapons from firing. We live in a universe that, if one of its innumerable atoms is split, can release an immense amount of energy. We live on a planet which, if hearts are united, can use that energy for peace.

Yet some of us are not compelled to give God—who created the universe and everything within it—a standing ovation; to stand, glorify and praise Him.[571] We are deluded, deceived and forgetful of God, the one who created us: "O mankind, what has deceived you concerning your Lord, the Generous?"[572]

God is truly great.

If we do not feel the urge to praise our creator and connect with Him, there is something wrong with our hearts. We have a spiritual disease that requires spiritual medicine. This disease is the ego; the medicine is Islam.

To take this medicine, and therefore be eligible for Divine mercy and God's special love, we have to believe, internalise, understand and submit to the implications of the following profound statement:

> *"There is no deity worthy of worship except God (Allah), and Muhammad is His final servant and messenger."*

It is my hope that this book has helped you to start the process of healing.

May God guide and shower you with His special love.

Afterword
Don't Hate, Debate
Dialogue with Islam

To use a colloquialism, the Internet is phat. There's a play on words here, because according to slang, 'phat' means 'excellent', and phonetically it can mean 'big or large'. They both apply to the Internet. It can be an excellent source of information, but it can also be too big to access all the authentic and valid information about a particular topic. Besides its positive value, it is also a large abyss of lies, misinformation and misrepresentations. The Internet can also be quite unforgiving. I personally have experienced the dark side of the Internet many times. All of my mistakes, misunderstandings and errors are there for everyone to laugh at, but what makes me content is that it also provides a source for people to learn. I'm a true believer in espousing contrasting views, because in this context the truth always prevails. This book is actually a product of learning from my failures and errors. Now, does that mean this book is perfect? Obviously not. However, it does lead me to a very important point. Whatever kind of reader you describe yourself to be (atheist, sceptic, agnostic, Muslim, secular, humanist, etc.) you will undoubtedly have more questions or would like further clarifications. This is why I have developed an online portal that will continue our conversation further. Any questions, comments, concerns or constructive feedback you have will be assessed at www.hamzatzortzis.com/thedivinereality.

This is quite unique for this type of publication because the book is not meant to be a monologue but a dialogue. The discussion does have ethical rules, which include no expletives (unless you're quoting someone to make a valid point), personal attacks or degrading speech. Aside from that, anything goes.

No one book covers everything on this topic, and some issues have been left out, mostly due to scope and priority. However, this does not mean that the Islamic tradition lacks answers.

I would advise interested parties to keep an open mind and to sincerely engage in a dialogue. You see, we have two spheres in our life: what can be called our drama, and the other is reality. We think our drama and reality are the same. This is simply not true. Our drama consists of our negative past experiences, limited intellects, ideas and perspectives. Reality is just what is, without any skewed perspective. However, we always skew reality because we superimpose our drama on it. This is why we find it hard to connect with other human beings, and this is precisely why our lives seem to be one giant circle, repeating the same mistakes in different ways. We all have done this before. We have had a couple of negative experiences in the past which destroy our ability to connect deeply with people in the present, thereby creating a future with the building blocks of the past; it is no wonder we repeat the same mistakes. We have to realise that the past does not equal the future. So whatever your experiences with religion, Islam and arguments for God and revelation, I ask you to not allow them to cloud your judgement when reflecting on what you have read in this book.

I would like to end this section by sharing some Qur'anic and prophetic advice on discussing, debating and dealing with others. God commands His noble Prophet Moses to speak mildly to Pharaoh while conveying the message of Islam to him: "And speak to him mildly; perhaps he might accept admonition."[573]

The exegete Al-Qurtubi explains that this verse implies that if Moses were commanded to speak softly and mildly to Pharaoh, who was an oppressor, then imagine how we must speak to others: "If Musa was commanded to speak mildly to Pharaoh then it is even more appropriate for others to follow this command when speaking to others and when commanding the good and forbidding the evil."[574]

God commands the Prophet Muhammad ﷺ to discuss using good words in the best possible manner: "Invite to the way of your Lord with wisdom and beautiful preaching, and argue with them in a way that is better."[575]

The grammarian Al-Zamakhshari comments on the above verse by asserting that this means we must engage with others without any harshness: "Arguing with them in a way that is better means using the best method of argumentation which is the method of kindness and gentleness without gruffness and harshness."[576]

Using good words in the context of discussion is one of the greatest virtues in the Islamic tradition. The Qur'an presents a beautiful example of comparing a good word with a tree with perpetual fruit and firm roots:

"Have you not considered how God presents an example, [making] a good word like a good tree, whose root is firmly fixed and its branches [high] in the sky? It produces its fruit all the time, by permission of its Lord. And God presents examples for the people that perhaps they will be reminded. And the example of a bad word is like a bad tree, uprooted from the surface of the Earth, not having any stability. God keeps firm those who believe, with the firm word, in the worldly life and in the Hereafter. And God sends astray the wrongdoers. And God does what He wills."[577]

It is my personal wish that by internalising some of these timeless values and teachings, we can all repel evil with good, and realise there is no need to hate, thereby facilitating close friendships even if we disagree.

"And not equal are the good deed and the bad. Repel evil by that deed which is better; and thereupon the one whom between you and him is enmity will become as though he were a devoted friend."[578]

Notes

[1] Narrated by Abu Dawud. I have referenced the Prophetic traditions by their compilers. For example, "Narrated by Bukhari" means that it is in the hadith book compiled by Bukhari. You can search for the various hadiths using online English and Arabic databases. Please note translations may vary.

[2] Al-Ghazali. (2015) The Remembrance of Death and the Afterlife. 2nd Edition. Translated with an Introduction and Notes by T. J. Winter. Cambridge: Islamic Texts Society, p. 8.

[3] You can watch some of these debates at www.hamzatzortzis.com [Accessed 3rd October 2016].

[4] Prophetic traditions are authentic and verified words, statements, actions and consent of the Prophet Muhammad ﷺ.

[5] Bullivant, S. (2015). Defining 'Atheism'. In: The Oxford Handbook of Atheism. Oxford: Oxford University Press, pp. 11-21.

[6] Schweizer, B. (2010). Hating God: The Untold Story of Misotheism. New York: Oxford University Press, p. 28.

[7] Ibid, p. 216.

[8] Ibid, pp. 217-218.

[9] Ibid, pp. 217-218.

[10] Dawkins, R. (2006) The God Delusion. London: Bantam Press, p. 14.

[11] Narrated by Muslim.

[12] The Qur'an, Chapter 52, Verse 36. Throughout this book I have used various Qur'anic translations. The translations I have used most frequently are the translation by Professor Abdel Haleem [See Abdel Haleem, M. A. S. (2005 & Reissue Edition, 2008) The Qur'an: A New Translation. New York: Oxford University Press] and the translation by Sahih International [available at: www.quran.com].

[13] "Who but a fool would forsake the religion of Abraham?" The Qur'an, Chapter 2, Verse 130.

[14] Crone, P. Atheism (pre-modern). In: Encyclopaedia of Islam, THREE, Edited by: Kate Fleet, Gudrun Krämer, Denis Matringe, John Nawas, Everett Rowson. Available at: http://dx.doi.org/10.1163/1573-3912_ei3_COM_23358 [Accessed 1st October 2016].

[15] Ibid.

[16] Al-Ghazali. (2007) Kimiya-e Saadat: The Alchemy of Happiness. Translated by Claude Field. Kuala Lumpur: Islamic Book Trust, p. 22. The translator refers to physicists; however, in the original context it refers to those who reject God's providence.

[17] The Qur'an, Chapter 10, Verse 99.

[18] The Qur'an, Chapter 2, Verse 256.

[19] Idris, J. (2012). An Islamic View of Peaceful Coexistence. Available at: www.jaafaridris.com/an-islamic-view-of-peaceful-coexistence [Accessed 1st October 2016].

[20] Bremmer, J. N. (2007). Atheism in Antiquity. In: M. Martin, ed., The Cambridge Companion to Atheism, 1st Edition. New York: Cambridge University Press, p. 11.

[21] Hyman, G. (2007) Atheism in Modern History. In: M. Martin, ed., The Cambridge Companion to Atheism, p. 29.

[22] Addison, J. (1753). The Evidence of the Christian Religion. London, pp. 224-223.

[23] Hyman, G. (2007) Atheism in Modern History, p. 31.

[24] Bradlaugh, C. (1929). Humanity's Gain from Unbelief and Other Selections from the Works of Charles Bradlaugh. London: Watts & Co. The Thinkers Library, No. 4.

[25] Ibid, p. 23.

[26] Ibid, p. 1.

[27] Modernizing the Case for God. Time Magazine, 7 April 1980, pp. 65-66. Available at: http://content.time.com/time/magazine/article/0,9171,921990,00.html [Accessed 2nd October 2016].

[28] Crick, F. (1982). Life Itself: Its Origin and Nature. London: Futura Publications, pp. 117-129.

[29] Hitchens, C. (2007). God Is Not Great: The Case Against Religion. New York: Atlantic Books, p. 13.

[30] Harris, S. (2006). The End of Faith: Religion, Terror and the Future of Reason. London: The Free Press, p. 227.

[31] Dawkins, R. (2006). The God Delusion, p. 20.

[32] Cited in William, P. S. (2009). A Sceptic's Guide to Atheism. Milton Keynes: Paternoster, p. 41.

[33] Ibid p. 44.

[34] Office for National Statistics. (2011). Religion in England Wales 2011.[online] Available at: http://www.ons.gov.uk/ons/rel/census/2011-census/key-statistics-for-local-authorities-in-england-and-wales/rpt-religion.html#tab-Changing-picture-of-religious-affiliation-over-last-decade. [Accessed 1st October 2016].

[35] Biotechnology Report. Fieldwork January 2010 – February 2010. Bruxelles: TNS Opinion & Social, p. 203. Available at: http://ec.europa.eu/public_opinion/archives/ebs/ebs_341_en.pdf [Accessed 1st October 2016].

[36] The history of atheism in China has its own complexities and cannot be equated with Western atheism. Chinese atheism is not due to Darwinism or a Dawkins type of new atheism. Atheism in China is based on a unique set of cultural, political and intellectual factors. It has to be studied on its own.

[37] Zuckerman, P. (2007). Atheism: Contemporary Numbers and Patterns. In: M. Martin, ed, The Cambridge Companion to Atheism, p. 61.

[38] Ibid, p. 55.

[39] WIN-Gallup International. (2012). Global Index of Religiosity and Atheism, p. 16. Available at: http://www.wingia.com/web/files/news/14/file/14.pdf [Accessed 2nd October 216].

[40] Some of ideas in this chapter have been inspired by and adapted from Craig, W.L. The absurdity of life without god. Available at: http://www.reasonablefaith.org/the-absurdity-of-life-without-god [Accessed 23rd November 2016].

[41] Schopenhauer, A. (2014). Studies in Pessimism: On the Sufferings of the World. [ebook] The University of Adelaide Library. Chapter 1. Available at: https://ebooks.adelaide.edu.au/s/schopenhauer/arthur/pessimism/chapter1.html [Accessed 2nd October 2016].

[42] The Qur'an, Chapter 12, Verse 87.

[43] The Qur'an, Chapter 99, Verses 6 to 8.

[44] The Qur'an, Chapter 45, Verse 22.

[45] The Qur'an, Chapter 50, Verse 35.

[46] The Qur'an, Chapter 10, Verse 26.

[47] The Qur'an, Chapter 36, Verses 55 to 58.

[48] The Qur'an, Chapter 17, Verse 70.

[49] The Qur'an, Chapter 3, Verse 191.

[50] The Qur'an, Chapter, 32, Verse 18.

[51] Nasr, S. H. (2004). The Heart of Islam: Enduring Values for Humanity. New York: HarperSanFrancisco, p. 275.

[52] The Qur'an, Chapter 57, Verses 20 to 21.

[53] Cited in BBC (no date) Radio 4 - in our time - greatest philosopher - Ludwig Wittgenstein. Available at:

http://www.bbc.co.uk/radio4/history/inourtime/greatest_philosopher_ludwig_wittgenst
ein.shtml [Accessed 1st October 2016].

[54] Cited in Pollan, S. M. and Levine, M, (2006) It's All in Your Head: Thinking Your Way
to Happiness. New York: HarperCollins, p. 4.

[55] Williams, M. (2015) The Life Cycle of the Sun. Available at:
http://www.universetoday.com/18847/life-of-the-sun/ [Accessed 2nd October 2016].

[56] The Qur'an, Chapter 3, Verse 90.

[57] Dawkins, R. (2006) The Selfish Gene. 30th Anniversary edition. Oxford: Oxford
University Press.

[58] The Qur'an, Chapter 7, Verse 128.

[59] The Qur'an, Chapter 39, Verse 29.

[60] Mogahed, Y. (2015) Reclaim Your Heart. 2nd Edition. San Clemente, CA: FB
Publishing, p. 55.

[61] The Qur'an, Chapter 11, Verse 105.

[62] The Qur'an, Chapter 25, Verse 75.

[63] The Qur'an, Chapter 59, Verse 19.

[64] Dawkins, R. (2001) River Out of Eden: A Darwinian View of Life. London: Phoenix, p.
155.

[65] Basic assumptions of science (no date) Available at:
http://undsci.berkeley.edu/article/basic_assumptions [Accessed 14th November 2016].

[66] Darwin Correspondence Project (2016) Available at:
https://www.darwinproject.ac.uk/letter/DCP-LETT-13230.xml [Accessed 4th October
2016].

[67] O'Hear, A. (1997) Beyond Evolution: Human Nature and the Limits of Evolutionary
Explanation. New York: Oxford University Press, p. 60.

[68] Gray, J. (2014) The Closed Mind of Richard Dawkins. Available at:
https://newrepublic.com/article/119596/appetite-wonder-review-closed-mind-richard-
dawkins [Accessed 4th October 2016].

[69] Francis, C. (1994) The Astonishing Hypothesis: The Scientific Search for the Soul. New
York: Charles Scribner's Sons, p. 262.

[70] Pinker, S. (1997) How the Mind Works. New York: W. W. Norton, p. 305.

[71] Harris, S. (2010) The Moral Landscape. New York: Free Press, p. 66.

[72] The Qur'an, Chapter 41, Verse 53.

[73] The Qur'an, Chapter 47, Verse 24.

[74] The Qur'an, Chapter 11, Verse 51.

[75] The Qur'an, Chapter 3, Verse 190.

[76] Taken and adapted from Searle, J. (1989). Reply to Jacquette. Philosophy and Phenomenological Research, 49(4), 703.

[77] The response to this objection has been inspired by and adapted from Kane B. (2014) Philosophy of mind 4.2 - objections to functionalism. Available at: https://www.youtube.com/watch?v=ZmEk1lq_Wgk [Accessed 24th October 2016].

[78] Searle, J. (1984) Minds, Brains and Science. Cambridge, Mass: Harvard University Press, pp. 32-33.

[79] Searle, J. (1990) Is the Brain's Mind a Computer Program? Scientific American 262: 27.

[80] Ibid, p. 30.

[81] Ibid. For responses to other objections and more detail on this topic please see: Searle, J. (1980) Minds, Brains, and Programs. Behavioral and Brain Sciences 3, 417-424; Searle, J. (1980) Intrinsic Intentionality. Behavioral and Brain Sciences 3: 450-456; Searle, J. (1989). Reply to Jacquette. Philosophy and Phenomenological Research, 49(4), 701-708; Searle, J. (1990) Is the Brain's Mind a Computer Program? Scientific American 262: 26-31; Searle, J. (1992) The Rediscovery of the Mind. Cambridge, MA: MIT Press.

[82] BBC Today. (2008). Available at: http://news.bbc.co.uk/today/hi/today/newsid_7745000/7745514.stm [Accessed 1st October 2016].

[83] Ibn Taymiyyah, A. (1991) Dar' Ta'arud al-'Aql wan-Naql. 2nd Edition. Edited by Muhammad Rashad Salim. Riyadh, Jami'ah al-Imam Muhammad bin Saud al-Islamiyah. Vol 8, p. 482.

[84] Al-Isfahani, Al-Raghib. (2009) Mufradat al-Qur'an al-Karim. 4th Edition. Edited by Ṣafwan Dawudi. Beirut: al-Dar al-Shamiyya, p. 640.

[85] Petrovich, O. (1997). Understanding the Non-Natural Causality in Children and Adults: A Case Against Artificialism. Psyche en Geloof, 8, 151-165.

[86] Zwartz, B. (2008). Infants 'Have Natural Belief In God'. Available at: http://www.theage.com.au/national/infants-have-natural-belief-in-god-20080725-3l3b.html [Accessed 4th October 2016].

[87] Bloom, P. (2007). Religion is Natural. Developmental Science, 10, 147-151.

[88] Kelemen, D. (2004) Are Children "Intuitive Theists"? Reasoning About Purpose and Design in Nature. Psychological Science, 15(5), 295-301.

[89] Järnefelt, E., Canfield, C. F. & Kelemen, D. (2015). The Divided Mind of a Disbeliever: Intuitive Beliefs About Nature as Purposefully Created Among Different Groups of Non-Religious Adults. Cognition 140:72-88.

[90] Ibid, 74.

[91] Ibid.

[92] Ibid, 79.

[93] Ibid, 81.

[94] Ibid, 82.

[95] Ibid, 83.

[96] Ibid, 84.

[97] Ibid.

[98] Corriveau, K. H., Chen, E. E. and Harris, P. L. (2015), Judgments About Fact and Fiction by Children From Religious and Nonreligious Backgrounds. Cogn Sci, 39: 353–382. doi:10.1111/cogs.12138.

[99] Barrett, J. L. (2012) Born Believers: The Science of Children's Religious Belief. New York: Free Press, pp. 35-36.

[100] Al-'Asqalani, A. (2000) Fath al-Bari Sharh Sahih al-Bukhari. 3rd Edition. Riyadh: Dar al-Salam, p. 316.

[101] Narrated by Muslim.

[102] Al-Ghazali. (2007) Kimiya-e Saadat: The Alchemy of Happiness. Translated by Claude Field. Kuala Lumpur: Islamic Book Trust, p. 10.

[103] Ibn Taymiyyah, A. (2004) Majmu' al-Fatawa Shaykhul Islam Ahmad bin Taymiyyah. Madina: Mujama' Malik Fahad. Vol 16, p. 324.

[104] Ibid. Vol 6, p. 73.

[105] Ibn Taymiyyah, A. (1991) Dar' Ta'arud al-'Aql wan-Naql. Vol 7, p. 219.

[106] The Qur'an, Chapter 16, Verse 69.

[107] The Qur'an, Chapter 10, Verse 24.

[108] The Qur'an, Chapter 52, Verses 35 and 36.

[109] The Qur'an, Chapter 28, Verse 56.

[110] The Qur'an, Chapter 14, Verse 10.

[111] Farfur, M. S. (2010) The Beneficial Message and The Definitive Proof in The Study of Theology. Translation and notes by Wesam Charkawi. Auburn: Wesam Charkawi, pp. 85-86.

[112] Gwynne, R. W. (2004) Logic, Rhetoric and Legal Reasoning in the Qur'an: God's Arguments. Abingdon: Routledge. 2004, p. ix.

[113] Ibid, p. 203

[114] Cited in Hoover, J. (2007) Ibn Taymiyya's Theodicy of Perpetual Optimism. Leiden: Brill, p. 31.

[115] The Qur'an, Chapter 52, Verses 35 and 36.

[116] Mohar, M. A. (2003) A word for word meaning of the Qur'ān. Vol III. Ipswich: JIMAS, p. 1713.

[117] This argument has been inspired by and adapted from Idris, J. (1994) The Contemporary Physicists and God's Existence. Available at: http://www.jaafaridris.com/the-contemporary-physicists-and-gods-existence/ [Accessed 23rd November 2016].

[118] Hilbert, D. (1964) On the Infinite. In: P. Benacerraf and H. Putnam (eds), Philosophy of Mathematics: Selected Readings. Englewood Cliffs, NJ: Prentice-Hall, p. 151.

[119] Quine: Terms explained. Available at: http://www.rit.edu/cla/philosophy/quine/underdetermination.html [Accessed 23rd October 2016].

[120] American Physical Society. (1998) Focus: The Force of Empty Space. Available at: http://physics.aps.org/story/v2/st28 [Accessed 23rd November 2016].

[121] Leibniz, G. W. (1714) The Principles of Nature and Grace, Based on Reason. 1714. Available at: http://www.earlymoderntexts.com/assets/pdfs/leibniz1714a.pdf [Accessed 4th October 2016].

[122] Krauss, L. M. (2012) A Universe from Nothing: Why is there Something Rather Than Nothing. London: Simon & Schuster, p. 170.

[123] Ibid.

[124] Ibid, p. 105.

[125] Albert, D. (2012) 'A Universe From Nothing,' by Lawrence M. Krauss. Available at: http://www.nytimes.com/2012/03/25/books/review/a-universe-from-nothing-by-lawrence-m-krauss.html?_r=0 [Accessed 1st October 2016].

[126] Craig, W.L. (2012) A Universe from Nothing. Available at: http://www.reasonablefaith.org/a-universe-from-nothing [Accessed 9th October 2016].

[127] Analogies adapted from Craig, W.L. (2012) A Universe from Nothing. Available at: http://www.reasonablefaith.org/a-universe-from-nothing [Accessed 9th October 2016].

[128] Krauss, L. A (2012) Universe from Nothing, p. 174.

[129] Sober, E. (2010). Empiricism. In: Psillos, S and Curd, M, ed, The Routledge Companion to Philosophy of Science. Abingdon: Routledge, pp. 137-138.

[130] Krauss, L. (2012) A Universe from Nothing, p. xiii.

[131] Ibid p. 147.

[132] iERA. (2013) Lawrence Krauss vs Hamza Tzortzis - Islam vs atheism debate. Available at: http://www.youtube.com/watch?v=uSwJuOPG4FI [Accessed 10th September 2016].

133 Tony Sobrado. (2012) How the Universe Came from 'Nothing', Richard Dawkins and Lawrence Krauss discuss. Available at: https://youtu.be/CXGyesfHzew?t=921 [Accessed 2nd October 2016].

134 Cited in Al-Bayhaqi, A. (2006) Kitab al-Asma was-Sifat. Edited by Abdullah Al-Hashidi. Cairo: Maktabatu al-Suwaadi. Vol 2, p. 271.

135 This example has been taken from Green, A. R. The Man in the Red Underpants. 2nd Edition. London: One Reason, pp. 9-10.

136 This example has been adapted from Idris, J. (2006) Contemporary Physicists and God's Existence (part 2 of 3): A Series of Causes. Available at: http://www.islamreligion.com/articles/491/ [Accessed 2nd October 2016].

137 Idris, J. (2006) Contemporary Physicists and God's Existence (part 2 of 3): A Series of Causes. Available at: http://www.islamreligion.com/articles/491/ [Accessed 2nd October 2016].

138 Cited in Goodman, L. E. (1971) Ghazali's Argument From Creation (I). International Journal of Middle East Studies, Vol 2, Issue. 1, 83.

139 Flew, A. (2007) There is a God: How the World's Most Notorious Atheist Changed His Mind. New York: HarperOne. 2007, p. 165.

140 Narrated by Bukhari.

141 Cited in Al-Bayhaqi, A. (2006) Kitab al-Asma was-Sifat. Vol 2, p. 270.

142 Wali-Allah, S. (2003) The Conclusive Argument from God (Hujjat Allah al-Baligha). Translated by Marcia K. Hermansen. Islamabad: Islamic Research Institute, p. 33.

143 The Qur'an, Chapter 112, Verses 2 and 3.

144 Lennox, J. C. (2009) God's Undertaker: Has Science Buried God? Oxford: Lion Books, p. 183.

145 Hoover, J. (2004) Perpetual Creativity in the Perfection of God: Ibn Taymiyya's Hadith Commentary on God's Creation of this World. Journal of Islamic Studies 15(3): 296.

146 The Qur'an, Chapter 42, Verse 11.

147 The Qur'an, Chapter 58, Verse 7.

148 This is an estimate based on the number of hydrogen atoms that are contained in the estimated total number of stars in the observable universe. The number is higher if other atoms are included.

149 The Qur'an, Chapter 24, Verse 45.

150 Al-Tahawi. (2007) The Creed of Imam Al-Tahawi. Translated from Arabic, Introduced and Annotated by Hamza Yusuf. California: Zaytuna Institute, p. 50.

151 The Qur'an, Chapter 2, Verse 20.

152 Al-Qurtubi, M. (2006) Al-Jaami' al-Ahkaam al-Qur'an. Edited by Dr. Adullah Al-Turki and Muhammad 'Arqasusi. Beirut: Mu'assasa al-Risalah. Vol 1, pp. 338-9.

153 Inspired and adapted from Craig, W. L. The coherence of Theism - part 2. Available at: http://www.bethinking.org/god/the-coherence-of-theism/part-2 [Accessed 13th November 2016].

154 Swinburne, R. (2004) The Existence of God. 2nd Edition. New York: Oxford University Press, pp. 52-72.

155 The Qur'an, Chapter 11, Verse 107.

156 Al-Ghazali, M. (2005) Ihyaa 'Ulum al-Deen. Beirut: Dar Ibn Hazm, p. 107.

157 Randhawa, S. (2011) The Kalam Cosmological Argument and the Problem of Divine Creative Agency and Purpose. Draft version. Available at: http://www.academia.edu/29016615/The_Kal%C4%81m_Cosmological_Argument_and_the_Problem_of_Divine_Creative_Agency_and_Purpose [Accessed 22nd October 2016].

158 Analogy adapted from Wainwright, W. J. (1988) Philosophy of Religion. 2nd. Edition. Belmont, CA: Wadsworth Publishing.

159 The Qur'an, Chapter 3, Verse 97.

160 The Qur'an, Chapter 35, Verse 15.

161 Ibn Kathir, I. (1999) Tafsir al-Qur'an al-'Adheem. Edited by Saami As-Salaama. 2nd Edition. Riyadh: Dar Tayiba. Vol 6, p. 541.

162 Hossein, S. (1993) An Introduction to Islamic Cosmological Doctrines. Albany: State University of New York Press, pp. 197-200.

163 Al-Ghazali, M. (1964) Fada'ih al-Batiniyya. Edited by Abdurahman Badawi. Kuwait: Muasassa Dar al-Kutub al-Thiqafa, p. 82.

164 Craig, W. L. (2008) Reasonable Faith: Christian Truth and Apologetics. 3rd Edition. Wheaton, Illinois: Crossway Books, p. 109.

165 Godwin, S. J. (no date) Transcript of the Russell/Copleston radio debate. Available at: http://www.scandalon.co.uk/philosophy/cosmological_radio.htm [Accessed 4th October 2016].

166 Adapted from Craig, W.L. Reasonable Faith. Available at: http://www.reasonablefaith.org/defenders-1-podcast/transcript/s04-01 [Accessed: 24th October 2016].

167 Eaton, G. (2001) Remembering God: Reflections on Islam. Lahore: Suhail Academy, pp. 18-19.

168 New Scientist: The Collection. The Big Questions. Vol I, Issue I, p. 51.

169 Koch, C. (2012) Consciousness: Confessions of a Romantic Reductionist. Cambridge, Massachusetts: MIT Press, pp. 23-24.

170 Chalmers, D. (2010) The Character of Consciousness. Oxford: Oxford University Press, p. 5.

171 Alter, T. (2014) Hard Problem of Consciousness. In: Bayne, T., Cleeremans, A., and Wilken, P. (ed.). The Oxford Companion to Consciousness. Oxford: Oxford University Press, p. 340.

172 The following 5 points have been taken and adapted from Chalmers, D. (2010) The Character of Consciousness, pp. 11-13.

173 Discover Magazine. (2016) What is Consciousness? | DiscoverMagazine.com. Available at: http://discovermagazine.com/1992/nov/whatisconsciousn149. [Accessed 1st October 2016].

174 Revonsuo. A. (2010) Consciousness: The Science of Subjectivity. Hove, East Sussex: Psychology Press, p. 202.

175 Manzoti, R. and Moderato, P. (2014) Neuroscience: Dualism in Disguise. In: Lavazza, A. and Robinson, H. (ed.). Contemporary Dualism: A Defense. Abingdon: Routledge, p. 82.

176 Ibid.

177 Chalmers, D. (2010) The Character of Consciousness, p. 105.

178 Levine, J. (2011) The Explanatory Gap. In: Bayne, T., Cleeremans, A., and Wilken, P. (ed.). The Oxford Companion to Consciousness. Oxford: Oxford University Press, p. 280.

179 Stoljar, D. (2016) "Physicalism", The Stanford Encyclopedia of Philosophy. Edward N. Zalta (ed.). Available at: http://plato.stanford.edu/archives/spr2016/entries/physicalism [Accessed 4th October 2016].

180 Jackson, F. (1986) What Mary Didn't Know. The Journal of Philosophy, Vol 83, No. 5: 291-295.

181 Chalmers, D. (2010) The Character of Consciousness, p. 108.

182 Ibid, p. 109.

183 The above discussion has been taken and adapted from the relevant lecture and seminar discussion that was held during my postgraduate degree (Masters in Philosophy). Patterson, S. (2016) Week 6: Responses to the Modal and Knowledge Arguments. Lecture notes distributed in Philosophy of Mind at Birkbeck College, University of London on 16th November 2016.

[184] Gertler, B. (1999) A Defense of the Knowledge Argument. Philosophical Studies. 93 (3):317-336.

[185] McConnell, J. (1994). In Defense of the Knowledge Argument. Philosophical Topics, 22(1/2), 157-187.

[186] Chalmers, D. (2007) Phenomenal Consciousness and the Explanatory Gap. In: Alter, T. and Walter, S. (ed). Phenomenal Concepts and Phenomenal Knowledge: New Essays on Consciousness and Physicalism. New York: Oxford University Press. A version of this essay can be found online at: http://consc.net/papers/pceg.pdf [Accessed 21st November 2016].

[187] Chalmers, D. (2010) The Character of Consciousness, p. 111.

[188] Churchland, P. (1988) Matter and Consciousness: A Contemporary Introduction to the Philosophy of the Mind. Cambridge: MIT Press, pp. 43-39.

[189] Ibid.

[190] Ibid.

[191] Revonsuo, A. (2010) Consciousness: The Science of Subjectivity, pp. 180-181.

[192] Ibid, p. 21.

[193] Ibid, p. 22.

[194] Ibid, p. 24.

[195] Lund, D. (2014) Materialism, Dualism and the Conscious Self. In: Lavazza, A. and Robinson, H. (ed.). Contemporary Dualism: A Defense. Abingdon: Routledge, p. 57.

[196] Solomon, R. (2005) Introducing Philosophy: A Text with Integrated Readings. 8th Edition. Oxford: Oxford University Press, p. 416.

[197] Block, N. (1980) Troubles with Functionalism. In: Block, N. (ed.). Readings in the Philosophy of Psychology. Cambridge, MA: Harvard University Press. Vol 1, pp. 268-205.

[198] Van Gulick, R. (2008) Functionalism and Qualia. In: Velmans, M. and Schneider, S. (ed.). The Blackwell Companion to Consciousness. Oxford: Blackwell Publishing, p. 381.

[199] Revonsuo, A. (2010) Consciousness: The Science of Subjectivity, p. 39.

[200] Ibid, p. 26.

[201] Ibid, pp. 29-30.

[202] Ibid, p. 30.

[203] Sober, E. (2010) Empiricism. In: Psillos, S. and Curd, M. The Routledge Companion to Philosophy of Science, pp. 137-138.

[204] Eccles, J. C. (1989) Evolution of the Brain, Creation of the Self. Abingdon: Routledge, p. 241.

205 Sober, E. (2000) Philosophy of Biology. 2nd Edition. Boulder, CO: Westview Press, p. 24.

206 Seager, W. and Allen-Hermanson, S. (2015) "Panpsychism", The Stanford Encyclopedia of Philosophy (Fall 2015 Edition), Edward N. Zalta (ed.). Available online at: http://plato.stanford.edu/archives/fall2015/entries/panpsychism/.

207 Feser, E. (2006) The Philosophy of Mind. Oxford: OneWorld, p. 138.

208 Moreland, J. P. (2008) Consciousness and the Existence of God: A Theistic Argument. Abingdon: Routledge, p. 35.

209 Ibid, p. 192.

210 Taliaferro, C. (2006) Naturalism and the Mind. In: Craig, W. L. and. Moreland, J. P. (ed.). Naturalism: A Critical Analysis. Abingdon: Routledge, pp. 148-9.

211 Ibid p. 150.

212 The Qur'an, Chapter 2, Verse 255.

213 The Qur'an, Chapter 67, Verse 14.

214 Taliaferro, C. (2014) The Promise and Sensibility of Integrative Dualism. In: Lavazza, A. and Robinson, H. (ed.). Contemporary Dualism: A Defense. Abingdon: Routledge, pp. 202-203.

215 The Qur'an, Chapter 17, Verse 85.

216 The Qur'an, Chapter 30, Verse 8.

217 Analogy adapted from Collins, R. (2002) God, Design and Fine-Tuning. Adapted version. Available at: http://home.messiah.edu/~rcollins/Fine-tuning/Revised%20Version%20of%20Fine-tuning%20for%20anthology.doc [Accessed 24th October 2016]

218 The Qur'an, Chapter 55, Verses 5 to 7.

219 The Qur'an, Chapter 3, Verse 190.

220 The Qur'an, Chapter 55, Verse 5.

221 The Qur'an, Chapter 16, Verse 12.

222 Tibawi, A.L. (ed. and tr.). (1965) Al-Risala al-Qudsiyya (*The Jerusalem Epistle*) "Al-Ghazali's Tract on Dogmatic Theology". In: The Islamic Quarterly, 9:3–4 (1965), 3-4.

223 Ibn Abi Al-'Izz. (2000) Commentary on the Creed of At-Tahawi. Translated by Muhammad 'Abdul-Haqq Ansari. Riyadh: Institute of Islamic and Arabic Sciences in America, p. 9

224 Collins, R. (2009) The Teleological Argument. In: Craig, W. L. and Moreland, J. P. The Blackwell Companion to Natural Theology. West Sussex: Wiley-Blackwell, p. 212.

225 Ibid.

[226] John Leslie. (2001) Infinite Minds: A Philosophical Cosmology. Oxford: Clarendon Press, p. 205.

[227] Collins, R. The Teleological Argument, p. 212.

[228] Cited in Jammer, M. (1999) Einstein and Religion. Princeton, NJ: Princeton University Press, p. 150.

[229] Dawkins, R. (1999) Unweaving the Rainbow. London: Penguin, p. 4.

[230] Ward, P. D. and Brownlee, D. (2004) Rare Earth: Why Complex Life Is Uncommon in the Universe. New York, NY: Copernicus Books, p. 16.

[231] Ibid, pp. 221-222.

[232] 'No Jupiter, no advanced life? ' - evolution may be impossible in Star Systems without a giant planet (2012). Available at: http://www.dailygalaxy.com/my_weblog/2012/11/would-advanced-life-be-impossible-in-star-systems-without-a-jupiter-.html [Accessed 2nd October 2016].

[233] Rasio, F.A. and E.B. Ford. (1996) Dynamical instabilities and the formation of extrasolar planetary systems. Science 274: 954-956.

[234] Ward, P. D. and Brownlee, D. (2004) Rare Earth: Why Complex Life Is Uncommon in the Universe. New York, NY: Copernicus Books, pp. 238 – 239.

[235] Ibid, p. 227.

[236] Ibid, p. 223.

[237] Ibid.

[238] Inspired by and adapted from Collins, R. The Fine-Tuning Design Argument. PowerPoint Presentation. Available at: http://home.messiah.edu/~rcollins/Fine-tuning/Fine-tuning%20powerpoint%20final%20version%2010-3-08.ppt [Accessed 24th October 2016].

[239] Ibid.

[240] Craig, W. L. (2008) Reasonable Faith: Christian Truth and Apologetics, p. 161.

[241] Davies, P. (1993) The Mind of God: Science and the Search for Ultimate Meaning. London: Penguin, p. 169.

[242] Cited in Flew, A. (2007) There is a God, p.119.

[243] Ibid.

[244] Barnes, L. A. (2011) The Fine-Tuning of the Universe for Intelligent Life. Sydney Institute for Astronomy. Available at: http://arxiv.org/PS_cache/arxiv/pdf/1112/1112.4647v1.pdf [Accessed 5th October 2016].

[245] Adapted from Collins, R. (2009) The Teleological Argument, pp. 262-265.

[246] I am grateful to Abu Hurayra for his contribution in responding to these objections.

[247] Dawkins, R. (2006) The God Delusion, p. 158.

[248] Both points have been adapted from Professor William Lane Craig's treatment on the issue. Craig, W. L. (2009) Dawkins's Delusion. In: Copan, P. and Craig, W. L. (ed.). Contending with Christianity's Critics: Answering New Atheists & Other Objectors. Nashville, Tennessee: B & H Publishing Group, p. 4.

[249] The Qur'an, Chapter 112, Verses 1 to 4.

[250] Flew, A. (2007) There is a God, p. 111.

[251] Collins, R. (2002) God, Design and Fine-Tuning. Adapted version. Available at: http://home.messiah.edu/~rcollins/Fine-tuning/Revised%20Version%20of%20Fine-tuning%20for%20anthology.doc [Accessed 24th October 2016].

[252] Adapted from Collins, R. (2009) The Teleological Argument, p. 276.

[253] Ibid.

[254] Markham, I. S. (2010) Against Atheism: Why Dawkins, Hitchens, and Harris are Fundamentally Wrong. West Sussex: Wiley-Blackwell, p. 34.

[255] The arguments presented in this chapter, including some of the ideas, have been inspired by and adapted from Craig, W. L. Can We Be Good Without God? Available at: http://www.reasonablefaith.org/can-we-be-good-without-god [Accessed: 24th October 2016]; Craig, W. L. (2008) Reasonable Faith: Christian Truth and Apologetics Wheaton, Illinois: Crossway Books, pp. 172-183.

[256] Ibid.

[257] The Qur'an, Chapter 7, Verse 28.

[258] Mackie, J. L. (1990) Ethics: Inventing Right and Wrong. London: Penguin. 1990, p. 15.

[259] Akhtar, S. (2008) The Qur'an and the Secular Mind. Abingdon: Routledge, p.99.

[260] The Qur'an, Chapter 2, Verse 163.

[261] The Qur'an, Chapter 59, Verses 22 to 24.

[262] Darwin, C. (1874) The Descent of Man and Selection in Relation to Sex. 2nd Edition, p. 99. Available at: http://www.gutenberg.org/ebooks/2300 [Accessed 4th October 2016].

[263] National Geographic (1996). Sharks in Love. Available at: http://video.nationalgeographic.com/video/shark_nurse_mating [Accessed 24th October 2016].

[264] Cited in Linville, M. D. (2009) The Moral Argument. In: Craig, W. L. and Moreland, J. P. (ed.). The Blackwell Companion to Natural Theology. West Sussex: Wiley-Blackwell, p. 400.

[265] The Qur'an, Chapter 21, Verse 22.

266 Al-Mahalli, J. and As-Suyuti, J. (2007) Tafsir Al-Jalalayn. Translated by Aisha Bewley. London: Dar Al Taqwa, p. 690; Mahali, J. and As-Suyuti J. (2001) Tafsir al-Jalalayn. 3rd Edition. Cairo: Dar al-Hadith, p. 422. You can access a copy online at: https://ia800205.us.archive.org/1/items/FP158160/158160.pdf [Accessed 1st October 2016].

267 Avveroes. (2001) Faith and Reason in Islam. Translated with footnotes, index and bibliography by Ibrahim Y. Najjar. Oxford: One World, p. 40.

268 The Qur'an, Chapter 7, Verse 28.

269 For more on the Divine nature of the Qur'an, please read: Khan, N. A. and Randhawa, S. (2016) Divine Speech: Exploring the Qur'an as Literature. Texas: Bayyinah Institute and Zakariya, A. (2015) The Eternal Challenge: A Journey Through The Miraculous Qur'an. London: One Reason.

270 The Qur'an, Chapter 29, Verse 46.

271 Narrated by Tirmidhi.

272 The problem of evil and suffering argument has been expressed in a number of different ways. Some of the arguments use the words good, merciful, loving or kind interchangeably. Despite the varying use of words, the argument remains the same. Instead of using the word good, terms such as merciful, loving, kind, etc., can also be used. The problem of evil assumes that the traditional concept of God must include an attribute that would imply God does not want evil and suffering to exist. Hence, using alternative words such as merciful, loving and kind do not affect the argument.

273 This assumption has been adapted from Professor William Lane Craig's treatment on the problem of evil. Moreland, J. P. and Craig, W. L. (2003). Philosophical Foundations for a Christian Worldview. Downers Grove, Ill, InterVarsity Press. See chapter 27.

274 Shaha, A. (2012) The Young Atheist's Handbook, p. 51.

275 This part of the story shows God's mercy. All children enter paradise—which is eternal bliss—regardless of their beliefs and actions. Therefore, God inspiring the man to kill the boy is to be understood through the lens of mercy and compassion.

276 The Qur'an, Chapter 18, Verses 65 to 82.

277 Ibn Kathir, I. (1999) Tafsir al-Qur'an al-'Atheem. Vol 5, p. 181.

278 Ibid.

279 Ibn Taymiyyah, A. (2004) Majmu' al-Fatawa Shaykhul Islam Ahmad bin Taymiyyah. Vol 14, p. 266.

280 Ibn Taymiyyah, A. (1986) Minhaj al-Sunnah. Edited by Muhammad Rashad Salim. Riyadh: Jami'ah al-Imam Muhammad bin Saud al-Islamiyah. Vol 3, p142.

281 Cited in Hoover, J. (2007) Ibn Taymiyya's Theodicy of Perpetual Optimism. Leiden: Brill, p.4.

282 The Qur'an, Chapter 51, Verse 56.

283 The Qur'an, Chapter 67, Verse 2.

284 The Qur'an, Chapter 39, Verse 7.

285 Narrated by Tirmidhi.

286 The Qur'an, Chapter 2, Verse 214.

287 The Qur'an Chapter 2, Verse 286.

288 The Qur'an, Chapter 5, Verse 100.

289 Al-Bayhaqi's Shu'ab al-Iman, traced back to Al-Hasan Al-Basri, who ascribes it to the Prophet Muhammad ﷺ. The scholars have graded this Prophetic tradition as *hasan*; its level of authenticity is good.

290 The Qur'an, Chapter 57, Verse 20.

291 Narrated by Muslim.

292 Narrated by Bukhari.

293 Narrated by Muslim.

294 Narrated by Bukhari.

295 Anyone that attempts suicide bombing or engages in terrorism and dies as a result is not considered a martyr. These evil acts are forbidden in Islam.

296 Narrated by Muslim.

297 Narrated by Ahmad.

298 Narrated by Muslim.

299 Ibid.

300 Ibid.

301 Gauch, H. G, Jr. (2012) Scientific Method in Brief. Cambridge: Cambridge University Press, p. 98.

302 Farhad, A. (2013) Richard Dawkins - science works bitches! Available at: https://youtu.be/0OtFSDKrq88?t=73 [Accessed 2nd October 2016].

303 Russell, B. (1935) Religion and Science. Oxford: Oxford University Press, p. 8.

304 Adapted from DPMosteller. (2011) Has science made belief in god unreasonable, J. P. Moreland. Available at: http://www.youtube.com/watch?v=TU9iiCqHxbE [Accessed 2nd October 2016].

305 Sober, E. (2010). Empiricism. In: Psillos, S and Curd, M, ed, The Routledge Companion to Philosophy of Science, pp. 137-138.

306 Darwin, C. The Descent of Man and Selection in Relation to Sex. 2nd Edition, p. 99. Available at: http://www.gutenberg.org/ebooks/2300 [Accessed 4th October 2016].

307 iERA (2013) Lawrence Krauss vs Hamza Tzortzis - Islam vs atheism debate. Available at: https://youtu.be/uSwJuOPG4FI?t=4161 [Accessed 18th October 2016]

308 Johnson, R. (2013) Rational Morality: A Science of Right and Wrong. Great Britain: Dangerous Little Books, pp. 19-20.

309 Craig, W.L. (2011) Is Scientism Self-Refuting. Available at: http://www.reasonablefaith.org/is-scientism-self-refuting [Accessed 4th October 2016].

310 McMyler, B. (2011) Testimony, Truth and Authority. New York: Oxford University Press, p. 3.

311 Lackey, J. (2006) Introduction. In: Lackey, J. and Sosa, E. (ed.). The Epistemology of Testimony. Oxford: Oxford University Press, p. 2.

312 McMyler, B. (2011) Testimony, Truth and Authority, p 10.

313 Coady, C. A. (1992) Testimony: A Philosophical Study. Oxford: Oxford University Press, p. 82.

314 See Shapiro, J. A. (2011) Evolution: A View from the 21st Century. New Jersey: FT Press; and Pigliucci, M. and Muller, G. B. (ed). (2010) Evolution: The Extended Synthesis. Cambridge, MA: MIT Press; and Godfrey-Smith, P. (2014) Philosophy of Biology. Princeton, NJ: Princeton University Press.

315 Barker, G. and Kitcher, P. (2013) Philosophy of Science: A New Introduction. Oxford: Oxford University Press. 2014, p. 17.

316 Annas, J. and Barnes, J. (1994). Sextus Empiricus: Outlines of Scepticism. New York: Cambridge University Press, p. 123.

317 Hume, D. (2002) Of scepticism with regard to reason. In: Epistemology: Huemer, M, ed, Contemporary Readings. Abingdon: Routledge, pp. 298-310. Originally published in Hume, D. (1902) Sceptical doubts concerning the operations of understanding. In: Selby-Bigge, L. A., ed, An enquiry concerning human understanding. In: Enquiries concerning human understanding and concerning the principles of morals, 2nd edition. Oxford: Clarendon Press, pp. 298-310.

318 Ibid, p. 305.

319 Ibid, pp. 304-5.

320 Rosenburg, A. (2012) Philosophy of Science: A Contemporary Introduction. New York: Routledge, p. 182.

321 Okasha, S. (2002) Philosophy of Science, A Very Short Introduction. Oxford: Oxford University Press, p. 77.

322 Stewart, R. B. (ed.). (2007) Intelligent Design: William A. Dembski & Michael Ruse in Dialogue. Minneapolis, MN: Fortress Press, p.37.

323 Moreland, J. P. (2009) The Recalcitrant Imago Dei. London: SCM Press, p. 4.

324 IDquest (2008) Richard Dawkins admits to intelligent design. Available at: https://www.youtube.com/watch?v=BoncJBrrdQ8 [Accessed 2nd October 2016].

325 iERA (2013) Lawrence Krauss vs Hamza Tzortzis - Islam vs atheism debate. Available at: http://www.youtube.com/watch?v=uSwJuOPG4FI#t=7247 [Accessed 2nd October 2016].

326 Hume, D. (1902). An Enquiry Concerning Human Understanding, section 88. Available at: http://www.gutenberg.org/files/9662/9662-h/9662-h.htm [Accessed 4th October 2016].

327 Fricker, E. (2006) Testimony and Epistemic Autonomy. In: Jennifer Lackey, J and Sosa, E, ed, The Epistemology of Testimony. Oxford: Oxford University Press, p. 244.

328 Lehrer, K. (2006). Testimony and Trustworthiness. In: Jennifer Lackey, J and Sosa, E, ed, The Epistemology of Testimony, p.145.

329 Ibid, p.149.

330 Ibid, p.150.

331 Ibid.

332 Ibid.

333 Ibid, p.151.

334 Ibid, p.156.

335 Ibid, pp. 156-157.

336 McMyler, B. (2011) Testimony, Truth and Authority, p 66.

337 Ibid, p 69.

338 Hume, D. (1902) An Enquiry Concerning Human Understanding, section 91. Available at: http://www.gutenberg.org/files/9662/9662-h/9662-h.htm [Accessed 4th October 2016].

339 Ibid, section 99.

340 Lipton, P. (2004) Inference to the Best Explanation. 2nd ed. Abingdon: Routledge, p.56.

341 Ibid, pp. 64-65.

342 Harman, G. (1965) The Inference to the Best Explanation. The Philosophical Review, 74(1), 88-95. Also available at: http://people.hss.caltech.edu/~franz/Knowledge%20and%20Reality/PDFs/Gilbert%20H.%20Harman%20-%20The%20Inference%20to%20the%20Best%20Explanation.pdf [Accessed 4th October 2016].

[343] The Qur'an, Chapter 96, Verse 1.

[344] The Magnificent Qur'an: A Unique History of Preservation. (2010). London: Exhibition Islam, pp. 145-204.

[345] Al-Suyuṭi. J. (2005) Al-Itqan fi 'Ulum al-Qur'an. Madina: Mujamma Malik Fahad, p. 1875.

[346] Shafi, M. (2005) Ma'riful Qur'an. 2nd Edition. Translated by Muhammad Jasan Askari and Muhamad Shamim. Karachi: Maktaba-e-Darul-Uloom. Vol 1, pp. 139-149.

[347] Usmani, M. T. (2000) An Approach to the Quranic Sciences. Translated by Dr. Mohammad Swaleh Siddiqui. Revised and Edited by Rafiq Abdur Rehman. Karachi: Darul Ishaat, p. 260.

[348] Cited in Irwin, R. (1999) The Penguin Anthology of Classical Arabic Literature. London: Penguin Books, p. 2.

[349] Ibn Khaldun, A. The Muqaddimah. Translated by Franz Rosenthal. Chapter 6, Section 58. Available at:
http://www.muslimphilosophy.com/ik/Muqaddimah/Chapter6/Ch_6_58.htm
[Accessed 9th October 2016].

[350] Ibn Rasheeq, A. H. (2000) Al-'Umda fee Sina'atu al-Sh'iar wa Naqdihi. Edited by Dr. Al-Nabwi Sha'lan. Cairo: Maktabu al-Khaniji, p. 89.

[351] Al-Qutaybah, A. (1925) 'Uyun al-Akhbar. Beirut: Dar al-Kutub al-Arabi. Vol 2, p. 185.

[352] Kermani, K. (2006) Poetry and Language. In: Rippin, A. (ed.). The Blackwell Companion to the Qur'an. Oxford: Blackwell Publishing, p. 108.

[353] Abdul-Raof, H. (2003) Exploring the Qur'an. Dundee: Al-Makhtoum Institute Academic Press, p.64.

[354] Personal interview with Professor Angelika Neuwrith in German. A copy of the recording is available on request.

[355] Islahi, A. A. (2007) Pondering Over the Qur'an: Tafsir of Surah al-Fatiha and Surah al-Baqarah. Vol 1. Translated by Mohammad Saleem Kayani. Kuala Lumpur: Islamic Book Trust, pp. 25-26.

[356] Cited in Islahi, A. A. (2007) Pondering Over the Qur'an: Tafsir of Surah al-Fatiha and Surah al-Baqarah. Vol 1, p. 26.

[357] Palmer, E. H. (tr.). (1900) The Qur'an. Part I. Oxford: Clarendon Press, p. lv.

[358] Draz, M. A. (2000) Introduction to the Qur'an. London: I. B. Tauris, p. 90.

[359] Zammit, M. R. (2002) A Comparative Lexical Study of Qur'anic Arabic. Leiden: Brill, p. 37.

360 Waliyyullāh, S. (2014) Al-Fawz al-Kabīr fī Uṣūl at-Tafsīr. The Great Victory on Qur'ānic Hermeneutics: A Manual of the Principles and Subtleties of Qur'anic Tafsīr. Translated, Introduction and Annotated by Tahir Mahmood Kiani. London: Taha, p.160.

361 Arberry, A. J. (1998) The Koran: Translated with an Introduction by Arthur J. Arberry. Oxford: Oxford University Press, p. x.

362 Usmani, M. T. (2000) An Approach to the Quranic Sciences, p. 262.

363 Al-Suyuṭi. J. (2005) Al-Itqan fi 'Ulum al-Qur'an. Madina: Mujamma Malik Fahad, p. 1881.

364 Ibid.

365 Lawrence, B. (2006) The Qur'an: A Biography. London: Atlantic Books, p 8.

366 Gibb, H. A. R. (1980) Islam: A Historical Survey. Oxford University Press, p. 28.

367 Van Gelder, G. J. H. (2013) Classical Arabic Literature: A Library of Arabic Literature Anthology. New York: New York University Press, pp. 31-33.

368 McAuley, D. E. (2012) Ibn 'Arabi's Mystical Poetics. Oxford: Oxford University Press, p.93.

369 Ibid, p. 94.

370 Cited in D. E. (2012) Ibn 'Arabi's Mystical Poetics. Oxford: Oxford University Press, p.94.

371 Bonebakker, S. A. (1984) Hatimi and his Encounter with Mutanabbi: A Biographical Sketch. Oxford: North-Holland Publishing Company, p.47.

372 Ibid, p.15; and see Ouyang, W. (1997) Literary Criticism in Medieval Arabic Islamic Culture: The Making of a Tradition. Edinburgh University Press.

373 Ibid, p. 44.

374 Mabillard, A. (1999) Shakespearean sonnet basics: Iambic pentameter and the English sonnet style. Available at: http://www.shakespeare-online.com/sonnets/sonnetstyle.html [Accessed 5th October 2016].

375 Holland, P. (2013) Shakespeare, William (1564–1616). Oxford Dictionary of National Biography. Oxford University Press. Available at: http://dx.doi.org/10.1093/ref:odnb/25200 [Accessed 9th October 2016].

376 Cited in Abdel Haleem, M. (2005) Understanding the Qur'an: Themes & Styles. London: I. B. Tauris, p. 184.

377 Abdul-Raof, H. (2003) Exploring the Qur'an. Dundee: Al-Maktoum Institute Academic Press; Abdul-Raof, H. (2001) Qur'an Translation: Discourse, Texture and Exegesis. Richmond, Surrey: Curzon.

378 Abdel Haleem, M. (2005) Understanding the Qur'an: Themes & Styles, p. 185.

379 Ibid, p. 188.

380 Chowdhury, S. Z. (2010) Introducing Arabic Rhetoric. Updated Edition. London: Ad-Duha, p. 99.

381 Ibid.

382 The Qur'an, Chapter 108, Verses 1 to 3.

383 Robinson, N. (2003) Discovering The Qur'an: A Contemporary Approach to a Veiled Text, 2nd Edition. Washington: Georgetown University Press, p. 254.

384 Cited in Qadhi, Y. (1999) An Introduction to the Sciences of the Qur'an. Birmingham: Al-Hidaayah, p. 269. The original translation has been amended; the name Allah has been replaced with God.

385 Kermani, K. (2006) Poetry and Language. In: Rippin, A. (ed.). The Blackwell Companion to the Qur'an. Oxford: Blackwell Publishing, p. 110.

386 The Qur'an, Chapter 16, Verse 103.

387 Ibn Kathir, I. (1999) Tafsir al-Qur'an al-'Atheem. Vol 4, p. 603.

388 Vanlancker–Sidtis, D. (2003) Auditory recognition of idioms by native and nonnative speakers of English: It takes one to know one. Applied Psycholinguistics 24, 45–57.

389 Ibid.

390 Hyltenstam, K. and Abrahamsson, N. (2000), Who can become native-like in a second language? All, some, or none? Studia Linguistica, 54: 150–166. doi: 10.1111/1467-9582.00056.

391 Ali, M. M. (2004) The Qur'an and the Orientalists. Ipswich: Jam'iyat Iḥyaa' Minhaaj Al-Sunnah, p. 14.

392 Kermani, K. (2006) Poetry and Language, p. 108.

393 Usmani, M. T. (2000) An Approach to the Quranic Sciences, p. 261.

394 Draz, M. A. (2001) The Qur'an: An Eternal Challenge. Translated and Edited by Adil Salahi. Leicester: The Islamic Foundation, p. 83.

395 Lings, M. (1983) Muhammad: his life based on the earliest sources. 2nd Revised Edition. Cambridge: The Islamic Texts Society, pp. 53-79.

396 Islamic Awareness (no date) The text of the Qur'an. Available at: http://www.islamic-awareness.org/Quran/Text/ [Accessed 1st October 2016].

397 Arberry, A. J. (1967) Poems of Al-Mutanabbi. Cambridge: Cambridge University Press, pp. 1-18.

398 For example these can include reproductions of Picasso's art. Available at: http://www.sohoart.co/artist/Pablo-Picasso.html [Accessed 6th October 2016].

399 See Textual Integrity of the Bible. Available at: http://www.islamic-awareness.org/Bible/Text/ [Accessed 7th October 2016].

400 The Qur'an, Chapter 18, Verse 109.

401 The name Muhammad is mentioned four times and Ahmad (another one of his names) is mentioned once. See http://corpus.quran.com/search.jsp?q=muhammad and http://corpus.quran.com/search.jsp?q=ahmad [Accessed 24th October 2016].

402 "Muhammad is not the father of any one of you men; he is God's messenger and the seal of the Prophets: God knows everything." The Qur'an, Chapter 33, Verse 40.

403 The Qur'an, Chapter 81, Verse 22.

404 The Qur'an, Chapter 53, Verse 2.

405 The Qur'an, Chapter 48, Verse 29.

406 Lings, M. (1983) Muhammad: His Life Based on the Earliest Sources, p. 34.

407 Ibid, p. 52.

408 Ibid, pp. 53 – 79.

409 Watt, W. M. (1953) Muhammad at Mecca. Oxford: Oxford University Press, p. 52.

410 Narrated by Bukhari.

411 Narrated by Muslim.

412 Narrated by Muslim.

413 Burj Khalifa. (2016) Facts & figures. Available at: http://www.burjkhalifa.ae/en/the-tower/factsandfigures.aspx [Accessed 1st October 2016].

414 Carrington, D. (2014) Saudi Arabia to Build World's Tallest Tower, Reaching 1 Kilometer into the Sky. Available at: http://edition.cnn.com/2014/04/17/world/meast/saudi-arabia-to-build-tallest-building-ever/ [Accessed 1st October 2016].

415 Zakariya, A. (2015). The Eternal Challenge: A Journey Through The Miraculous Qur'an. London: One Reason, pp. 69-70.

416 Narrated by Ibn Abi Shaybah.

417 Narrated by Tabarani, in the chapter Kitab al-Fitan. The Islamic scholars have graded the authenticity of this tradition as weak. However, it does not mean it is impossible that the Prophet ﷺ said these words. There is still a relatively high possibility.

418 For example, see Brody, G., Stoneman, Z., and Sanders, A. Effects of Television Viewing on Family Interactions: An Observational Study. Family Relations 29, no. 2 (1980): 216–20.

419 Draper, J. W. (1905) History of the Intellectual Development of Europe. New York and London: Harper and Brothers Publishers. Vol 1, pp. 329-330.

420 See M. M Azami. (1978) Studies in Early Hadith Literature. Indianapolis, Indiana: American Trust Publications.

421 Narrated by Abu Dawud and Tirmidhi.

422 Narrated by Bukhari in Al-Adab al-Mufrad.

423 Narrated by Tirmidhi.

424 Narrated by Bukhari.

425 Ibid.

426 Narrated by Muslim.

427 Narrated by Tirmidhi.

428 Ibid.

429 Narrated by Bukhari and Muslim.

430 Narrated by Tirmidhi.

431 Narrated by Bukhari, Muslim, Tirmidhi and Ibn Majah.

432 Narrated by Muslim.

433 Narrated by Ibn Hibban.

434 Narrated by Ibn Majah.

435 Narrated by Ahmad.

436 Ibid.

437 Narrated by Abu Dawud and Tirmidhi.

438 Narrated by Bukhari, Tareekh al-Kabeer.

439 Narrated by Tabarani.

440 Narrated by Bukhari.

441 Ibid.

442 Narrated by Ahmad and Tirmidhi.

443 Narrated by Bukhari.

444 Narrated by Bukhari, Muslim and Ahmad.

445 Narrated by Bukhari and Muslim.

446 Narrated by Bukhari.

447 Narrated by Muslim.

448 Narrated by Bukhari.

449 Ibid.

450 Narrated by Ibn Majah.

451 Narrated by Muslim.

452 Narrated by Tirmidhi.

453 Narrated by Muslim.

454 Ibid.

455 Ibid.

456 Narrated by Bukhari.

457 Narrated by Bukhari and Muslim.

458 Narrated by Bukhari.

459 Ibid.

460 Ibid.

461 Narrated by Bukhari and Muslim.

462 Narrated by Bukhari.

463 Narrated by An-Nasai.

464 Narrated by Muslim.

465 Narrated by Ahmad.

466 Cited in Ibn Musa Al-Yahsubi, Q. I. (2006) Muhammad Messenger of Allah: Ash-Shifa of Qadi 'Iyad. Translated by Aisha Abdarrahman Bewley. Cape Town: Madinah Press, p. 55.

467 Narrated by Bukhari and Muslim.

468 Ibid.

469 Narrated by Al-Bayhaqi, Ibn Hibban, Tabarani and Abu Nu'aym.

470 Narrated by Muslim.

471 As-Sallabee, M. A. (2005) The Noble Life of the Prophet. Vol 3. Riyadh: Darussalam, pp. 1707 & 1712.

472 Narrated by Tirmidhi.

473 Ibid.

474 Narrated by Tirmidhi.

475 Ibid.

476 Ibn Qayyim, S. (1998) Zaad al-Ma'ad. Edited by Shuayb Al-Arnaout and Abdul Qadir Al-Arnaout Vol 3. Beirut: Mu'assasa al-Risalah, pp. 50-51. An online copy can be accessed at: http://ia801308.us.archive.org/0/items/FP37672/03_37674.pdf [Accessed 1st October 2016].

477 Narrated by Bukhari.

478 Narrated by Bukhari, Muslim and Ahmad.

479 Narrated by Bukhari and Muslim.

480 Narrated by Ibn Maajah and al-Haakim.

481 Narrated by Tirmidhi.

482 Narrated by Bukhari and Muslim.

[483] Narrated by Tirmidhi.

[484] Ibid.

[485] The Qur'an, Chapter 5, Verse 8.

[486] The Qur'an, Chapter 4, Verse 135.

[487] The Qur'an, Chapter 90, Verses 12 to 18.

[488] Ibn Hisham, A. (1955) as-Sira an-Nabawiyya. Cairo: Mustafa Al-Halabi & Sons. Vol 1, pp. 501-504.

[489] Armstrong, K. (1997) A History of Jerusalem: One City Three Faiths. New York: Ballantine Books, p. 245.

[490] Cohen, A. (1994) A World Within: Jewish Life as Reflected in Muslim Court Documents from the Sijill of Jerusalem (XVIth Century). Part One. Philadelphia: The Center for Judaic Studies, University of Pennsylvania, pp. 22-23.

[491] Tabari, M, S. (1967) Tarikh Tabari: Tarikh ar-Rusul wal- Muluk. Edited by Muhammad Ibrahim. Vol 3. 3rd Edition. Cairo, Dar al-Ma'aarif, p. 609. On online copy can be accessed at: https://ia802500.us.archive.org/21/items/WAQ17280/trm03.pdf [Accessed 1st October 2016].

[492] Cited in Walker, C. J. (2005). Islam and the West: A Dissonant Harmony of Civilisations. Gloucester: Sutton Publishing, p. 17.

[493] Narrated by Yahya b. Adam in the book of al-Kharaaj.

[494] Reported by Al-Tabarani in Al-Mu'jam Al-Awsat.

[495] Al-Qaraafi, A. (1998) Al-Furuq. Vol 3. 1st Edition. Edited by Khalil Al-Mansur. Beirut: Dar al-Kutub al-Ilmiyyah, p. 29. An online copy can be accessed at: http://ia600203.us.archive.org/27/items/Forwq_Qarafy/Forwq_Qarafy_03.pdf [Accessed 1st October 2016].

[496] The Qur'an, Chapter 21, Verse 107.

[497] The Qur'an, Chapter 7, Verse 156.

[498] Cited in Walker, C. J. (2005) Islam and the West: A Dissonant Harmony of Civilisations, p. 17.

[499] Dozy, R. (1913). A History of Muslims in Spain. London: Chatto & Windus, p. 235.

[500] Arnold, T. (1896) The Preaching of Islam: A History of the Propagation of the Muslim Faith. Westminster: Archibald Constable & Co., p. 56.

[501] The Qur'an, Chapter 2, Verse 256.

[502] Bonner, M. (2006) Jihad in Islamic History. Princeton: Princeton University Press, pp. 89-90.

503 Hallaq, W. B. (2009). Sharia: Theory, Practice and Transformations. New York: Cambridge University Press, p. 332.

504 Ibn Zanjawiyah, H, S. (1986) Kitab al-Amwaal. Edited by Shakir Fiyadh. Makkah: Markaz al-Malik Faisal, pp. 169-170.

505 Mansel, P. (1995). Constantinople: City of the World's desire, 1453-1924. London: Penguin Books, p. 15.

506 The Qur'an, Chapter 49, Verse 13.

507 Hafiz ibn Hibban reported in al-Sahih, via his isnad, from Fadalah ibn Ubayd and Baihaqi.

508 Gibb, H. A. R. (2012) Whither Islam? A Survey of Modern Movements in the Moslem World. Abingdon: Routledge, p. 379.

509 Toynbee, A. J. (1948) Civilization on Trial. New York: Oxford University Press, p. 205.

510 Robinson, V. (1936). The Story of Medicine. New York: Tudor Publishing Company, p. 164.

511 Sabry, W. M., & Vohra, A. (2013). Role of Islam in the management of Psychiatric disorders. Indian Journal of Psychiatry, 55(Suppl 2), S205–S214. http://doi.org/10.4103/0019-5545.105534.

512 Badri, M. (2013). Abu Zayd Al-Balkhi's Sustenance of the Soul: The Cognitive Behavior Therapy of a Ninth Century Physician. Surrey: International Institute of Islamic Thought.

513 Narrated by Bukhari.

514 The Qur'an, Chapter 10, Verse 24.

515 The Qur'an, Chapter 96, Verses 1 to 5.

516 The Qur'an, Chapter 39, Verse 9.

517 The Qur'an, Chapter 88, Verses 17 to 20.

518 The Qur'an, Chapter 3, Verses 190 and 191.

519 See Steffens, B. (2007) Ibn Al-Haytham: First Scientist. Greensboro, NC: Morgan Reynolds Publishing.

520 Lindberg, David C. (1992). The Beginnings of Western Science. Chicago: The University of Chicago Press, pp. 362-363.

521 Steffens, B. (2007) Ibn Al-Haytham: First Scientist, p. 27.

522 For details see Al-Djazairi, S. E. (2005) The Hidden Debt to Islamic Civilisation. Oxford: Bayt Al-Hikma Press; Saliba, G. (2007) Islamic Science and the Making of the European Renaissance. Massachusetts: MIT Press.

---

[523] Saliba, G. (2007) Islamic Science and the Making of the European Renaissance. Massachusetts: MIT Press, p. 1.

[524] Arnold, T. (1896) The Preaching of Islam, p. 112.

[525] Hewlett Packard. Carly Fiorina Speeches. Technology, Business and Our Way of Life: What's Next. (2001). Available at: http://www.hp.com/hpinfo/execteam/speeches/fiorina/minnesota01.html [Accessed 10th September 2016].

[526] Smith, A. (1869). The Essays of Adam Smith. London: Alex Murray, p. 353.

[527] Ibn Qayyim, S. (2005) Al-Wabil al-Sayib. Edited by Abdullah Qaa'ir and Bakr Abu Zayd. Makkah: Dar Alim al-Fawa'id, p. 109. You can download an online copy at: http://www.ajurry.com/vb/attachment.php?attachmentid=26489&d=1363130186 [Accessed 1st October 2016].

[528] The Qur'an, Chapter 47, Verse 19.

[529] The Qur'an, Chapter 7, Verse 180.

[530] The Qur'an, Chapter 4, Verse 48.

[531] The Qur'an, Chapter 25, Verses 68 and 70.

[532] The Qur'an, Chapter 23, Verses 99 and 100.

[533] The Qur'an, Chapter 3, Verse 117.

[534] The Qur'an, Chapter 8, Verse 51.

[535] This is based on the following authentic tradition narrated by Ahmad and Ibn Hibban: "There are four (who will protest) to God on the Day of Resurrection: the deaf man who never heard anything, the insane man, the very old man, and the man who died during the *fatrah* (the interval between the time of Jesus (upon whom be peace) and the time of Muhammad ﷺ. The deaf man will say, 'O Lord, Islam came but I never heard anything.' The insane man will say, 'O Lord, Islam came but the children ran after me and threw stones at me.' The very old man will say, 'O Lord, Islam came but I did not understand anything.' The man who died during the *fatrah* will say, 'O Lord, no Messenger from You came to me.' He will accept their promises of obedience, then word will be sent to them to enter the Fire. By the One in Whose hand is the soul of Muhammad, if they enter it, it will be cool and safe for them." There are other hadiths and verses of the Qur'an that indicate that God will not allow anyone to enter hell until people have been given the correct message of Islam.

[536] Al-Ghazali, M. A. (1993) Fayasl al-Tafriqa Bayn al-Islam wa-l-Zandaqa. Edited by M. Bejou. Damascus, p. 84. An online copy is available at: http://ghazali.org/books/fiysal-bejou.pdf [Accessed 21st November 2016].

537 Ibid.

538 The Qur'an, Chapter 3, Verse 113. This verse refers to the 'people of the book'. However, the principle applies to all groups of people.

539 Ibid.

540 Narrated by Bukhari.

541 The Qur'an, Chapter 7, Verse 55.

542 The Qur'an, Chapter 40, Verse 1.

543 The Qur'an, Chapter, 20, Verse 14.

544 The Qur'an, Chapter 2, Verse 29.

545 The Qur'an, Chapter 7, Verses 191 to 194.

546 The Qur'an, Chapter 35, Verse 3.

547 The Qur'an, Chapter 96, Verses 6 and 7.

548 The Qur'an, Chapter 92, Verses 8 to 12.

549 The Qur'an, Chapter 14, Verse 34.

550 Fromm, E. (1956). The Art of Loving. New York: Harper & Row, pp. 58-59.

551 Al-Ghazali. (2011) Al-Ghazali on Love, Longing, Intimacy & Contentment. Translated with an introduction and notes by Eric Ormsby. Cambridge: The Islamic Texts Society, p. 25.

552 The Qur'an, Chapter 7, Verse 156.

553 The Qur'an, Chapter 55, Verses 1 and 2.

554 The Qur'an, Chapter 85, Verse 14.

555 Narrated by Abu Dawud.

556 Al-Ghazali. (2011) Al-Ghazali on Love, Longing, Intimacy & Contentment, p. 23.

557 The Qur'an, Chapter 3, Verse 31.

558 The Qur'an, Chapter 51, Verse 56.

559 Obedience to the Prophet Muhammad ﷺ is as a result of obeying God, as He commands us to do so.

560 The Qur'an, Chapter 3, Verse 132.

561 Al-Ghazali. (2011) Al-Ghazali on Love, Longing, Intimacy & Contentment, pp. 120-121.

562 Ibid, p. 123.

563 Mahali, J and Al-Suyuti J. (2001) Tafsir Al-Jalalayn, p. 302.

564 The Qur'an, Chapter 11, Verses 118 and 119.

565 The Qur'an, Chapter 25, Verses 43 and 44.

566 Twenge JM & Kasser T. Generational changes in materialism and work centrality, 1976-2007: Associations with temporal changes in societal insecurity and materialistic role modeling. Personality and Social Psychology Bulletin. 2013,. 39 (7) 883-897; DOI: 10.1177/0146167213484586.

567 Opree SJ, Buijzen M, & Valkenburg PM. Lower life satisfaction related to materialism in children frequently exposed to advertising. Pediatrics. 2012, 130 (3) e486-e491; DOI: 10.1542/peds.2011-3148.

568 The Qur'an, Chapter 59, Verse 19.

569 The Qur'an, Chapter 39, Verse 29.

570 Cited in Riffat, H. (1968) The Main Philosophical Idea in the Writings of Muhammad Iqbal (1877 – 1938). Durham theses, Durham University. Available at: http://etheses.dur.ac.uk/7986/2/7986_4984-vol2.PDF?UkUDh:CyT [Accessed 6th October 2016].

571 The structure and content of this chapter have been adapted from Reminders From Hamza Yusuf. (2016) Best of Hamza Yusuf. Available at: https://youtu.be/KUzjHU-g7E0 [Accessed 24th October 2016].

572 The Qur'an, Chapter 82, Verse 6.

573 The Qur'an, Chapter 20, Verse 44.

574 Al-Qurtubi, M. (2006). Al-Jaami' al-Ahkaam al-Qur'an, p. 65.

575 The Qur'an, Chapter 16, Verse 125.

576 Al-Zamakhshari, J. (2009) Tafsir al-Kashshaaf 'an Haqa'iq at-Tanzil. Edited by Khalil Shayhaa. Beirut: Darul Marefah, p. 588.

577 The Qur'an, Chapter 14, Verses 24 to 27.

578 The Qur'an, Chapter 41, Verse 34.

Lightning Source UK Ltd.
Milton Keynes UK
UKOW05f1146240117

292754UK00001B/262/P